T0083642

VITA GRIFFINI FILII CONANI

Vita Griffini Filii Conani

THE MEDIEVAL LATIN LIFE OF
GRUFFUDD AP CYNAN

edited and translated
by
Paul Russell

UNIVERSITY OF WALES PRESS
CARDIFF
2005

British Library in Cataloguing-in-Publication Data
A catalogue record for this book is available from the British Library.

ISBN 978-0-7083-1893-5

Printed by CPI Antony Rowe, Chippenham, Wiltshire

In memoriam patris mei

Contents

Preface

It is my pleasure to acknowledge the generous financial support of the Neil Ker Memorial Fund of the British Academy in the publication of this volume. A late draft of this work was awarded the Legonna Celtic Research Prize in 2003; I am grateful to the Council of the National Library of Wales and the judges for their kindness.

Many people have helped in the preparation of this edition. Thomas Charles-Edwards and Huw Pryce read drafts of the edition. I am grateful too for the helpful comments of the reader appointed by the University of Wales Press. David Dumville, Pierre-Yves Lambert, Patrick Sims-Williams, Jonathan Coe and Morfydd Owen have offered suggestions and ideas on particular points. Many people, in particular Beverley Smith, Alex Woolf, John Koch, Nerys Ann Jones and Charles Insley, have offered comments at lectures on this text in Aberystwyth, Bangor, Cambridge, Edinburgh and Oxford. This work could not have been completed without the help of librarians and archivists; in particular, I am grateful to Ann Daniels in the Melville Richard's Archive of Welsh Place Names for answering queries about names; to Fiona Wilkes and Julian Reid at Merton College, Oxford, who at various times allowed me access to the college's manuscripts; in particular, I am grateful to Maredudd ap Huw in the National Library of Wales, Aberystwyth, for his unstinting support and friendship in answering queries with such a wealth of detail and expertise. The text was the subject of a graduate reading class in Oxford in Trinity Term 2002; the comments of those present, especially Arkady Hodge, Fiona Edmonds, Kathleen Hutson and Max Lieberman, were of particular value, coming as they did from a wide range of different interests. A number of people helped in the final stages of the production of this book: the staff of the University of Wales Press have been extremely supportive and helpful; Simon Ó Faoláin prepared the map. This work would not even have started without the help and generous support of Daniel Huws. Not only did he check the text and answer numerous queries about difficult sections, but it was he who initially suggested to me in the context of Welsh law manuscripts that Peniarth 434 'might be worth a look'.

As ever, my wife, Felicity, and my son, Ben, have been a constant source of support and love. The work is dedicated to the memory of my father who saw its beginning but not its completion.

Illustrations

Abbreviations

For full bibliographical details, see Bibliography. For sigla of the manuscripts of *HGK* and *VGC*, see pp. 3–4.

AC	*Annales Cambriae*
AP	*Armes Prydein*
BBCS	*Bulletin of the Board of Celtic Studies*
BL	London, British Library
BT	*Book of Taliesin*
ByS	*Brenhinedd y Saeson*
ByT (Pen. 20)	*Brut y Tywysogyon* (Peniarth 20 version)
ByT (Pen. 20 tr.)	*Brut y Tywysogyon* (Peniarth 20 version, translation)
ByT (RB)	*Brut y Tywysogyon* (Red Book of Hergest version)
CBT	*Cyfres Beirdd y Tywysogion*
CMCS	*Cambridge Medieval Celtic Studies* (vols. 1–25); *Cambrian Medieval Celtic Studies* (vols. 26–)
CMRW	E. Owen, *Catalogue of Manuscripts relating to Wales in the British Museum*
DMLBS	*The Dictionary of Medieval Latin from British Sources*
EC	*Études celtiques*
EHR	*The English History Review*
EWGT	*Early Welsh Genealogical Tracts*
GPC	*Geiriadur Prifysgol Cymru*

HGC	*The History of Gruffydd ap Cynan*
HGK	*Historia Gruffud vab Kenan*
J	Law manuscript: Oxford, Jesus College MS, 57
L	Law manuscript: London, British Library, Cotton MS, Titus D.ix
LTWL	*The Latin Texts of the Welsh Laws*
MPW	*A Mediaeval Prince of Wales*
NLW	Aberystwyth, National Library of Wales
NLWJ	*National Library of Wales Journal*
O	Law manuscript: Aberystwyth, NLW, Peniarth MS, 36A
ODNB	*Oxford Dictionary of National Biography*
OLD	*The Oxford Latin Dictionary*
Q	Law manuscript: Aberystwyth, NLW, Wynnstay MS, 36
R	Law manuscript: Aberystwyth, NLW, Peniarth MS, 31
RC	*Revue celtique*
RMWL	J. G. Evans, *Report on Manuscripts in the Welsh Language*
THSC	*Transactions of the Honourable Society of Cymmrodorion*
Tr	Law manuscript: Cambridge, Trinity College MS, O.vii.1
VGC	*Vita Griffini filii Conani* (the text edited and translated in this volume)
VSBG	*Vitae Sanctorum Britanniae et Genealogiae*
W	Law manuscript: London, British Library, Cotton MS, Cleopatra A.xiv
WHR	*The Welsh History Review*
X	Law manuscript: London, British Library, Cotton MS, Cleopatra B.v

Introduction

Background

The Middle Welsh life of Gruffudd ap Cynan, the king of Gwynedd who died in 1137, is an important source for the history of Wales, the Irish Sea and Ireland in the eleventh and twelfth centuries, but it has long been recognized that the surviving Middle Welsh version is a translation of a Latin original which was thought to have been lost.[1] The Middle Welsh life was edited and translated into English by Arthur Jones in 1910 (*HGC*), but modern scholars have the benefit of Simon Evans's monumental edition of the text published in 1977 (*HGK*), followed by his English translation of the text in 1990 (*MPW*) which included the Welsh text.[2] A striking feature of this text is that only one medieval manuscript has survived and that is fragmentary, NLW, Peniarth MS 17, pp. 1–16. There was a renaissance in interest in Gruffudd ap Cynan in sixteenth-century north Wales and many more copies have survived from that period.[3] Both editions of the Welsh text, therefore, supplement the gaps in the Peniarth 17 text with material from NLW, Peniarth MS 267, probably the earliest of the surviving sixteenth-century versions. Even though it is clear that the sixteenth-century manuscripts belong to a different branch of the manuscript tradition, as a whole it seems to have been very close and therefore the

---

[1]   On the evidence for a lost Latin original, see below, pp. 15–17

[2]   The Welsh text in *MPW* is not an exact reprint of the text in *HGK*. On occasions, emendations or changes suggested in the notes in *HGK* have been incorporated into the text of *MPW*; for example, compare the text of *MPW* 23. 13 with that of *HGK* 1. 10–11 (cf. *VGC* §2/2 below and the note).

[3]   As an example of the traffic in manuscripts of *HGK*, in 1655 Meredith Lloyd asked Robert Vaughan for a loan of his copy of the Welsh life of Gruffudd ap Cynan; interestingly he called it *Hanes Griffith ap Cynan*; see N. Lloyd, 'Meredith Lloyd', *Journal of the Welsh Bibliographical Society*, 11 (1975–6), 133–92: pp. 165, 185–6. Robert Vaughan also seems to have had a copy of the Latin life; see his own library catalogue (Aberystwyth, NLW MS, 9095B; see D. Huws, 'Robert Vaughan', in Huws, *Medieval Welsh Manuscripts* (Cardiff and Aberystwyth, 2000), 294 under the shelfmark Z.2.3.8: 'Thelwalls translation of Griffith ap Conans life'; on Vaughan, see Huws, *MWM*, 287–302; Evans, 'Vaughan, Robert Powell', *ODNB*.

supplementary material provides a reasonably reliable guide to the contents of the lacunae in Peniarth 17.[4]

Another aspect of the sixteenth-century rebirth in interest in Gruffudd ap Cynan was the creation of a Latin translation of the Welsh text. Some ten manuscripts of this Latin translation have survived, some of which have been preserved in manuscripts side by side with the Welsh text.[5] They are testament to an increasing humanistic interest in this text in the sixteenth century and, given that one version of the Latin text, BL, Cotton Vitellius C.ix, was copied for Dr John Dee, perhaps also to an interest on the part of the Elizabethan court in aspects of earlier British history as a means of justifying imperial ambitions.[6] These Latin versions have recently been surveyed by Ceri Davies.[7] The main focus of this volume is on the earliest of them, the version preserved in NLW, Peniarth MS 434. This version has been heavily annotated and corrected. The text edited here is the underlying, original text in this manuscript, and in what follows it will be demonstrated that this text is not a translation of the Welsh text but represents a late copy of the medieval Latin life of Gruffudd ap Cynan which predated the Middle Welsh translation.

The underlying text of Peniarth 434 was heavily altered and annotated in the sixteenth century and it appears that the intention of most of the changes was to bring it into line with the Welsh text. Fair copies of Peniarth 434, therefore, look exactly like translations of the Welsh text. One such text is NLW MS, Peniarth 276 which was published by R. Williams in 1866.[8] Another, probably the earliest, is BL, Cotton Vitellius C.ix, which is in the hand of Maurice Kyffin and was eventually owned by Dr John Dee; it is printed in Appendix 3.[9]

---

[4]   See *HGK*, pp. cclxxxii–iv. For some instances where the text of Peniarth 17 may not preserve the best readings, see below, p. 42.

[5]   There are three manuscripts in which the Welsh and Latin texts are found side by side: Cotton Vitellius C.ix (B and *B*), Wynnstay 10 (Ch and *F*) and Llanstephan 150 (Dd and *Dd*). For the sigla, see below, p. 3–4.

[6]   P. French, *John Dee* (London, 1972), 188–207; W. H. Sherman, *John Dee: The Politics of Reading and Writing in the English Renaissance* (Amherst, 1995), 148–200; R. J. Roberts, 'Dee, John', *ODNB*; P. Russell, '"Divers evidences antient of some Welsh princes": the Welsh manuscripts and books of Dr John Dee', *Journal of Celtic Studies*, 5 (2005), forthcoming.

[7]   C. Davies, 'The sixteenth-century Latin translation of *Historia Gruffud vab Kenan*', in K. L. Maund (ed.), *Gruffudd ap Cynan: A Collaborative Biography* (Woodbridge, 1996), 157–64.

[8]   'Life of Griffith ap Cynan', ed. R. Williams. The Latin text printed there seems to be that of Peniarth 276, but it has been silently corrected in at least one place: on p. 31, ll. 15–16, the text *filii Catmani . . . filii Caswallani* is not found in the manuscript; it has been restored to correspond to the facing Welsh text where this section of the genealogy is found. For brief discussion, see *HGK* pp. cclxxxv (and n. 139). It was thought to be in the hand of Nicholas Robinson, bishop of Bangor, but this now seems unlikely, see below, p. 15, for further discussion.

[9]   For a full list of the manuscripts, see below, pp. 3–4. For Cotton Vitellius C.ix, see pp. 10–11 and Plate 7. For discussion of the relationship between these fair copies, see pp. 11–15.

The Manuscripts

What follows is not intended to be a full discussion of all the Latin manuscripts of the life of Gruffudd ap Cynan. Simon Evans produced a detailed survey in *HGK*, pp. cclxxiv–cclxxxix. Peniarth 434 will be discussed in some detail, as will Cotton Vitellius C.ix, being the two manuscripts which figure most significantly in this volume.

The Welsh version of the life of Gruffudd ap Cynan is preserved in the following manuscripts:[10]

A   NLW, Peniarth MS 17, pp. 1–16 (*saec.* xiii2)[11]
B   BL, Cotton Vitellius C.ix, fols. 144r–54v (*saec.* xvi2)
C   NLW, Peniarth MS 267, pp. 331–86 (*saec.* xviimed)
Ch   NLW, Wynnstay MS 10, pp. 167–87 (*saec.* xvi2) (copy of C)
D   NLW MS 3075 (= Mostyn 39), pp. 97–121 (*saec.* xvi2)
Dd   NLW, Llanstephan MS 150, fols. 1–40 (*saec.* xvii2) (copy of B)
E   Cardiff Central Library MS 2.388, pp. 7–17 (*saec.* xviii2)
F   NLW, Panton MS 2, pp. 397–428 (*saec.* xviii2)
Ff   NLW, Panton MS 26, pp. 75–160 (*saec.* xviii2) (copy of Ch)
G   NLW MS 53 (= Williams MS 258), pp. 122–42 (*saec.* xviii2) (copy of F)
Ng   NLW MS 119 (= Williams MS 324), pp. 25–106 (*saec.* xviii2) (copy of Ff)
H   NLW MS 13211 (= Llyfr Thelwall), pp. 1–7a (*saec.* xvi2)[12]
J   NLW MS 13215, pp. 283–300 (*saec.* xvi2–xvii1)

According to Evans, there were also some named manuscripts which are no longer extant, such as the Book of Sir Richard Wynn and the Book of Plas y Ward.[13] Evans's analysis of the relationship between these manuscripts is presented in Figure 1.[14] The important point to note is that A (the Peniarth 17 fragment) is independent of the others.

The Latin version of the life of Gruffudd ap Cynan is preserved in the following manuscripts:

---

[10] The sigla for the manuscripts of both the Welsh and the Latin versions are those used by Evans in *HGK*. Evans's distinction between roman capitals for the Welsh text and italic capitals for the Latin is maintained.
[11] This manuscript is fragmentary; it breaks off at a point corresponding to *HGK* 23. 23. The continuation of the text in *HGK* is taken from C (Peniarth 267).
[12] The last two manuscripts were only discovered when *HGK* was reaching its final stages and they were not allocated sigla by Evans; I have allocated them the next two letters (omitting I). For NLW 13215, see *Handlist*, IV, 506–8, which offers an end date of 'late XVII cent.', but nothing seems to have been added after the death of Edward Lhuyd in 1709 (I am grateful to Maredudd ap Huw for this information).
[13] *HGK*, pp. cclxxi– cclxxiii.
[14] *HGK*, p. cclxxiii.

A   NLW, Peniarth MS 434, pp. 1–54 (1575 × 85)
B   BL, Cotton MS Vitellius C.ix, fols. 133r–43v (*saec.* xvi2)
C   Cardiff Central Library MS 4.101 (The Book of Sir John Wynn), fols. 81–8 (*saec.* xvi/xvii)
Ch   Cambridge, Trinity College MS O.v.24, fols. 1–10 (*saec.* xvii1)
D   BL, Additional MS 19712, fols. 1–10 (*saec.* xvi–xvii)
Dd   NLW, Llanstephan MS 150, fols. 1–43 (*saec.* xviii)[15]
E   Cardiff Central Library MS 3.11, pp. 155–84 (*saec.* xvi2)[16]
F   NLW, Wynnstay MS 10, pp. 147–66 (*saec.* xvii2)[17]
Ff   Oxford, Bodley, Jones MS 57, fols. 5–15 (*saec.* xvii)
G   NLW, Peniarth MS 276, pp. 1–12 (*saec.* xvi2)

Fig 1 The relationship between the surviving manuscripts of the Welsh version (cf. *HGK* p.cclxxiii)

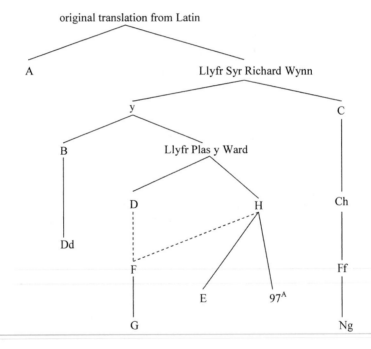

---

[15] This manuscript is dated to the end of the seventeenth century in *HGK*, p. cclx, but Daniel Huws has identified the hand as that of an amanuensis of Moses Williams, and so eighteenth-century in date.

[16] This manuscript does not contain a complete text; it breaks off at a point corresponding to the end of *VGC* §32/9. There is a picture of the first page of *VGC* in this manuscript (p. 155) in *The History of the Gwydir Family*, 70. For discussion of the contents of this manuscript and the sources of the texts, see H. Pryce, 'The church of Trefeglwys', and the end of the "Celtic" charter tradition in twelfth-century Wales', *CMCS*, 25 (Summer 1993), 15–54: pp. 18–22, 53–4.

[17] For discussion of the contents of this manuscript and the sources of the texts, see Pryce, 'Church of Trefeglwys', 18–22, 53–4.

The relationship between these manuscripts is considered below.[18] The present work is primarily concerned with manuscript *A* (Peniarth 434) which is the archetype of all the other copies. The following description is partly dependent on the brief description in *HGK*, pp. cclxxiv–cclxxv and on Daniel Huws's notes on the manuscript.[19]

NLW, Peniarth MS 434. Folio, 28 folios; paper (approx. 305mm × 210mm, but showing signs of trimming and repair) now all guarded as single leaves; the paper has a pot watermark similar to Briquet 12783 (1564–9); paginated 1–56, interleaved, with modern flyleaves; dated *c*.1575–85 (Plates 1–5). The beginning is wanting and the early pages, pp. 1–19, have subsequently been damaged by rodents. The outer top corner of these pages has suffered some loss of text; it is worst on p. 1 and the damage decreases until p. 20 where the text is complete. The first page and the last page (Plate 5) are heavily stained, suggesting that they were the outside pages of the manuscript for some time before binding. Most of the pages show damp staining on the outer five centimetres. The surviving text of p. 1 begins *dicto Hybernice Swrth* . . . The first surviving line of p. 1 is in an italic hand, which Daniel Huws has identified as that of Edward Thelwall. The same hand wrote most of the glosses. There are many surviving documents signed by him in the years when he was on the commission of the peace, 1583–1600 (always with his italic signature 'Edward' (or 'Ed') 'Theloal'), among the gaol files for Denbighshire in the records of Great Sessions. In addition, there are a number of examinations written in his own secretary hand, for example, Great Sessions 4/7/4/28–9 and 4/7/5/47–8, all dated 1588 (including a few words of Latin in his italic hand).[20] The rest of the main text (pp. 1–54) is in the notably assured secretary hand of his amanuensis. The text was then heavily edited throughout by Thelwall; his alterations and annotations form the apparatus of the edition below. The same combination of hands with the same *modus operandi* worked on another manuscript, Peniarth 256, a copy of the Latin text of the Welsh laws (Redaction E).[21] Thomas Wiliems later made further emendations to the text of Peniarth 434 in black ink, marking his contributions by a marginal sign which resembles a flower (see Plate 3). They are collected in section (b) of the apparatus, as are all later notes. Among these is a series of numbers in pencil added interlinearly in the middle of the recto of each folio. They are Alfred Horwood's foliation of the manuscript which he probably had bound and interleaved in the nineteenth century.[22] There is a note by Horwood on the flyleaf of the manuscript to this effect.

---

[18] See pp. 11–15.

[19] See also the *Handlist*, I, 15 (where all the corrections and annotations are attributed to Thomas Wiliems), and E. Bensley, 'Catalogue of Peniarth Manuscripts which are wholly or partly in Latin' (TS, NLW), 85, 'a draft of the Welsh [*sic*] life of Gruffudd ap Cynan'.

[20] For the records of Great Sessions for Wales preserved in the National Library of Wales, Aberystwyth, see G. Parry, *A Guide to the Records of Great Sessions in Wales* (Aberystwyth, 1995).

[21] See below, pp. 17–25, for further discussion.

[22] On Alfred Horwood, see below, p. 6.

On p. 56, apparently in the hand of Edward Thelwall, is the note 'to my L of B[angor]', possibly Nicholas Robinson (d. 1585); on p. 23 'Ricar Myles's book' (s. xvi/xvii). It is perhaps the manuscript referred to as in the possession of Hugh Hughes, vicar of Bangor, in 1760, and at Wig, Llandegái in 1788.[23] It was bought at a sale of the books and manuscripts of Alfred J. Horwood in 1888 by Egerton Phillimore and given by him to W. R. M. Wynne of Peniarth. There is a note by Phillimore on p. i:

> This book was bought by me of Mr Wm Ridler (Bk seller) of 45 Holywell St. Strand in the summer of 1884. He had bought it with other MSS (including a MS of Welsh poetry, that I also bought of him) at the sale of the collection of Alfred J. Horwood Esq., of the Temple. Given Octr 21st 1888 (Sunday) to WRM Wynne, Esq., of Peniarth, as a companion MS to his Hengwrt MS 155, also a translation of the Welsh Life of Gruffudd ap Cynan, and said to be in the autograph of Bishop Robinson.[24]

A section of a letter from Phillimore to W. R. M. Wynne has also been pasted into the manuscript. It is worth quoting in full if only to highlight the negative attitude towards the Latin versions of the life of Gruffudd ap Cynan:[25]

	Ty'n Rhôs
Tuesday October 30th	Cemmes Road R. S. O
1888	Montgomeryshire

P.S. Of course this requires no answer

Dear Wynne,

  Re MSS 155 & 406, many thanks. For you leisurely to consider the suggestions I ventured to make was just what I wanted. I am sure you thanked me most effusively for the MS! It was in my eyes of merely archaeological value: if it had been in Welsh, then it would have been "quite a different pair of shoes". I wish that, some time or other, you would look up the signature of Bp. Robinson at Peniarth mentioned in the Catalogue (under MS 155) and see whether it most tallies with the hand of that MS. or the one I gave you. The latter looks to me by far the older hand.

  I see that there is (or was) at Brogyntyn a MS. of the original Welsh Life of Griffith ap Cynan (found in your MSS. 105 and 406). You might well add that fact into my MS. note at the beginning of the MS. I gave you. It was collated for the text (mainly itself taken from your MS. 406) in the Myvyrian Archaeology: see vol. ii (in oak case in your inner Hall), p. 583 (notes) and the note after "AMEN" on p. 605. Acording to the same authority, there was also then a MS. at Downing and a Plas y Ward MS., written by Edwd Thelwall in 1574. This too you might add to my note.

                          E. G. B. Phillimore[26]

---

[23] A. Llwyd, *A History of the Island of Mona* (Rhuthin, 1833), 72.

[24] The latter manuscript is probably Peniarth 276 (*G*).

[25] The punctuation and underlining are original.

[26] Signature is in red ink in Wynne's hand. The second paragraph is also sidelined in the same red ink. The remainder of the letter is cut off at this point. Part of the next line is visible 'I'm sure [. . .'. On the verso of this fragment, part of the continuation reads: '. . .] is not exactly parallel: for his MSS. (of which he hardly realizes the value, perhaps) are kept just like books, in open cases in the big Library at Shirburn – a room which the family don't use – whereas your MSS. must [. . .] your living [. . .'.

The manuscript in the 'far older hand' is the present manuscript, Peniarth 434, while the other manuscript mentioned is probably Peniarth 276.[27] There is also a note on p. i in Phillimore's hand:

> This MS contains a draft of the Latin Translation of the Welsh Life of Gruffudd ap Cynan (see Hengwrt MSS 275 and 406).
> Note: There is a MS of the original Life in the Cottonian Collection at the British Museum ( ) and of the translation in the Additional MS . . . at the same place.

The gaps were never filled. The Welsh version in the Cottonian collection is presumably that preserved in Cotton Vitellius C.ix (B). The Latin version preserved among the Additional Manuscripts is BL, Additional MS. 19712 (D).

On p. 55 there is a Latin poem on weights and measures. Bensley described it as 'the table of grains, scruples and drachms, etc.'.[28] The end of some of the lines has been lost where the edge of the page has been damaged:

> Grana quarter quinque scrupu[li] pondere su[me
> In drachmam scropulus transit ter multiplicatus
> Si solidam quaeris tres drachmas dimidiabis
> Hexagonum solido differunt in nomine solo[29]
> Constat ex sex solidos, vel ter tribus uncia drach[mis
> Uncia pars librae duodena quis ambigit eff[. . .

It is an extract from the *Schola Salernitana*, a verse rendering of the *Regimen Sanitatis Salernitanum*; it corresponds, with some minor variations, to lines 1588–91 and 1593–4 in de Renzi's edition.[30] Inserted at the back of the manuscript and marked as p. 57 is a money order dated 28 October 1806, in pursuance of a Royal sign manual for the payment of an annuity to Diana Hotham for £100 for the quarter ending on 10 October 1806 and signed by William Wynn.

Edward Thelwall was the eldest son of Simon Thelwall (1526–86) and died on 29 July 1610.[31] In 1583 he became the fourth husband of Catrin o'r Berain (Katheryn of Berain, 1534/5–91) and she his third wife.[32] Through his marriage to her he became stepfather to Sir John Salusbury of Lleweni whose father had been Catrin's first husband.[33] The Thelwall family was also closely associated

---

[27] *HGK*, pp. cclxxiv– cclxxv. On the Downing manuscript, see *HGK*, pp. cclxxxvii– cclxxxviii.
[28] Bensley, 'Catalogue', 85.
[29] This line was added interlinearly in a lighter brown ink.
[30] *Collectio Salernitana*, V, 44; the missing letters are restored from de Renzi's edition.
[31] *Dictionary of Welsh Biography*, 932–3, s.n. Thelwall; see also H. R. Woudhuysen, *Sir Philip Sydney and the Circulation of Manuscripts, 1558–1640* (Oxford, 1996), 318–20.
[32] See J. Ballinger, *Katheryn of Berain, as a study in a North Wales Family History* (London, 1929), 26–7.
[33] See E. A. J. Honigmann, *Shakespeare* (Manchester, 1985), 92, 109–11 (and the family tree on p. 149). Robert Chester dedicated to the son the 1601 volume, *Loues Martyr*, in which Shakespeare's 'The Phoenix and the Turtle' was published. See also *Dictionary of Welsh Biography*, 889–90, s.n. Salusbury; Woudhuysen, *Sir Philip Sydney*, 319. The Thelwalls and the Salusburys were already related as Simon Thelwall, Edward's father, had married Alice Salusbury of Rug whose brother had married into the Llewenni branch of the family; see Jones, *The Wynn Family of Gwydir*, 123.

with the Wynns of Gwydir, who traced their genealogy back to Gruffudd ap
Cynan, and these links were strengthened by Edward's marriage to Catrin; her
previous husband (married before 1573) had been Maurice Wynn of Gwydir and
by marrying him she had become stepmother to Sir John Wynn, and so Edward's
marriage to Katrin made him Wynn's stepfather. Thelwall was prominent in
local public life and, along with other members of his family, is recorded as
serving on the commission of the peace in Denbighshire from 1583 until 1600.[34]
He was also known for his learning and command of languages, and his father
and he had amassed a considerable library; one item known to have been there
was a copy of Philip Sydney's *Old Arcadia*, now Oxford, Jesus College MS 150.[35]
He was included in a list of *gwyrda clodforus* who helped Thomas Wiliems in
the preparation of his Latin–Welsh dictionary.[36] On his death in 1610, several
poets composed *marwnadau* to him, six of which are preserved in BL
Additional MS. 14965, fols. 240r–248r:

'Oer och Iesu yw'r chwesir' (Siôn Cain), fols. 240r–241r
'Diliw fu'ch oes dolef chwyrn' (Rhisiart Phylip), fols. 241r–242v
'Mawr gwyn yng Nghymru ganoes' (Huw Machno), fols. 242v–244r
'Y cur i bawb yw cau'r bedd' (Morys Berwyn), fols. 244r–245r
'Trwy Iesu y daeth i'n tristau' (Richard Cynwal), fols. 245r–246v
'Dyffryn Clwyd aerwy hyd Ial' (Siôn Phylip), fols. 246v–248r[37]

All conventionally praise his ancestry and his fairness on the bench, but the
awdl farwnad of Siôn Phylip also hints at his learning though lamenting its loss
(fol. 247v37–40):

Pob deddf a chyneddf lle'r achwynnyd;
Pob kronigl disigl yna/i/ dwyswyd;
Pob iaith o wythiaith a waethwyd in mysg;
Y ddysc dda a'r addysc a ddiwreiddiwyd.

every law and custom where there was complaint;
every firm chronicle was there made firm;
every language of eight languages has been made worse among us;
great learning and education has been pulled up by the roots.

---

[34] J. R. S. Phillips, *The Justices of the Peace in Wales and Monmouthshire, 1541–1689* (Cardiff, 1957), 58–62; see above, p. 5, for discussion of the surviving documents in his hand.
[35] Woudhuysen, *Philip Sydney*, 318–19.
[36] *Rhagymadroddion*, 114; see also C. Davies, 'The sixteenth-century Latin translation', 160.
[37] Two other *cywyddau* in this manuscript refer to Thelwall, namely: 'Llaw Dduw fyth yn llwyddo fydd' (Harri Hywel) fol. 262r–262v, and 'Y carw rhudd cei air y rhawg' (Simwnt Fychan) fols. 269r–270r. There are also two other poems referring to Edward Thelwall extant: 'Tri achos noter uchod' (Simwnt Fychan), BL, Additional MS. 31080, fol. 216r; Cardiff Central Library MS. 2.201, pp. 163–5; Aberystwyth, NLW, Llanstephan MS. 124, pp. 129–30, and 'Yr aer gwâr eurawg eryr" (Siôn Cain), Aberystwyth, NLW, Peniarth MS. 117, pp. 215–18.

He was Welsh tutor to Edward, Lord Herbert of Cherbury, who said of Thelwall in his autobiography:

> my Parents thought fitt to send mee to some place where I might learne the Welch tongue, as beleeving it necessary to enable mee to treat with those of my freinds and Tennants who understood noe other Language; wherevpon I was recommended to Mr Edward Thellwall of Placeward in Denbighshire. This Gentleman I must remember with honor as having of himselfe acquired the exact knowledge of Greeke Lattaine Frensh Italian and Spanish, and all other Learning, Having for that purpose neither gone beyond seas nor soe much as had the benefitt of any Vniversityes. Besides, he was of that rare Temper in governing his Choller, that I neuer sawe him angry during the tyme of my stay there, and haue heard soe much of him for many years before when occasion of offence was given him. I haue seen him redden in the Face, and after remaine for a while Silent, But when he spake, his words were so calme and gentle, That I found he had digisted his Coller . . .[38]

Edward, Lord Herbert, married Mary, daughter of Sir William Herbert, heir to the Earl of Pembroke.[39] Sir William was a friend of Dr John Dee, and took a house in Mortlake in 1581 presumably to be near Dee. In that period Mary, his daughter, is mentioned in Dee's diary as a 3 year old playing with Dee's son, Arthur.[40] The links between the Thelwalls, Wynns and Dee are of significance for the subsequent manuscript transmission of the Latin version of the life of Gruffudd ap Cynan.[41] As far as can be determined, Thelwall's scribal activity seems to be the product of the early 1570s with no evidence that it continued into his later life when, as we have seen, other matters occupied his time; for example, there are numerous references to his transcriptions made in 1574 of 'Interdictio papae adversus Lewelinum . . .' and 'Literae Lewelini . . .'.[42]

[38] *The Life of Edward*, 14–15; for a modernized text, see *The Autobiography of Edward*, 37–8.
[39] There were ongoing links between the Herberts and the Thelwalls: the brothers of Edward Herbert and Edward Thelwall, Sir Henry and Simon respectively, were neighbours in Essex and shared the Mastership of the Revels in 1629; see Woudhuysen, *Philip Sydney*, 319, n. 5. On Sir William Herbert, see C. Maginn, 'Herbert, Sir William', *ODNB*.
[40] *The Diaries of John Dee*, 23 (s.d. 22, 23 January 1582)
[41] See below, pp. 10–11, on the discussion of Cotton Vitellius C.ix. For links with the Wynns, see *The History of the Gwydir Family*, I. 1–13 (and nn. 77–9); J. G. Jones, *The Wynn Family of Gwydir* (Aberystwyth, 1995), 107, 123 (and the family tree of the Wynns, after p. 280).
[42] See NLW 13211 (*Handlist*, IV, s.n.), also reported in Lhuyd's *Parochialia*, I, 99, Wynnstay 10 (William Maurice's copy), fols. 195v–6v, NLW 1995 (Panton 26), NLW 13215, p. 303 (*Handlist*, IV, s.n.), NLW 3075, pp. 127–34, and BL Additional MS. 14980, fol. 123, etc. A reference in Lhuyd's *Parochialia*, I, 127, if it is reliable, suggests that Edward Thelwall's scribal activity may have begun as early as 1570.

BL, Cotton MS, Vitellius C.ix, fols. 133r–143v;[43] paper.[44] The paper has three pot watermarks, all different from the one in Peniarth 434, and none easily identifiable. The text is printed below in Appendix 3. The edges of the pages show damage from the Cottonian fire of 23 October 1731, though there is only slight damage to the text. The manuscript contains some thirty-five texts, mainly of historical interest, and was compiled in the sixteenth century by or for the antiquarian Arthur Agard (1540–1615, Deputy Chamberlain in the Exchequer). Our text is the first of a group of three texts copied in the same hand, the other two being a copy of the Welsh life of Gruffudd ap Cynan (B above; fols. 144r–154v) and a copy of the text *Am ddiwedd Arthur* (fols. 155r–157v).[45] The hand of this group of texts does not reappear in the manuscript and it looks as if these quires were bound in a composite volume as a group from elsewhere. The hand has been identified by Daniel Huws as that of Maurice Kyffin, who acted as an amanuensis for Dr John Dee;[46] there is an autograph translation by Maurice Kyffin preserved in BL, Cotton Caligula A.vi, fol. 42r. Our text is entitled *Vita Griffini* *filij*/ *Conani, Regis Venedotiae vel Northwalliae*.[47] Above this in a different hand is *Vita Griffini Regis Venedo*[. . .] | *Iurisperito in Latinum conversa*.[48] The gap can be filled by reference to *Dd* (Llanstephan 150) which seems to represent an indirect copy of this manuscript and has preserved the inscription in full; in *Dd* it reads *Vita Griffini Regis Venedotiae a Thelwallo* | *juris perito in Latinum conversa*.[49] There are notes in Cotton Vitellius C.ix in the Welsh sections described above (fols. 144r–57v) in the hand of Dr John Dee, suggesting that parts of the manuscript were in his possession in the second half of the sixteenth

---

[43] The modern foliation includes three folios at the beginning. The original foliation of the manuscript is visible on some pages. The folio references for this manuscript in *RMWL*, II, 1022, have confused the two foliations; it correctly has *VGC* beginning on fol. 133 but then reverts to the older foliation for *HGK* and the text on Arthur which should begin on fols. 144 and 155 respectively. The references are consistent in *CMRW*, 17

[44] See *CMRW*, 17, *RMWL*, II, 1022 (dated to 'circa 1575'), *HGK* pp. cclvii–cclviii, cclxxv. See also *A Catalogue of the Manuscripts in the Cottonian Library*, 425: 'Codex chartaceus, in folio, constans foliis 325 . . . item 9 Vita Griffini, filii Conani, regis Venedotiae vel Northwalliae, a Thelwallo jurisperito Latine versa . . . 130'. For image, see Plate 7.

[45] For details of the last text, see *HGK* p. cclvii, n. 28; for details of the edition, see *Am ddiwedd Arthur*.

[46] Maurice Kyffin was a regular visitor to the Dee household; see *The Diaries of John Dee*, 11 (s.d. 25 October 1580), 45 (s.d. 14 June 1582), 264 (s.d. 7 February 1594); see also *Dictionary of Welsh Biography*, 538, s.n. Kyffin, Morris; Williams, 'Kyffin, Maurice', *ODNB*. It is tempting to think that on one of those dates, or on some other visit (the diaries of Dee are by no means complete), Kyffin delivered his copy of Peniarth 434 to Dee.

[47] The *filij* has been added above in a later hand; see Appendix 3.

[48] The edge of the page has been damaged by fire.

[49] Llanstephan 150 (*s.* xvii2) (*Dd*) contains a copy of the three Welsh texts in Cotton Vitellius C.ix; see *RMWL*, II. ii, 727, *HGK*, pp. cclx, cclxxvi. They are bound in a different order, the Welsh text coming first, but as the manuscript is not continuously foliated it is not clear that the difference in order is significant. The date of *Dd*, eighteenth century, makes it certain that there was at least one intermediate copy between it and *B*, labelled *β* in the stemma in Figure 2; see below, pp. 13–14, for further discussion.

century.[50] In addition, fols. 3–57 of the same manuscript contain a text in Dee's secretary hand, *Correctiones et supplementa Sigeberti Gemblicensis ex manuscriptis per J. Dee*. These works are not noted in any of the contemporary catalogues or lists of Dee's library.[51] Dee's interest in Gruffudd ap Cynan was of long standing; in Dublin, Trinity College MS 634 (E.5.22) there is a marginal note on fol. 2r: 'Mr Simon Thelwall in Northwales hath the historie, of the life of Griffith ap Kynan ap Jago prince of Northwales'.[52] It is not clear whether these words refer to a Latin or a Welsh text; they may refer to the folios preserved in Cotton Vitellius C.ix or more likely to Peniarth 434. It is possible that these folios came into the possession of Arthur Agard during the plundering of Dee's library after his departure to the Continent in September 1583 or during its dispersal after his death in 1609.[53]

The relationship between the surviving manuscripts of the Latin version

The surviving manuscripts of the Latin version of the life of Gruffudd ap Cynan are listed above. The two manuscripts of central importance for this volume have been discussed in detail. What follows takes the priority of Peniarth 434 (*A*) for granted as it will be shown that all the other versions are directly or indirectly fair copies of it. The surviving manuscripts all date from the late sixteenth and early seventeenth centuries.[54] The following discussion is summarized in the stemma in Figure 2. The manuscripts can be divided into two groups: *B*, *Dd*, *E*, *F*, *Ff* and *G* on the one hand and, on the other, *C*, *Ch* and *D*. There are two criteria for the split. First, the omission of sentence §32/11, *Quoties tentarunt Powisiae incolae, at non potuerunt*, is shared by all the manuscripts in the first group while the sentence is retained in the second.[55] Secondly, the first group shows no indication that the annotations of Thomas Wiliems were present in manuscript *A* when the archetype of this group was

---

[50] See *John Dee's Library Catalogue*, 163 (DM 35). For discussion of Dee's interest in Welsh manuscripts, see Russell, "Divers evidences antient".

[51] There are lists dating from 1556 and 1557 and a catalogue of 1583; see *John Dee's Library Catalogue*.

[52] See *John Dee's Library Catalogue*, 19, n. 15 (the manuscript in question is *John Dee's Library Catalogue*, DM 18). This note is undatable but another note by Dee on fol. 36v of the same manuscript also relates to manuscripts in Wales; it refers to Archdeacon Crowley and is datable to after 1559.

[53] Sherman, *John Dee*, 30–1.

[54] Evans discusses the relationship between these manuscripts at *HGK*, pp. cclxxviii–cclxxxii, but his discussion is skewed by his assumption that they represent a translation of the Welsh text and he is predominantly concerned with trying to establish which Welsh text was used as the basis for the translation. Nevertheless, there is much of importance in what he says, although in some cases the line of argument has to be reversed.

[55] For the style of reference to the text of *VGC* edited in this volume, see p. 50.

Fig 2 The relationship between the surviving manuscripts of the Latin version

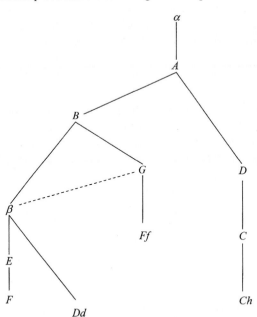

copied, but they have been incorporated into the manuscripts of the second group. The archetype of the second group, therefore, was copied later than the archetype of the first group.

We may take the sub-groups in chronological order. The first group of manuscripts (*B*, *Dd*, *E*, *F*, *Ff* and *G*), which does not contain Thomas Wiliems' annotations, is more complicated to unravel. Some of the relationships considered here have already been noted by Evans; for example, he noted that there was a close relationship between *E* and *F* and between *Ff* and *G*.[56] The difficulty with this group is that the texts are very similar and therefore the evidence for deciding upon their relationship is exiguous. One item of textual evidence, however, can give some room for manoeuvre. At *VGC* §14/2 the basic text reads *Gwrgeneus filius Caecilii*.[57] In *B* there is a gloss in the right margin giving further genealogical detail, *mab Ithel mab Gwerystan etc.* In *Dd* this has been incorporated into the text *verbatim*, and likewise in *E*, *F* and *G* where it has been Latinized as *filii Ithel filii Gwerystan etc.* On that evidence *B* is the archetype of this group and is a fair copy of *A*. The title and the surrounding texts are also important. In *B* *VGC* is followed by a copy of *HGK* and a text on the death

[56]   *HGK*, p. cclvvviii, n. 108.
[57]   The text of this phrase in the edition below is composite: the latter part has been lost where the page was damaged; the gap has been filled from *B* and is identical in the other manuscripts as well.

of Arthur, all in the same hand.[58] In *Dd* the same three texts are copied; as the manuscript is presently bound, they are not in the same order but this may be not significant as there is no continuous foliation in *Dd*. The title of the text is identical in both *B* and *Dd* in that they both have the double title including the reference to Edward Thelwall; this enables us to use the title in *Dd* to restore the section of the title in *B* lost in the Cottonian fire.[59] The title in *Dd* has been further annotated, *In Lat. trad. per N. R. ep. B.* 'translated into Latin by Nicholas Robinson, bishop of Bangor'. Both this and part of the title have also been given a further annotation referring to another copy in *Cod. Seb.*, referring to the library of Sir John Sebright which was sold in London in 1807.[60] In other words, *Dd* seems to be a more or less exact copy of *B*. As we shall see, *E* seems to be a copy of *Dd*, but that presents a problem in that *Dd* was copied in the eighteenth century by an amanuensis of Moses Williams, while *E* belongs to the second half of the sixteenth century. Evidence for the status of *E* is presented below, but it looks as if *E* was copied from the exemplar of *Dd* indicated in the stemma in Figure 2 by *β*.

G is also a copy of *B*, but the process of copying has not been quite so faithful. It is striking that the text of *VGC* in *G* is surrounded by several hundred blank pages; there are one hundred and forty numbered pages before the text and a similar amount after it.[61] It looks as if the intention had been to copy the other texts from *B* as well, but that project was never realized and the pages remained empty. The main title in *G* is copied from *B*, but the surtitle which attributes the translation to Thelwall has been omitted. There is an ownership note by Robert Vaughan of Hengwrt in the top left-hand corner. The scribe of *G* was not averse to making the occasional change of wording and adjustment to the Latin spelling and to the spelling of the Welsh names;[62] for example, at *VGC*, §12/3 (= *B*, fol. 135r31) *profecti* has been misread as *praefecti*; at the end of *VGC*, §17/2 (= *B*, fol. 137r17) he added another main verb, *appulit*; at *VGC*, §17/7 (= *B*, fol. 137r28) he replaced the adverb *assidue* with *quotidie*; at *VGC*, §32/9 (= *B*, fol. 142v22) he corrected the spelling *discenderet* to *descenderet*. In most respects, however, it is clearly a copy of *B*. *Ff* may be dealt with easily. This is a copy of *G* and does not differ in any significant way from it.[63]

E and *F* remain to be discussed. At first glance *E* looks like a copy of *G*; for example, it shares all the readings unique to *G* listed above.[64] However, in terms

---

[58] See p. 10 above for details.

[59] See p. 10 above, and also *HGK*, p. cclxxvi.

[60] This may well be *E*; see *HGK*, p. cclxxvi; Huws, *Medieval Welsh Manuscripts*, 298.

[61] *HGK*, p. cclxxviii.

[62] This manuscript has been thought to be in the hand of Nicholas Robinson, bishop of Bangor (see *HGK*, p. cclxxvii, n. 105; 'Life of Griffith ap Cynan', ed. Williams, 131), but there is no evidence to indicate that this is so. For a discussion of Robinson's role in the production of *VGC*, see p. 15 below.

[63] *HGK*, p. cclxxvii, attributed erroneously to Robert Vaughan.

[64] *HGK*, pp. cclxxvi–cclxxvii.

of its title and heading, it is clearly derived from β (represented by *Dd*), especially in having *In Lat. trad. per N. R. ep. B*. For the explanation we need to return briefly to β and *Dd*. Subsequent to its copying from *B*, β was collated with *G* and at various points, notably in the cases listed above where *G* has altered the text, the *G* reading has been added interlinearly; the interlinear arrangement of these additions was preserved in *Dd*. The text of *E* can be best explained as being a fair copy of β after β had been collated with *G*. *F* is a copy of *E*. It was subsequently collated with another text, probably a Welsh text of *HGK*, perhaps *Ch* with which it is bound in NLW, Wynnstay 10.[65]

We may now turn to the other smaller group, *C*, *Ch* and *D*, which is distinguished by two features: it has retained *VGC*, §32/11, and it is derived from *A* after Thomas Wiliems had made his annotations to that manuscript, with the result that these have been incorporated into the text. In short, *D* is the archetype of this group.[66] *C* is a reworked copy of it, and *Ch* is a copy of *C*. But this rather bald summary conceals some very interesting developments. *D* is a fair copy of *A* (including Thomas Wiliems's notes). But there is one other difference between the two groups of manuscripts and that has to do with the genealogies at the beginning of the text. As will be discussed below, the genealogies in the Peniarth 434 (*A*) version of *VGC* differ from the genealogies in *HGK* in two places where in error they have omitted sections of the genealogy (the missing sections are restored in brackets, [ ]): §2/1, *fil. Cadwaledri Benedicti, fil. Cadwallawn* [*fil. Catmani, fil. Iacobi, fil. Beli, fil. Runi, fil. Maglocuni, fil. Caswallani*] *manus oblongae*, §2/2 *fil. Gurwsti*, [*fil. Riwalloni, fil. Regatae, filiae Lyri, fil. Rudi, fil. Bladudi, fil. Llywelit*] *fil. Bruti Ysgwydwyn*. The latter gap was noticed by Thelwall and he added the omitted section above (p. 2.2-).[67] That section then found its way into the fair copies and thus all nine derivative manuscripts have the second section of genealogy restored. However, Thelwall failed to notice the first gap, and so the same gap is preserved in the fair copies; that section of genealogy has not been restored in *B* or in any of its descendants, nor was it restored in *D*. However, after *D* was copied by William Lloyd, an amanuensis of Wynn, it was subject to very heavy annotation and alteration. Much of that alteration was stylistic; for example, the opening sentence about Edward reigning in England and Therdelach in Ireland was turned into an ablative absolute construction as opposed to the temporal clause of the original.[68] Another annotation restored the text of the missing section of the genealogy interlinearly, presumably from a Welsh text as no other Latin text could have supplied the information. *C* is a fair copy of the very untidy product which *D*

---

[65] *HGK*, p. cclxxvii; cf. also pp. cclviii–cclix.
[66] For *D*, see *HGK*, pp. cclxxv–cclxxvi; for *C* and *Ch*, *HGK*, p. cclxxv.
[67] Where the early pages of Peniarth 434 (*A*) are damaged along the top edge, line references are counted from the bottom of the page which has remained intact; this is indicated by a minus sign after the line number.
[68] See below, pp. 40–1, for further discussion on the stylistic features of the annotations in this manuscript.

had become; *C* is in the hand of Sir John Wynn himself and he may have been responsible for the annotation in *D* by William Lloyd.[69] Subsequently, the manuscript was annotated by Thomas Wiliems. There is a nice symmetry in the way that, just as *A* was heavily annotated and fair copies were made of it, so *D* was heavily annotated and a fair copy, *C*, was made of it. *Ch* requires little discussion; it is a copy of *C*. The above discussion is summarized in the stemma in Figure 2.

In a number of the manuscripts considered above, the creation of a Latin translation of *HGK* has been attributed to Nicholas Robinson, but the textual history shows that such an attribution seems to be secondary; *B* attributes the translation to Thelwall, and *Dd* (representing *β*) has that heading to which is added an attribution to Robinson, while in *E*, which is a copy of *β*, the Thelwall attribution has been silently removed but the Robinson attribution preserved.[70] Given that *A*, demonstrably the archetype of the other versions, is partially in the hand of Edward Thelwall and fully glossed and annotated by him, it is certain that the attribution to Robinson is incorrect. The reattribution to Robinson in manuscripts containing an attribution to Thelwall seems to have occurred in those manuscripts which passed through the hands of the Wynn family, and it is possible that there was a deliberate attempt on their part to write Thelwall out of the story. One possibility is that Thelwall's marriage to Katrin o'r Berain, which made him stepfather to Sir John Wynn, and the simultaneous marriage of Simon, Edward Thelwall's son, to Jane Wynn, daughter of Katrin o'r Berain and Maurice Wynn and stepsister to Sir John Wynn, brought the Thelwall family into too close a relationship for the liking of Sir John and gave rise to personal dislike.

The evidence for an original Latin life of Gruffudd ap Cynan

It has always been assumed that there was a lost Latin life lying behind the extant Middle Welsh life. Apart from a general assumption that any life of a Welsh king composed in the twelfth century was probably in Latin, there are a number of features of the Welsh text which point in the same direction.

(a) Welsh names, and especially place names, are characteristically made up of elements which are also attested as common nouns or as adjectives; as such, their 'meaning' would be perspicuous to a speaker of Welsh. However, in *HGK* they are frequently subject to etymological analysis; for example, *y lle a elwir yg*

---

[69] For a discussion of the stylistic changes wrought on the text, see C. Davies, 'Sixteenth-century Latin translation', 161–5, who thinks it is a feature of *C* alone when in fact the changes have already been added in *D*; cf. also Jones's comments (*HGC*, 11–12).

[70] For previous discussion, see *HGK*, pp. cclxxx–cclxxxii, Davies, 'Sixteenth-century Latin translation', 159–61.

Kymraec Gvaet Erw, neu y Tir Gvaetlyt, 'the place called in Welsh Gwaed Erw, or the Bloody Field' (*HGK*, 9. 4–5 = *MPW*, 61. 16–17); *E menyd, hagen, y bu e vrwyder endaw a eilw kiudaut e wlat Menyd Carn. Sef yu henne menyd e garned* 'However, the mountain on which the battle was fought the people of the land call Mynydd Carn, namely the mountain of the cairn' (*HGK*, 16.13–14 = *MPW*, 68. 36–69. 1). Such a practice is perfectly reasonable within a Latin text, even perhaps in a Latin text intended predominantly for Welsh speakers, but it makes no real sense in a Welsh text where common Welsh words are explained by other common Welsh words.[71] The technique can be paralleled in Latin by the practice of, for example, Giraldus Cambrensis: *Kairarvon, id est castrum de Arvon* (*Itinerarium Kambriae*, 124), *Porthmaur Meneviae, id est Portu magno, usque Ridhelic quod Britannice Vadum salicis* (*Descriptio Kambriae*, 165).[72] From an earlier period and slightly further afield, we may compare how Asser deals with place names in his Life of Alfred explaining English names both in Latin and Welsh: *in orientali parte saltus qui dicitur Seluudu, Latine autem sylva magna Britannice Coit Maur* 'in the eastern part of Selwood Forest (*sylva magna* [great wood] in Latin, and *Coit Maur* in Welsh)' (*Asser's Life of King Alfred*, 55. 7–8 = *Alfred the Great*, 84 (§55)), *Snotengaham adiit, quod Britannice Tigguocobauc interpretatur, Latine autem speluncarum domus* '(the Viking army) reached Nottingham (which is called *Tig Guocobauc* in Welsh, or *Speluncarum Domus* [house of caves] in Latin' (*Asser's Life of King Alfred*, 30. 2–5 = *Alfred the Great*, 77 (§30)).

(b) In one instance, *a Remys y gan Remo* (*HGK*, 4. 13), where the origin of the name for modern Rheims is explained as coming from Remus, brother of Romulus, the name preserved in the Welsh text is *Remo*, apparently preserving the ablative case of the original Latin *a Remo*. In the preceding phrase, *Ruvein y gan Romulus*, *Romulus* has been restored to the nominative. The Latin text edited here is damaged in places and this section is missing, but it can be restored from the later copies as *a Remo Rhemi* (see below §5/11).[73]

(c) Merlin's prophecy about Gruffudd ap Cynan (*HGK*, 5. 20 = *MPW*, 58. 6–12; cf. §8/2 below) is preserved in the Welsh text in both Welsh and Latin.[74] If the text had originally been composed in Welsh, there would have been no reason for the prophecy to be in Latin. The metrical patterns of the Welsh version suggest it is the original, but *VGC* only has the Latin version. It may well be that in text perceived to be in Latin the Welsh version has fallen out in the course of transmission.

[71] See *HGK*, pp. ccxxvii–ccxxviii; *HGC*, 14–16.
[72] For discussion of Giraldus, see S. Zimmer, 'A medieval linguist', *EC*, 35 (2003), 313–50; these examples are to be found on pp. 325 and 328 respectively.
[73] On the background to this, see below, p. 50.
[74] See the discussion in the notes to §8.

(d) The use of cumbersome cross-referencing phrases which work more satisfactorily in Latin than in Welsh, for example, *dywededigyon . . . uchof* (*HGK*, 15. 2–3): *praedicti* (§18/3), *a dywetpvyt uchof* (*HGK*, 17. 3 (varr. *uchot*)): *prius nominatum* (§19/2), etc.

One further point is suggestive rather than central to the argument:

(e) Evans pointed to the title *Historia*, as opposed to *Hanes* or *Buchedd*, as in-dicating a Latin origin.[75] The title in *VGC* is *Vita* (see Notes, title (p. 125)) and matches the use of *Vita* in, for example, Einhard's Life of Charlemagne. It is sug-gested in the Notes that *buchedd* might have been felt to be too hagiographical.

Digression: the early manuscript tradition of Latin Redaction E of the Welsh laws

Before going on to consider the relationship between Peniarth 434 and the Welsh text of the life of Gruffudd ap Cynan in greater detail, a digression is in order, since the key to that relationship lies in the interrelationship of the three earliest extant manscripts of Redaction E of the Latin laws of medieval Wales. Since Hywel Emanuel's edition of the Latin laws in 1967 (*LTWL*), they are con-ventionally divided into five redactions. The fifth of these redactions, Latin E, is preserved in three manuscripts: [76]

Lat E1   Cambridge, Corpus Christi College MS, 454 (s. xv¹)
Lat E2   Oxford, Merton College MS, 323 (s. xvi²) (written by Dr John Dee)[77]
Lat E3   NLW, Peniarth MS, 256 (s. xvi²)

Emanuel printed the text of E1 as his main text and added variants from E2 and E3 in the apparatus.[78] He claimed that the three manuscripts represented three versions of the same archetype; for him the relationsip between the manu-scripts was as presented in Figure 3.[79] However, it emerges that there are signi-ficant differences between the three versions which cannot be explained by a common archetype. For our purposes, Peniarth 256 (E3) is the crucial version.[80] It is heavily annotated and Daniel Huws has identified the hand of the annotator

---

[75] *HGK*, 35, n. 1; for further discussion, see B. F. Roberts, 'Ystoria', *BBCS*, 26 (1974–5), 13–20.
[76] For details, see *LTWL*, 408–13. Later manuscripts of this redaction all derive from one of these three manuscripts; see *LTWL*, 413–18; aspects of Emanuel's discussion of the later manuscripts are in need of revision, but they do not affect the current discussion.
[77] This manuscript is listed as DM 160 in *John Dee's Library Catalogue*, 182.
[78] *LTWL*, 434–509.
[79] *LTWL*, 418 (simplified).
[80] For a description of the manuscript see *LTWL*, 412–13; see also *RMWL* I.i, 1072, T. Lewis, 'Bibliography of the laws of Hywel Dda', *Aberystwyth Studies*, 10 (1928), 151–82: pp. 164–5.

Fig 3 Emanuel's stemma for the relationship between the early manuscripts of Redaction E

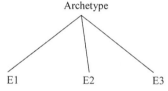

as that of Edward Thelwall and the main hand of the basic text (probably an amanuensis) as the same hand which wrote the bulk of the main text of Peniarth 434.[81] In other words, the same hands were involved in the production of both these manuscripts and the production seems to have been carried out in the same way.

The basic text of Peniarth 256 (E3) underlying all the annotation and correction is essentially a copy of Cambridge, Corpus Christi College MS, 454 (E1), a manuscript of the Parker collection.[82] The text of Oxford, Merton College MS, 323 (E2) is more closely related to that of Peniarth 256 than Emanuel realised. In all respects it is a fair copy of Peniarth 256 written by Dr John Dee ignoring all the deletions but incorporating all the additions.[83] Peniarth 256 was also copied

[81] See Plate 6. The link with Thelwall is supported by a note on fol. 6 (inverted) 'Simon Thelwall –
     2s', a money account relating to Simon Thelwall of Plas y Ward (d. 1586), possibly representing
     earlier use of the manuscript.

[82] The prologue of this manuscript is defective: the text ends with one line to spare at the bottom of
     fol. 1r; the verso is blank, and one folio is missing before the text apparently resumes at the top of
     fol. 2r (present foliation). It is not clear whether the prologue was copied into Peniarth 256 as the
     Peniarth manuscript is lacking at least its first folio; the text begins *et ciphus aureus* (corresponding
     to *LTWL*, 436. 23). Merton 323 acquired another prologue, and Peniarth 225 (a copy of Peniarth
     256 made by Thomas Wiliems in 1594) has several empty pages at the beginning before the laws of
     court. Presumably Peniarth 256 did not have a prologue, or at least not a complete prologue which
     was worth copying. Emanuel printed both the defective prologue from E1 and the prologue in E2
     (*LTWL*, 434–5). I hope to provide a full discussion of the manuscript tradition of Latin E
     elsewhere. For a text and translation of the prologues to Latin E1 and E2, see P. Russell, *The
     Prologues to the Medieval Welsh Lawbooks* (Cambridge, 2004), 31–7.

[83] See Plate 8. The date of the Merton manuscript is by no means clear. Emanuel (*LTWL*, 411), who
     did not recognise the main hand as that of Dee but did accept that the manuscript had belonged to
     him, notes that the Merton manuscript does not figure in Dee's own catalogue compiled by him
     and dated 6 September 1583, and so was written after that date (Emanuel's word is 'acquired').
     Huws, 'Texts', in Charles-Edwards et al. (eds), *Lawyers and Laymen* (Cardiff, 1986), 136, suggests
     that Dee wrote the manuscript between 1585 and 1588, since in his pedigree in the margin of fol. 1r
     the births of his first four children are recorded in the first block of writing, including Michael
     Pragensis who was born in Prague in 1585, while the births of the other four children, born
     between 1588 and 1595, are later additions. Dee's interest in the 'matter of Britain,' and his own
     place within it came to a peak in the period from 1570 up to about 1583, and it is likely that the
     copying of the Merton manuscript was within this period; see R. J. Roberts, 'John Dee and the
     matter of Britain' *THSC* (1991), 129–43. Furthermore, Dee left England on 21 Sept. 1583 for the
     continent, not to return until 22 Nov. 1589 (*Diaries of John Dee*, 104, 246, respectively). Since it is
     unlikely that the copying of the text took place outside the country, it was probably copied before
     1583 but not included in his 1583 catalogue. The note of the births of his first four children is in
     red ink and could well have been added later than the copying of the main text. Indeed, he may
     well have taken the copied manuscript text with him and added the pedigree subsequently after the
     birth of Michael; it seems likely, to judge from the annotation on the 1583 catalogue, that he took
     his four Welsh printed books to the continent with him (*John Dee's Library Catalogue*, 49) and he

by Thomas Wiliems in Peniarth 225 in about 1594, and by William Maurice in Wynnstay 38 in 1662.[84]

Peniarth 256 was written by three hands:

A   Edward Thelwall (main text: fols. 1r–v, 33–34r, 53–4, 56)
B   amanuensis of A (main text: all not written by hands A and C)
C   amanuensis of A (main text: fols. 2r–v, 34v, 36r–v)

The manuscript was subsequently heavily glossed and edited by hand A (Edward Thelwall). In other words, it looks as if Peniarth 256 (E3) and Merton 323 (E2) stand in the same relationship to each other as do Peniarth 434 and, for example, the Cotton Vitellius C.ix version of *VGC*. Emanuel's stemma should, therefore, be revised as in Figure 4.

Fig 4 The revised stemma for the early manuscripts of Redation E

Archetype
|
E1
|
E3
|
E2

The nature of the editing and glossing in Peniarth 256 is worth examining in greater detail. It would appear that the glossing and editing hand (probably Edward Thelwall) worked on the manuscript on several separate occasions. The layers can be distinguished by ink colour. The main text is in a brown ink varying from a pale to a very dark brown upon which three levels of additions are discernible:[85] a first layer in a pale brown ink, a second in dark brown ink (in places almost black), and a third layer in the same pale brown colour as the first layer; for example, the first layer of glossing can be clearly seen at Peniarth 256, fol. 59v12–16 (= *LTWL*, 504. 1–3) on the six instances where *ceidwaid* are required (glosses are in brackets): *In sex locis debent esse ketweit* (gl. *.i. tutores uel conseruatores*): *videlicet, kadw tir a daiar* (gl. *.i. tueri terram*), *kadw cyn colli* (gl. *.i. custodire secum ante perdicionem*), *kadw geni a meithrin* (gl. *.i. attestari nativitatem et educationem*), *kadw guesti* (gl. *.i. tueri commorationem*), *kadw breint* (gl. *.i. conseruare libertatem*), *kadw alltudiaeth* (gl. *.i. propugnare exilium*);

may well have packed some of his Welsh manuscripts. The manuscript was still in Dee's possession in 1600 when he added on one of the flyleaves at the front of the manuscript a calculation about a prognosticated reform of Welsh law in 666 years after their creation by his ancestor, Hywel Dda (Huws, 'Texts', 136). For further discussion, see Russell, "'Divers evidences antient'".

[84]   See *LTWL*, 414, 417 respectively.

[85]   There are also two additions in red ink: on fol. 8v10 and 13 he added the word *numel(l)as* twice, the first case glossing *tauilhualeu* and in the second *kenlleuaneu*.

the second can be seen in the correction to the last gloss where the ending of *exilium* was deleted and it was changed to *ab exilatione*.[86] The second layer of glosses in a dark, almost black, ink, presumably represents a second visit to the manuscript, in some cases correcting his earlier efforts but in others writing fresh glosses.[87] The last layer is distinguishable from the first layer in that in places it overwrites the second layer of dark ink glosses; for example, at fol. 16r7 *Pro tecto lxxx denarios nisi fuerint tigna* (= *LTWL*, 453. 11–12), *pro* is deleted and replaced by *in*, and the rest apart from *tecto* is also deleted and *scilicet sunt octaginta sex columnae* added in a dark ink; subsequently, in a light brown ink *ipsius aulae* over *sunt octaginta* was added, *columnae* was deleted and *tigna* was added above it in a slightly darker ink.[88] In short, alterations to the manuscript were carried out over a period of time and seem to be the result of several visits.

Different types of annotation can also be distinguished. Welsh terms were glossed in Latin (see the example above on *ceidwaid*) and occasionally in Greek; for example, on fol. 11v11–13 (= *LTWL*, 448. 11–12) *naw affeith* is glossed by *novem accessoria*, the latter word being glossed by Greek συναιτία. Longer sections of text in Welsh are usually deleted completely; for example, the triad on *teir meuylwryaeth* at fol. 21r17–20 (= *LTWL*, 459. 12–14), or the section on 'nines' at fol. 52ʳ14–20 (= *LTWL*, 495. 20–5). Some sections of text have been rewritten perhaps after collation with another text; this is discussed in detail below. There are a few instances where Thelwall makes his own comment; for example, in a passage on the *edling* (fol. 1v1 = *LTWL*, 437. 10) he adds a comment in the top margin to the effect that the *edling* is like a prince in England or the Dauphin in France: *ut princeps in Anglia vel Delphinus in Francia* (the last word then deleted and *Gallia* added).[89]

For our purposes the question of whether he was collating his base text with other manuscripts is of particular interest. All the indications suggest that he was doing this with several other manuscripts. A survey of the annotation of Peniarth 256 shows that almost all of it derives from the Blegywryd and Cyfnerth redactions. In many cases, it is impossible to tell which, as the text is much the same in both and Thelwall's annotation is translated into Latin, thus preventing direct access to the Welsh text. An important passage, however, is found on fol. 23v4–17; the text (corresponding to *LTWL*, 461. 23–33) is as follows:

Ex tribus fit *dirwy*: viz., pugna, furto, *treis*. Duplex autem fit *dirwy* in curia et in ecclesia, et duplex *camlvry*. Que ecclesia si matrix fuerit, de pugna que in cemiterio eius agitur xiiii libras habebit. Si vero extra in villa, septem. Quarum medietas abbati cedet si

---

[86] Cf. also Peniarth 256, fol. 10r16–19, for a heavily glossed section on the cook, where two levels of glossing can be discerned.

[87] For example, the glosses at fol. 32v10 are in different colours and may well represent two separate glossing sessions.

[88] For another example, see fol. 18r20 (= *LTWL*, 455. 28).

[89] Only the last few words survive in this manuscript, but the comment was copied by Dr John Dee and survives intact in Merton 323, fol. 3r14–15 with a note by Dee added in the left margin.

legalis sit, id est, si ecclesiastica doctrina instructus, et litteratus; altera medietas presbiteris[90] et canonicis. Talis diuisio fit inter abbatem et presbiteros de pugna illorum qui ab abbate uel presbiteris refugium accipiunt. Sicque diuiditur omne quod tantummodo sancto, non altari nec alii oblatum, erogatur. ✗ Tres sunt lire legales: uidelicet, lira regis, optimatis, penkerd.

In the left-hand margin of this passage, Thelwall wrote, in black ink with a cross as a reference mark in the text before the final sentence of the above passage, *pagina fere hic deest quae est in Brytanico textu* 'almost a page is missing here which is in the Welsh text'. In other words, he had a manuscript in Welsh next to him which he was collating with our text and he found that at this point the texts did not match and that there was a passage in the Welsh manuscript which was not in our text. The passage has to do with triads. Two triads are given, the first on *dirwy*, the second on harps, and Thelwall's cross is inserted between the two triads. Not all the redactions of Welsh law contain triads and consideration of the arrangement of triads suggests that Thelwall had at his elbow a manuscript of the Blegywryd redaction; the Iorwerth redaction does not contain many triads and certainly does not contain these particular triads; while the Cyfnerth redaction does contain triads, there is no triad on harps in the Cyfnerth corpus and the triad on *dirwy* takes a different form.[91] Manuscripts of the Blegywryd redaction fall into two groups depending on the arrangement of triads. There is one group where the triads occur in several blocks throughout the text;[92] manuscripts L (BL Cotton MS, Titus D.ix (s. xiv[med])) and J (Oxford, Jesus College MS, 57 (*c*.1400)) are of this type. But in manuscripts such as O (NLW, Peniarth MS, 36A (*c*.1300)) or Tr (Cambridge, Trinity College MS, O.vii.I (*c*.1300)) the triads are arranged in a single big block. In terms of printed versions of the Blegywryd redaction, the former group is represented by the edition of J, the latter by the text edited as *Llyfr Blegywryd*.[93] The description given in Thelwall's marginal note, in which he describes the triad on *dirwy* and triad on harps being separated by about a page of text, best fits a manuscript of the L or J type and not one like O or Tr. This is well illustrated by a comparison of the page numbers of the two different printed texts of Blegywryd manuscripts: *Cyfreithiau Hywel Dda*, 32. 6–17 (*dirwy*) and 33. 15–18 (*telyn*), but *Llyfr Blegywryd* 42. 29–43. 13 (*dirwy*) and 18. 8–9 (*telyn*) respectively. In all the manuscripts of the former type, these two triads are approximately a manuscript page apart (depending on the size of the manuscript page), while in the latter

---

[90] The manuscript (fol. 23v11) has *presbitis* with *er* added above the *ti*.
[91] Cf. *Welsh Medieval Law*, ed. Wade-Evans, 123.
[92] For the sigla of Welsh law manuscripts employed in the following section, see the abbreviations listed above, pp. xiii–iv and for a full list, see Charles-Edwards, et al. (eds), *The Welsh King and his Court*, 576–77. For the dates of the manuscripts, see Huws, *Medieval Welsh Manuscripts*, 57–64.
[93] For the printed text of J, see *Cyfreithiau Hywel Dda*.

type of Blegywryd text the triads occur up to twenty pages apart and in reverse order.

There is another case where he is making use of a Blegywryd manuscript. At fol. 5v17 in a passage on the *hospicia* of the members of the court towards the end of the section on the entitlement of the *penteulu*, a cross has been inserted in the text and there is a faint marginal note on a damaged edge of the page which seems to read *hic deest* 'here something is missing'. Nothing more was added, but when this manuscript was copied by Dr John Dee in Merton 323 he copied this marginal query and pursued it, and at the equivalent point (fol. 6r right margin, ll. 10–17; see Plate 8) in his manuscript copy he added the following (corresponding to the printed text in *Llyfr Blegywryd*, 10. 26–11. 9):

> Haec omissa sunt per interpretem quae tamen in Britanico textu habentur. Os is kynted heuyt i deila yn gynt nor Distein, y traian hefyd a geiff. Y eistedua a uyd yn y tal issaf ir Neuad ar teulu y gyt ac ef. At y llaw asseu idaw at a drûs. Mab yr brenhin neu ney idau a dyly bot yn Benteulu.
>
> Or gat y Brenhin vn or teulu ar var gantaw hyt odis y Penntan; y Pennteulu bieu y wahaûd at gynhal y gyt ac ef, os myn. Ac ef bieu kymryt yr henuryat a vynho ar y deheu. Ac arall ar y asseu. March yn wosseb a dyly y gan y Brenhin. Rann deuvarch idau or ebrann.

Daniel Huws has identified the quoted text as one of the Blegywryd redaction and more specifically the text is closest to the reading of L which is known to have been in Dee's possession at some point as it contains a note in his hand (fol. 59).[94]

In sum, then, Edward Thelwall was annotating and correcting his text of the Redaction E of the Latin laws by reference to a Blegywryd manuscript similar to L or J. Precisely which manuscript it might have been is probably impossible to tell, partly because the annotations are always translated into Latin. One way of making progress on this would be to attempt to establish which of the relevant manuscripts might have been in the north in the second half of the sixteenth century. We know, for example, that Peniarth 31 (R) and Wynnstay 36 (Q), both of which are Blegywryd manuscripts and have the same arrangement of triads as L and J, belonged to Meredith Lloyd and were therefore in north Wales in the first half of the seventeenth century at least.[95] It is possible that one of these came into the possession of Edward Thelwall in the later sixteenth century.

However, even allowing for the vagaries of translation, not all the major annotations in Peniarth 256 can be matched with a Blegywryd text of this type, and it raises the question of whether he had another text to hand as well. One passage is particularly suggestive. It concerns the value of buildings and parts

---

[94] Huws, 'Texts', 136; Daniel Huws was not aware that Thelwall had already identified a gap in the text.

[95] N. Lloyd, 'Meredith Lloyd', 151, 184.

of buildings. It has the advantage of being a list of technical terms, and so is more amenable to analysis than a passage of translated Welsh. Three versions of the text are presented below (sentence numbering is editorial): (a) the text of E1 (*LTWL*, 453. 14–24 (Cambridge, Corpus Christi 454)), (b) the text of Peniarth 256 with all the annotations and corrections indicated as clearly as possibleb (cf. Plate 6), and (c) John Dee's fair copy in Merton 323 with the passages underlined which derive from the glossing and corrections in Peniarth 256.

(a) E1 (LTWL, 453. 14–24)

[1]De precio domorum
[2]Precium domus yemalis est: de qualibet furca que sustinet laquear, id est, *nenbren*, xx denarii. [3]Pro *nenbren* xl denarii. [4]Si denudetur, tercia pars tocius domus redditur. [5]Columpne, bancce, *ystlisseu, hinniogeu, gordrysseu, dupist, dor*, quodlibet istorum iiii denarios legales ualet. [6]Pro domo estiuali xl denarii si comburatur. [7]Et nota quod cum cuiuslibet predictarum domorum precio et precium dampni rerum intus perditarum redditur. [8]Precium auctumpnalis domus: xxiiii denarii. [9]Precium estiualis domus: xii denarii. [10]Furce estiualis domus uel auctumpnalis: denarius legalis. [11]*Dorglwid* ii denarii legales. [12]*Clwyt* i denarius legalis.

(b) E3 (Peniarth 256, fo. 16r–v)

[1]~~De precio domorum~~

.i. valet
[2]Precium domus yemalis est: de qualibet furca que sustinet laquear, id est, *nenbren*, ∧xxx

Beigkiau .i. . . .
xxx denudetur ~~Ceinciau~~ et
denarii. [3]Pro *nenbren* ~~xl~~ denarii. [4]~~Si denudetur,~~ tertia pars totius domus redditur. [5]~~Columpne,~~

.i. .... .i. .... .i. ostia .i. .... .i. ostiola .i. limen
et Talbeigkiau et styffyleu et doreu et kynhor gordrysseu trothwy Tubyst quodlibet eorum iiiid legal valet
~~bancce, ystlisseu, hinniogeu, gordrysseu, dupist, cor~~, ~~quodlibet~~ iiii denarios legales.

precium domus autumpnalis 24d Si aliqua per teretris perforetur Qua libet furca domus autumpnalis et aestivalis
aliter 12d tantum valet 12d unum valet denarium
[6]Pro domo estiuali xl denarii si comburatur. [7]Et nota quod cum cuiuslibet predictarum

omnium rerum intra predictas domos
domorum precio et precium ~~dampnum rerum intus predictarum~~ [16v] redditur. [8]~~Precium auctumpnalis domus: xxiiii denarii.~~ [9]~~Precium estiualis domus: xii denarii.~~ [10]~~Furce estiualis domus uel auctumpnalis: denarius legalis.~~

(c) E2 (Merton 323, fols. 13ᵛ–14ʳ; underlined passages derive from glosses in E3)

¹Precium domus yemalis est: de qualibet furca que sustinet laquear, .i., *nenbren*, xxx d.

.i. ....
²Pro *nenbren* <u>xxx</u> denarii. ³Si denudetur, tertia pars totius domus redditur. ⁴<u>*Beigkiav*</u>,

.i. ...... .i. ...... .i. .....i. ....
<u>Talbeigkiau et *styffyleu* et *doreu* et *kynhor gordrysseu* .i. ostiola *trothwy* .i. limen *Tubyst*</u>
quodlibet istorum <u>iiii denarios legales ualet</u>. ⁵<u>Precium domus autumpnalis 24d</u>. ⁶<u>Si aliqua per</u>
<u>terebro perforetur, aliter 12d tantum valet</u>. ⁷<u>Pro domo estiuali 12d quaelibet furcae domus</u>
<u>autumpnalis et aestivalis unum valet denarium</u>. [14r] ⁸Et nota quod cum cuiuslibet predictarum
domorum precio et precium <u>omnium rerum intra predictas domos</u> redditur.

Several observations may be made about this passage which are confirmed by
Thelwall's practice elsewhere. There are a number of other examples in this text
as well which suggest that, while he regarded the content of the Welsh texts to
have priority, the language of the text should be Latin; for example, the section
on 'nines' (*de novenario*), which in Cambridge, Corpus Christi 454, fol. 47r2–9
(= *LTWL*, 495. 19–26; Peniarth 256, fol. 52r14–20), is in Welsh, was deleted as
there was no equivalent passage in the Welsh text with which he was collating it.[96]
In our text the list of parts of a building (which is partly in Latin, partly in
Welsh) is deleted and replaced by another similar list. However, where possible,
a Latin gloss to the Welsh term is supplied, but in some instances he was unable
to provide a Latin rendering and so he left a hopeful .*i.* .... The last three
sentences are deleted completely, presumably because he realized that he had
already added this material a few lines earlier. The additional material is too
detailed and technical to have been created *ab initio* by Thelwall, and on the
basis of what we have already seen of his working practices there is a strong
presumption that he had another text to hand. The list of Welsh terms is our
best guide. Texts of the Iorwerth redaction do not have such a list. Blegywryd
texts do have a similar list but differ in the wording and order of items: for
example, *y colofneu, meinkeu, ystyffyleu, amhinogeu, trothwyeu, gordrysseu,
tubyst, doreu* . . . (Bleg 95. 5–13 (= *Cyfreithiau Hywel Dda* 83. 12–18)). Cyfnerth
texts look more promising in that for the most part they have the same wording
and order of items; as, for example, in the printed text: *Y meinkeu ar tal ueinkeu
ar ystyffyleu ar doreu ar kynhoreu ar gordrysseu are trothwyeu ar tubyst* . . .
(*Welsh Medieval Law*, 101. 19–21, printed from manuscript W (BL Cotton MS,
Cleopatra A.xiv)). But the closest by far is the reading of X (BL Cotton MS,
Cleopatra B.v (s. xiv^med), fol. 219v4–6): *e beigkyeu ar talbeigkyeu ar ystyfyleu ar
doreu ar kynhor ar gordrysseu ar trothwyeu ar tubyst*.[97] Manuscript X, therefore,

---

⁹⁶ It is otherwise only found in *LTWL* 244. 34–245. 3 (Lat B).
⁹⁷ On X, see *RMWL*, I, ii, 952, Huws, *Medieval Welsh Manuscripts*, 59, M.E. Owen, 'The laws of court
    from Cyfnerth', in T. M. Charles-Edwards et al. (eds), *The Welsh King and his Court* (Cardiff, 2000), 426,
    Ovendon, 'Jaspar Gryffyth and his books', *British Library Journal*, 20 (1994), 107–39: pp. 113, 118, 129.

or a manuscript very closely related to it, must be a strong candidate for the manuscript which Edward Thelwall had at his elbow. We also know that this manuscript was in north-east Wales in the sixteenth century and so geographically close to Thelwall. On the first page of the text of the laws there is an ownership note of Jasper Griffith, dated 1600, and there is also a couplet of a *cywydd* to St Anne. There are other instances of where Thelwall made use of a Cyfnerth text in Peniarth 256, for example, fol. 4r8–9 (= *LTWL*, 440. 9) = *Welsh Medieval Law*, 25. 5–15, fol. 25v10–12 (= *LTWL*, 463. 23–4) = *Welsh Medieval Law*, 45. 9–11, fol. 26r8–9 (= *LTWL*, 464. 4) = *Welsh Medieval Law*, 45. 15–19. Though it is not possible to establish which version of Cyfnerth is being used, as the text is more or less identical in all of them, the presumption is that he was making further use of X (or a manuscript closely related to it).

To sum up, the working practice of Edward Thelwall and his amanuenses seems to be as follows: a text is copied by his amanuenses, though Thelwall may copy the first page or so. The text is then heavily annotated and glossed with reference to similar Welsh texts by Thelwall. In the case of Peniarth 256 we can identify at least two different sources of that annotation, a Blegywryd text of the L and J type and a Cyfnerth manuscript, probably X or a close copy or ancestor of it.

The Peniarth 434 version of the life of Gruffudd ap Cynan

The above discussion of the relationship between the manuscripts of Latin redaction E of the Welsh laws has clarified the *modus operandi* of Edward Thelwall. In terms of layout, distribution and hands, Peniarth 434 is identical with Peniarth 256. Manuscripts such as Cotton Vitellius C.ix (version *B*) and Llanstephan 150 (version *D*) seem to be fair copies.[98] The question now concerns the underlying text of the manuscript. Among the manuscripts of Latin redaction E the underlying text of Peniarth 256 has survived in Cambridge, Corpus Christi 454. But, as far as is known, the underlying text of Peniarth 434 is not extant, and therefore the manuscript deserves closer scrutiny in order to establish the precise nature of the text and of its glossing and annotation.

(a) The underlying text

Three examples of increasing complexity may allow us to develop a view of the nature of this underlying text. The first consists of a single line of text. When William Rufus entered Gwynedd and carried out a systematic devastation and

[98] See above, p. 11–15.

pillaging of the country, the underlying text of the Peniarth 434 version comments in good Old Testament style: . . . *ut ne canem quidem ad parietem mingentem relinqueret* (p. 38. 5–6 (§25/1 below)) 'so that he might not leave even a dog pissing against a wall'. In Kings and Samuel *ad parietem mingentes* is used to refer to males and in particular to the slaughter of all males in contexts of complete devastation.[99] The further touch that not even male dogs were left alive strikingly emphasizes the level of destruction wreaked by William. However, the Old Testament allusion was removed by Thelwall who deleted *ad parietem mingentem* and added *ullum vivum* above, producing an appreciably blander clause, 'so that he might not leave even a dog alive'. Rather than attributing this to an over-sensitive sense of propriety, his correction matches the Middle Welsh text exactly: *hyt na bei en vyw kemeint a chi* 'so that there was not left alive so much as a dog' (*HGK*, 22. 14 = *MPW*, 74. 30–1). The suspicion is immediately aroused by this one example that Thelwall had a copy of the Welsh text beside him and was correcting the main text of Peniarth 434 by reference to it, exactly as he had been doing with the Latin law texts.

When in 1081, just before the battle of Mynydd Carn, Gruffudd is negotiating with Rhys ap Tewdwr for his support, he asks him who his oppressors are and Rhys replies in the following way (the text is reproduced first from Peniarth 434 with all the annotations and deletions in place; the second version is the fair copy from Cotton Vitellius C.ix)

(i) Peniarth 434, p. 24. 8–14 (§17/9–10 below) (Plate 2)

quae supra et infra sylvam sita est   satellitibus suis   is

Caradocus (inquit ille) filius Griffini de Gwenta ~~veh coet et is coet~~, cum ~~asseclis suis,~~ incolae

de   cum plurimis aliis ballistariis   Meiliricus filius Riwallani cum Powisianis et cum suis etiam   u anis

Morgannwc ~~vna cum~~ Normannis ~~et Trahaernus Rex cum habitantibus~~ Arwystli. Auditis vero

Trahaernus rex eorum qui Rhesi patriam tanta clade affecerunt

ex   ab eo

nominibus ~~oppressorum~~ ira indignationeque aestuans Griffinus quaerit quodnam illi laboris

illos eius hostes bellum gereret

praemium constitueret, si contra ~~hostes eius oppugnaret~~.

(ii) Cotton Vitellius C.ix, fol. 137r–v (the underlined sections indicate what has been incorporated from Thelwall's corrections):

Caradocus (inquit ille) filius Griffini de Gwenta <u>quae supra, et infra sylvam sita est</u>, cum <u>satellitibus suis</u>, incolis ~~de~~ Morgannwc, <u>cum plurimis aliis balistariis</u>, et

---

[99] For further discussion and the biblical references, see the notes to *VGC* below at §25/1. For further insular examples, see Dumville, 'Celtic-Latin texts in northern England', *Celtica*, 12 (1977), 24–6.

Normannis, <u>Meiliricus filius Riwallani cum Powisianis, et Trahaernus Rex cum suis etiam Arustlianis</u>.

Auditis vero nominibus <u>eorum, qui Rhesi patriam tanta clade affecerunt</u>, ira indignationeque <u>ex</u>aestuans Griffinus quaerit <u>ab eo</u> quodnam illi laboris praemium constitueret, si contra <u>illos eius hostes</u> secum <u>bellum gereret</u>.

We may note characteristic features of Edward Thelwall's technique, particularly the replacement of Welsh with Latin; for example, *Gwenta vch coet et is coet* is replaced by *Gwenta quae supra et infra sylvam sita est*; *cum habitantibus Arwystli* by *cum suis etiam Arustlianis*. Another tendency is to fill out the more laconic Latin phrases; for example, *oppressorum* is replaced by *eorum qui Rhesi patriam tanta clade affecerunt*; or to improve the style by using a compound verb, for example, *exaestuans* for *aestuans*. However, there are some more substantive additions: while in the underlying text Rhys talks of his three oppressors as Caradog from Gwent, the natives of Morgannwg together with the Normans, *una cum Normannis* (the last phrase has been expanded to *cum plurimis aliis ballistariis Normannis*), and Trahaearn, the additions merge the inhabitants of Morgannwg into the men supporting Caradog and then bring in Meilyr ap Rhiwallon and the men of Powys; these last do not figure in the base text at all.

The corresponding section of Middle Welsh text is presented below and it is immediately clear that the substantive additions (underlined below) are to be found in the Welsh text and were probably taken from there by Thelwall, translated, and added to our text:

'Caradauc m. Grufud', hep enteu, 'o Went Uch Coet ac is Coet a'e Wenhvyssyon, a gvyr Morgannvc, <u>a llawer o albryswyr</u> Nordmannyeit gantav; <u>Meilir m. Riwallaun a'e Bowyswyr</u> gantav, Trahaearn vrenhin a gwyr Arwystli. A phan gigleu Gruffud enw y ormeswyr, froeni o gyndared a oruc, a govyn idav pa beth a rodei er emlad drostav en erbyn y gwyr henne. (*HGK*, 14. 8–15 = *MPW*, 66. 29–67. 2).

The third and final example is the section recounting the battle of Mynydd Carn fought in 1081. The text is edited in full below (§18), and Plate 3 is an image of the latter part of this section but a number of instances of variation are selected and discussed here. The evidence is presented below (Thelwall's emendation may be assumed to replace the reading of *VGC* unless preceded by + in which case it is an addition to the *VGC* text):

VGC § 18	Thelwall's emendation	HGK reading (HGK, 14. 20–16. 26 = MPW, 67. 9–69. 16)
(a) 18/1 armisque aliis	plurimisque Venedotis	a llawer o Wyndit
(b) 18/4 advesperascit	+ et lux defectura	a'r dyd ysyd yn trengi
(c) 18/7 cuspidibus ferentes	+ cultellata	kyllellauc
(d) 18/7 conspiciunt	+ et hastatos scutatosque Venedotos	a'r Gwyndyt gleiuyauc tareanauc
(e) 18/9 in quo ne filius quidem patri pepercit	cuius famam post parentum mortem longe celebrabunt filii	ac ena y bu vrwyder dirvaur y chof y'r etiued wedy eu ryeni
(f) 18/11 subiugarent	pugnarent sibique cedere compellerent	en dwyssav en wychyr, ac eu gelynyon en darestung udunt
(g) 18/14 persequitur	et per totum diem posterum adeo acriter persecutus est	a'e hemlynvs wynteu . . . ac en hyt e dyd drannoeth
(h) 18/15 Rhesus subduxit	+ ne periculum proditionis a Griffino sibi intenderetur	ofynhav brat o barthret Gruffudd a oruc Rys
(i) 18/17 lapidum ingens cumulus	+ Garnedd	Sef yu henne menyd e garned
(j) 18/17 sub quo thesauros absconditos olim opinantur	heroem aliquem multis antea seculis sepeliri ferunt	a dan er honn y cladwt rysswr yg kynnoessoed gynt
(k) 18/20 susceptus regebat	reversus est ut eam quietam et pace felicem redderet ac gubernaret	y'u medu ac y'u thagneuedu

It is immediately clear that most of the changes and additions to the base text match the Welsh text. The modifications fall into a number of categories: in (b) and (c) the base text is augmented but not deleted; in (e) and (j) the base text is deleted and replaced by a different phrase; in (f), (g), (h) and (k) a short phrase, in some cases a single word, is deleted and replaced by a much longer phrase. However, in (a) the text is altered and in (d) text is added, but the alterations are more substantive than in the other instances; in both cases the men of Gwynedd, who are otherwise in the underlying text absent from the battle of Mynydd Carn, are added by Thelwall so that the text matches the factual details of the Welsh text. In (i) the name *Garnedd* is added to describe the *lapidum ingens cumulus*; however, the plural *montes* is used to describe the locality in *VGC* in contrast to the singular *Menyd Carn* of the Welsh text (*HGK*, 16. 14 = *MPW*, 68. 37). In some instances, adherence to the Welsh text results in the deletion of phrases of arguably greater literary merit than the replacements; for example, in (e) a battle in which not even a son spared his father (*in quo ne filius quidem patri pepercit*) seems much more savage with its connotations of civil war than a war which will be remembered by sons long after the death of their parents (*cuius famam post parentum mortem longe celebrabunt filii*), the replacement clause carried over from the Welsh text. A particularly interesting example of variation is found in (j) concerning what lies beneath the *carn* or *carnedd*. Our text states that there is hidden treasure but the Welsh text holds that it is the grave of a warrior. In this instance, it looks as if an error may have crept in during the transmission of the Welsh text: our Latin text would translate into Welsh as *cladwyt trysor* or the like, but all the extant Welsh texts have *cladwt rysswr* (*HGK*, 16. 15 = *MPW*, 69. 2–3), perhaps as a result of an early misreading (or indeed mishearing) of *cladwyt trysor* as *cladwyt rysswr*; if so, it presents us with valuable evidence for a stage of transmission of the Welsh text before the archetype of all the extant Welsh texts.

It seems clear then that the *modus operandi* of Edward Thelwall was to annotate the Latin text before him in such a way as to bring it into line with the Welsh text. As with the text of the Latin laws, the content of the Welsh text had priority but Latin was the language of preference. It is not surprising, therefore, that fair copies of this work look like translations of the Welsh text. In one sense that is indeed what they are, but they were not created by the usual process of sitting down with the Welsh text and a blank sheet of paper and translating it into Latin; they have rather arisen out of a modification of a pre-existing Latin text. Several questions then arise. Just as we can identify the Welsh text that Thelwall was using to annotate his Latin law text, is it possible to establish which version of the Welsh text of *HGK* he was using? Secondly, and more importantly for this volume, what can be established about the nature of the underlying Latin text and its relationship to the Welsh text?

A little progress can be made on the first question but largely negatively. It is almost certainly the case that he was not using Peniarth 17 since, where there is any difference in the reading between Peniarth 17 and the rest, he has a reading corresponding to the rest.[100] For example, at §6/2 the base text reads *Slani* as the name of the mother of Auloed, but Thelwall corrects it to *Alam*, the reading of all the other versions of *HGK* but not that of Peniarth 17, which has *Slani*. Any further progress can only depend on likelihoods. There is some evidence that Edward Thelwall made a copy of *HGK* at Plas y Ward in 1570 or 1574, and it is quite possible that this was the copy at his elbow when he was editing our manuscript.[101] That manuscript is now lost, though the Thelwall manuscript (NLW 13211) seems to be derived from it.[102]

As regards the nature of the underlying Latin text, in the analysis of three samples of text it has emerged that, in some episodes more than others, the base Latin text differs substantially from the Welsh version. It is also a little shorter: the text of *VGC* edited here is some 6,200 words long;[103] the Latin fair copies, which are in effect translations of the Welsh text, are about 6,900 long. This represents an expansion of some 10 per cent, though the degree of

---

[100] See Figure 1, above.

[101] *HGK*, pp. cclix, cclxvi, n. 66, cclxxii–cclxxiii, cclxxxviii.

[102] *HGK*, pp. cclxxxviii–cclxxxix.

[103] The figure includes the sections of text imported from Cotton Vitellius C.ix to fill the gaps where text has been lost from Peniarth 434; see below, p. 50, for details.

variation is greater since in many cases the changes involved deletion of the original text.

Several possibilities may be considered. The first is that it is indeed a translation of the extant Welsh text but executed badly. Thelwall's changes would then be regarded as corrections, bringing it back into line with the original. But even a poor translation would bear some relation to the Welsh, however incorrect. Poor translations might even omit sections, but the systematic omission of clauses, phrases, words goes far beyond that. In addition, a poor translation would rarely come up with totally different phrasing and grammatical structures; more commonly, a translation is poor by reason of its slavish adherence to the phrasing and structure of the original. Furthermore, there are many instances where the text is so different that it cannot be even a poor rendering of the Welsh; see, for example, several instances in the passage quoted above on the battle of Mynydd Carn (§18). If it is a rendering of a Welsh text, then it must have been a very different Welsh text to the extant version. It should also be pointed out that, even if it were a translation, it was done further back in the manuscript tradition. The Latin text preserved in Peniarth 434 is a copy in that it contains clear evidence of copying errors, for example, §17/2 *Theodrex* (for *Theodwr rex*); §18/3 ~~vix~~ *ex numero vix*, etc. Furthermore, it is clear that the exemplar from which the scribe was working was not totally legible. In a number of places he has simply given up on the text and left a gap (indicated in the edition below by < >) which was sometimes filled subsequently by Thelwall by reference to the Welsh version.[104]

Another, admittedly less likely, possibility is that the Welsh text is a straight translation of the original Latin, but our text represents a cut-down and modified Latin version, subsequently expanded again by Edward Thelwall to match the Welsh text. However, it is far from clear that there is any rationale for the modification. For example, it is difficult to imagine that, in a text originating from Gwynedd and whose transmission, both in the Welsh and Latin versions, is restricted to Gwynedd, the men of Gwynedd would be written out of the battle of Mynydd Carn; it is far more likely that they were originally not present but were added at a later stage.

A third possibility is that our Latin text is a translation of a different Welsh text which has not survived. That text would have been a little shorter and perhaps not so focused on Gwynedd. The process of polishing and expansion of the Welsh text would then be similar to the kind of process seen in the different versions of *Peredur*.[105] However, in effect, that simply pushes the difficulties

---

[104] See §§8/3, 9/1 (*bis*), 9/2, 10/1, 11/2 (*bis*), 13/3, 14/18, 15/5, 18/1 (*bis*), 18/5, 18/20 (*bis*), 21/2, 22/2, 23/17, 24/1, 25/1, 25/5 (*bis*), 29/1, 31/5, 33/5, 34/3. For the system of reference to the text, see below, p. 50. In most cases, no more than a word seems to be missing, and so they do not seriously affect the comparison of the lengths of the texts above (p. 29).

[105] Cf. P. W. Thomas, 'Cydberthynas y pedair fersiwn ganoloesol', in S. Davies and P. W. Thomas (eds), *Canhwyll Marchogyon* (Cardiff, 2000), 10–43.

outlined in the preceding paragraph a stage further back in the line of transmission. A possible stemma, as presented in Figure 5, highlights some of the
problems with this approach, in particular the complexity of the process of
translation to and fro between Latin and Welsh. A specific problem is that there
seems to be no evidence of a tradition of translating texts from Welsh into Latin
between the mid-thirteenth century, when our evidence begins, and the sixteenth
century, and so the creation of L^2 would probably have to be relatively late. [106]

Fig 5 A stemma to show how Peniarth 434 might derive from a different Welsh text
(L^1 = the original Latin text; L^2 = a secondary Latin text; W^1 = the first (now lost)
Welsh text; W^2 = the achetype of the extant Welsh texts.)

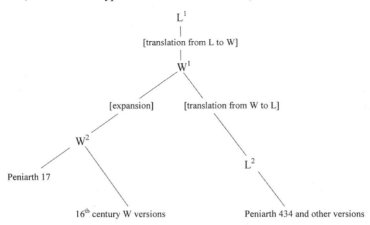

It is a good deal simpler and more economical, involving postulation of fewer intermediate stages, to suppose that Peniarth 434 represents a copy of the original
Latin composition (see Figure 6 overleaf). If so, the process of translation would
also involve expansion and modification; models to consider might perhaps be
the relationship between the Latin and Welsh lives of St David, or the reworking
of parts of *Ymborth yr Enaid* from Hugo of St Victor's *De Fructibus Carnis et
Spiritus*.[107] One advantage of this approach is that we are not put in the position
of postulating the existence of an intermediate, unattested Welsh text.

(b) Misunderstandings in HGK, *clarified in* VGC

The last hypothesis can be supported in a number of ways. One approach is to
consider cases where the Latin text is clearer than the Welsh text and it appears

---

[106] The translation of law texts from Welsh into Latin, as evidenced in the Blegywryd redaction,
predates our earliest manuscript evidence, and there is a marked gap in the manuscript evidence
from the surviving medieval text and the later copies which seem to begin in the late sixteenth
century at the earliest; see, for examples, the discussions on manuscripts in *LTWL*.

[107] *Rhigyfarch's Life of St David*, pp. xxix–xli; *The Welsh Life of St David*, pp. xxxix–lix; *Ymborth yr
Enaid*, pp. xliv–l.

Fig 6 A stemma to show how Peniarth 434 might be a descendant of the original Latin text of the Life of Gruffudd ap Cynan (L¹ = the original Latin text; W¹ = the archetype of the extant Welsh texts.)

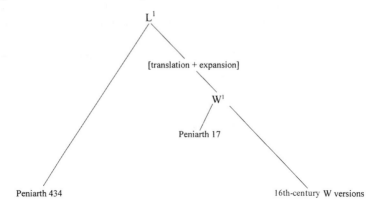

that the Welsh text has misunderstood the Latin text or failed to carry over details of the Latin sometimes because the grammar of Middle Welsh cannot render the Latin with sufficient precision of reference. The latter can occur in relative clauses where the Middle Welsh structures do not mark the antecedent as precisely as it is possible to do in Latin; for example, at §4/1 *qui e Scotia genus ducebat* 'who derived his ancestry from Scotland' must refer to King Olaf of Dublin, the maternal grandfather of Gruffudd, while the Welsh version *a hanoed gynt o deyrnas Prydein* is open to various interpretations depending on what is regarded as the antecedent of the relative *a*.[108] Similarly, at §5/1 the Welsh text is unclear as to whether Alanus is one of Harald's brothers or brother to the king, Harald's father, . . . *Harald Harfagyr a'e deu vroder yn veibeon y vrenhin Llychlyn. Ac Alyn y vrawt* . . . 'Harald Haarfager and his two brothers were sons of the king of Llychlyn. And Alyn his brother' (*HGK*, 3. 1–2 = *MPW*, 55. 10–11). But the Latin has *cuius fratrem* where the relative should refer to the closest masculine singular noun, namely the king of Llychlyn; the only doubt over this example is that *cuius fratrem* has been lost from Peniarth 434 through damage to the edge of the page and is restored from Cotton Vitellius C.ix, but there is only space for two words and there is no indication of amendment by Thelwall.[109]

Another structure which seems to cause difficulty is the use of *vel* 'or'. At §5/10 the Latin text provides two explanations of how Normandy was divided into twelve parts: *Hanc regionem in duodecim partes sunt partiti ad numerum*

---

[108] For further discussion, see the notes on §4/1.

[109] For further discussion, see the notes on §5/1 where the consequences of these different interpretations are considered. Cf. also §33/3 for another example of where a relative clause in the Latin text has been less than clearly rendered in the Welsh, and §6/4 where the relevant Latin text has been lost at the top of a damaged page, but the later copies are suggestive.

Baronum vel similitudinem ducum, qui in aliam Galliae partem Britanniam, vel Wallice Lydaw dictam, olim advenerant 'They divided this region into twelve parts, according to the number of "barons", or like the leaders who had formerly arrived in another part of Gaul, namely Brittany, or in Welsh *Llydaw*'. The Welsh text has merged the two explanations: *herwyd y barwnyeit a'r tywyssogyon . . .* 'according to the barons and leaders' (*HGK*, 4. 9 = *MPW*, 56. 19–20). It is possible that the confusion arose because in the exemplar used for the Welsh translation an abbreviation for *vel* was used, perhaps *l̵* or *u̵l̵*. Another confusion involving *vel* occurs at §10/6 but here the confusion has possibly arisen in the Welsh text: the Latin text has Gruffudd going off either to Robert of Rhuddlan or to Hugh of Chester, *Griffinus rursum per mare iter arripit vel versus castrum Rudlan versus Robertum Baronem nobilem et potentem, vel ad Hugonem Comitem Cestriae*, but the Welsh text has Robert as the nephew of Hugh, *nei i Hu yarll Caer* (*HGK*, 7. 15–16). Here there may have been a scribal confusion in an early version of the Welsh text between *nei* 'nephew' and *neu* 'or'.

A misunderstanding of a Latin technical term seems to lie behind §32/2 where Henry pays his allies, the king of Scotland, the Scots and the southern Welsh out of his treasury to support his attack on Gwynedd; the term used is *erogando* but this is understood as *dwyn ganthaw* 'take with him' rather than in its technical sense.

A striking example of how the Latin text is clearer than the Welsh is at §12/6 where the location of the battle of Gwaederw is described as *in loco vallis Kyning*. The Welsh version read this as *yg glynn kyving*, 'in a narrow glen' (*HGK*, 9. 4–5 = *MPW*, 61. 16–17), taking *Kyning* as the Welsh adjective *cyfyng*. It would be possible to take *Kyning* in *VGC* as an error for *Kyuing*, but the text does not use Welsh in this way; it always translates and explains it, and furthermore the spelling with a capital *K-* and the usage of *in loco vallis . . .* clearly suggests that the author is thinking in terms of a place name. If so, the text presents us with a possible location for the battle.[110]

Another aspect which is clarified is the status of Gellan. In the Welsh text his status is ambiguous as he is called *telynor pencerdd* (*HGK*, 21. 14 = *MPW*, 73. 34–5) which could mean 'harpist to the *pencerdd*', but *VGC cytharaedus, penkerd* (§23/16) makes it clear that *penkerd* is glossing *cytharaedus*.[111]

(c) Comparison of factual details in VGC *and* HGK

Another approach is to examine some of the factual details missing from our text in relation to the Welsh text and also vice versa, instances where our text has details which are missing in the Welsh text, and to consider whether they are more likely to have been deleted (if this Latin text is a later adaption) or to have been added subsequently in the Welsh version. A general feature of this

---

[110] For a suggested location, see the notes on §12/6.
[111] See J. E. C. Williams, 'Meilyr Brydydd and Gruffudd ap Cynan', in Maund, *Gruffudd ap Cynan*, 169.

Latin text is that it seems to be less focused on Gwynedd than the Welsh text.[112] For example, as we have seen above, the men of Gwynedd are not at Mynydd Carn (§§18/1, 18/7); at §10/2 the Welsh text is only concerned about the depredations of Trahaearn and Cynwrig upon Gwynedd, while in the Latin text the sentence begins by talking about Wales as a whole; at §22/8, when Gruffudd has escaped from prison and is careering around Gwynedd, he is described as *quasi erro quidam* 'like a runaway slave', perhaps conjuring up images of Spartacus, but this simile is not used in the Welsh text; at §25/3 William Rufus is cutting down forests and thus depriving the *imbecilliores* 'the incapacitated' of shelter, but in the Welsh text these people are described simply as *Gwyndyt* (*HGK*, 22. 16); at §31/1 the bishop of Bangor is not named, but he is identified as Erfyn (Hervé) in the Welsh text (*HGK*, 28. 4–5). Since, as can be seen from the discussion of the manuscripts, the manuscript tradition of this text, both in Latin and in Welsh, is firmly located in Gwynedd, it seems unlikely that details about Gwynedd would have been removed from the text in the course of transmission and translation. However, the converse seems a much more plausible account, that a sharper Gwynedd focus was added in the course of the translation of a Latin text on the life of Gruffudd ap Cynan which seemed to keep activities in Gwynedd at arm's length.

(d) The orthography of the names in VGC

Consideration of the orthography of the Welsh names might be of some help, even though we have to take into account that some of the names may have been modernized in the course of the transmission of the Latin text. The question is whether some or any of the orthographical patterns in the Welsh names can be regarded as plausible twelfth-century spellings. A breakdown of the orthography of the names is presented in Appendix 1; all the Welsh names attested in Peniarth 434 have been considered, omitting any names which only occur in the sections from Cotton Vitellius C.ix or in the later annotation. In the following discussion, the evidence of the genealogical section (§2) has been set aside since it is most likely to have been influenced by other sources; while it seems to preserve some relatively old spellings, we cannot tell whether they are original to this text or brought into it from other genealogical material.[113] It might be argued that the nature of the evidence, being only names, means that there might be a tendency towards archaism anyway. Even so, it seems worth considering the evidence from the non-genealogical sections. As might be expected, the evidence is very mixed and it seems likely that the names have been modernized at various stages in the course of transmission. The important

---

[112] For further details on the examples mentioned below, see the notes to the sections of text cited.

[113] See P. Sims-Williams, 'Historical need and literary narrative', *WHR*, 17 (1994) 20–6; P. E. Thornton, 'The genealogy of Gruffudd ap Cynan', in Maund, *Gruffudd ap Cynan*, 82–7.

evidence is that which shows spelling features which are not characteristic of the later period. Among the central vowels, the later pattern would be to use *y* for the reduced vowel /ə/ and for the central /ɨ/; occasional use of *i* is probably regarded as an older spelling, for example, *Kelliniauk* (§21/1) beside *Kelynnawk* (§12/1), *Evyonid* (§23/10) beside *Eivionyd* (§31/2). Note also the early use of *e* for /ei/ in *Evyonid* (§23/10). The spelling *-aw-* is regular in unaccented syllables in this text even though by the fourteenth century the vowel had been reduced to /o/, for example, *Meiriawn* (§10/3), etc. but cf. also *Rhiwallon* (§10/2). Among the fricatives, /v/ was by the fifteenth and sixteenth centuries regularly spelt *f*, though in the medieval period it was only common in final position; the *f* spelling only occurs once, *Sandef* (§23/2), and that in final position; elsewhere in this text the regular spelling is *v*, for example, *Arvon* (§21/2, 23/10), *Meivot* (§34/4), etc. The later spelling of the dental fricative /ð/ was *dd* but that only occurs twice in our text, *Bleddyn* (§12/4, 26/9), *Merwydd* (§§21/1, 14/1); the usual spelling is *d*, for example, *Kyndelo* (§18/1), *Arllechwed* (§31/2), though there is one example of *t*, *Rutlan* (§16/2), and two of *th*, *Meredith* (§26/5) and *Meirionyth* (§21/1). As for the dental stop /d/, the regular spelling would have been *d*, and our text frequently has that, but the *t* spelling is very common, especially in final position, for example, *Llwyt* (§14/7), *Dinieuyt* (§23/9), *Angharat* (§24/1), and almost certainly represents a preservation of an early spelling pattern. The patterns outlined in this paragraph are consistent with what is known of the systems of orthography prevalent in north Wales in the thirteenth century; we know virtually nothing about the orthography of Welsh in north Wales in the twelfth century. However, it is striking that, where one can penetrate the orthography of a thirteenth-century manuscript and see aspects of the orthography of its exemplar, it can appear remarkably archaic; for example, the exemplar of parts of the Black Book of Chirk (NLW, Peniarth MS, 29) seems to have been written in an orthography which, in some respects at least, resembles the orthography of Old Welsh.[114] In such an orthography the use of *i* for central vowels, *v* for /v/, *d* or *t* for /ð/, and *t* for /-d/ would not be out of place. The orthography of the Welsh names in Peniarth 434, then, shows a mixed pattern but it is consistent with a manuscript composed in the twelfth century and then undergoing modernization of its orthography in the course of transmission over the intervening period.

(e) The Latinity of VGC

Another way of looking at the text of *VGC* in Peniarth 434 is to consider its Latinity. At this stage of the argument, this is not so much to demonstrate that

---

[114] P. Russell, 'Scribal (in)competence in thirteenth-century north Wales', *NLWJ*, 29 (1995–6), 129–76, for other examples, see also P. Russell, 'What did medieval Welsh scribes do? The scribe of the Dingestow Court manuscript', *CMCS*, 37 (Summer 1999), 79–96.

the text cannot be sixteenth century in origin or conversely cannot be medieval, but rather to explore how, if at all, we might be able to detect modification of the text which has occurred in the later stages of transmission. However, we should bear in mind that comparison with sixteenth-century texts may be beside the point, as it is clear that the exemplar of the underlying text of Peniarth 434 was in places difficult to read to the extent that the copyist left gaps;[115] some of those gaps were subsequently filled by Thelwall either by recovering more of the text from the exemplar or by reference to the Welsh text. If what he was transcribing was either a relatively recent composition or a recent copy, we would not expect the exemplar to be illegible, unless some specific damage had occurred to it.

It may be useful to begin with a brief sketch of the Latinity of *VGC*. The overall impression is of a strong, powerful narrative which seems relatively simple and uncomplicated stylistically. There is little complex subordination. The narrative moves forward often by a simple pattern of ablative absolutes (or occasional *cum*-clauses) and main verbs, very often with subsequent action marked by gerunds in the ablative or present participles. For example, Harald Harfagyr's conquest of Ireland is described by a present participle and a pair of pluperfect main verbs followed by a pair of gerunds (the structural elements are underlined): *Verum non multo antea Haraldus Harfagyr exercitum ducens copiosum eam erat ingressus, totamque Hyberniam pertransierat summa crudelitate incolas mactando fugandoque* (§5/6).[116] Participles can be used similarly: *audito tanto belli apparatu* < > *in occursum Griffinus copias totius principatus collegit,* < > *in angustiis viarum insidias collocans, in quas subito incideret a montibus descendens exercitus* (§25/5), where *collocans* is used to describe the action following on from the main verb *collegit* ; we may also note in passing the striking word order of the final relative clause, with the subject delayed until the end of the sentence.[117]

The narrative is frequently paratactic in that within a sentence the action moves forward by a series of parallel clauses rather than by subordination, often concluding in a rhetorical climax; a good example is the fate of those servants kidnapped with Gruffudd who are sent on their way but not without some brutal treatment: *famulos vero eius tum etiam captos, amputatis singulorum pollicibus dextris, inhumanius afflictos, liberos dimiserunt* (§19/6); the *liberos*

---

[115] See above, p. 30.

[116] Cf. also §9/2 *monstrando . . . petendo*, §12/4 *expectando*, §12/8 *comprecando*, §23/3 *pugnando*, §26/11 *persequendo*, §29/6 *mulctando*, §30/4 *consolando*, §31/6 *gubernando*, §32/1 *erogando*, §35/2 *benedicendo*.

[117] For the editing conventions and an explanation of < >, see p. 50. Cf. also §5/6 *ducens*, §5/9 *deducens*, §12/4 *precurrens*, §12/8 *afferens*, §14/10 *insidens*, §15/2 *acquiescens*, §17/10 *aestuans*, §19/5 *adhibens*, §21/1 *adducens*, §22/1 *veniens*, §22/5 *pergens*, §25/6 *reformidans*, §27/1 *appropinquans*, §32/7 *ductans*, §32/9 *metuens*, §34/1 *cogitans*. Another feature of note in *VGC* is the use of *ab* + ablative absolute in §10/6 *ab hac congressione sic finita*, §18/15 *ab hoc bello terribili fortiter per Griffinum confecto*.

following on from *inhumanius afflictos* is not without irony. On a larger scale, the paratactic structure is very effective in narrating the sudden, unexpected and fast-moving nature of Gruffudd's rescue:

> iuvenis quidam Eiderniensis Kynwricus Hir nomine una cum sodalico modico Cestriam veniens ad necessaria coemenda, conspicit forte in palatio civitatis vinctum suum regem, quem in amplexibus abreptum clam e civitate subduxit, iterque in patriam vespere conatur, civibus iam caenantibus, atque domi apud se tacitus diebus nonnullis aluit (§22/1)

Here the basic structure is *veniens . . . conspicit* (note the delay of the object *regem*) . . . *quem . . . subduxit . . . iterque . . . conatur . . . atque . . . aluit*, and the process is marked by the historic presents but ending with the perfect to indicate the successful conclusion. In other cases, the rhetorical force is even greater: at the battle of Mynydd Carn the opposing kings are terrified at the sight of Gruffudd's forces:

> terrore ingenti continentur reges, stupentque dum copias Griffini faeroces, constipata militum agmina, splendentia vexilla, Danos bipennibus armatos, Hybernos iacula ferreis cuspidibus ferentes conspiciunt. (§18/7).

We may note the emphatic position of *terrore*, the framing of *reges* by the two main verbs, but in particular the ascending climax of the description of the forces which gradually becomes more detailed and more terrifying, possibly reflecting the increasing detail which would become visible as it approached.[118]

The ascending climax of the last example is a feature which is widespread in the text, particularly in the form of an ascending tricolon. When Trahaearn hears of the approach of Gruffudd's fleet, he is overcome: *qui audito classis regiae adventu, cepit tristitia affici, suspiria alta ducere, timore et tremore contabescere* (§15/3), and his distress is well captured by the ascending tricolon with the alliteration of the final part. Similarly, when Gruffudd leads an assault on the Norman castles on Anglesey, the Normans are described as *Francos loricatos, galeatos bipennibusque armatos* (§23/5). Later in the same passage the beseiged Normans are described in terms of ascending phrases: *Franci obsessi e muris, praesidiis, et turribus in eos iacula torserunt, sagittas emiserunt, saxa deiecerunt, aliisque sese instrumentis defensitarunt* (§23/12). The tricolon of defensive places is followed by four successive main verbs which between them encompass all possible means of defence.

The rhythm of the language is also the product of a very competent Latinist. For example, heavy endings are a marked feature of this text, and, while they

---

[118] This passage is discussed by Davies, 'Sixteenth-century Latin translation', 162–4. Although he is using the version preserved in *G*, a number of his comments are still valid, especially his point about the chiastic order of the elements in *copias Griffini faeroces, constipata militum agmina*. As examples of paratactic structure, compare also the description of Gruffudd rebuilding Gwynedd (§33/2).

do not always correspond to perfect classical *clausulae*, they nevertheless give sections of the narrative a powerful sense of beginning and ending;[119] see, for example, §5/1 *inter preliandum interfecit*, §5/5 *in Hyberniam pervenisse*, §8.1 *prophetasse dicitur*, etc., and especially combined with patterns of alliteration, for example, §2/3 *series sequitur*, §15/3 *timore et tremore contabescere.*[120]

On a larger scale, it is striking that, although the division into sections in the edition follows that of *HGK*, these largely keep to the paragraph division of the manuscript and there can be a real sense of climax at the end of a section of the narrative. It may be marked in a number of ways; some sections end with a biblical analogy, for example, §19/7 (a New Testament quotation, Matthew 26.31, after the kidnap of Gruffudd), §21/3 (help from God in answer the prayers of the people), §25/9 (Gruffudd restraining his ferocity like David towards Saul), §31/8 (the people of Gwynedd returning like the Israelites from Babylon). In some cases, the section ends on a rhetorical crescendo; for example, after the betrayal of Gruffudd at the battle of Bron yr Erw, there is a rhetorical lament beginning *Nemo miretur has humanarum rerum vicissitudines, ut interdum vincere, interdum fugere sit necesse . . .* (§14/13) which in an ascending tricolon goes on to compare his fate with three great figures who suffered betrayal at the hands of their own people, Iudas Maccabaeus, Julius Caesar and, coming closer to home, last but not least, Arthur (§14/14–18). At the battle over the castle at Aberlleiniog (§23/15–17), Gruffudd's *pencerdd* Gellan falls and is given, as it were, a prose *marwnad* beginning *quanta scientiarum varietate, quanto eloquentiae splendore perpolitum esse oporteret . . .* in which the author in high rhetorical style laments his own lack of skill in praising him, though he admits that he would fail even if he had the eloquence of Cicero or the poetical genius of Homer. The most striking example comes at the point in the narrative where Gruffudd has finally seen off all his enemies and Henry has retreated for the last time (§32/10–12). In a highly rhetorical tricolon marking the end of his troubles, repeating *quoties* and *non potuerunt*, he lists his vanquished opponents, each one ending the clause in emphatic position:

> O Deus bone, <u>quoties</u> Griffinum subvertere conati sunt comites, ac <u>non potuerunt</u>. <u>Quoties</u> tentarunt Powisiae incolae, at <u>non potuerunt</u>. <u>Quoties</u> aggressi sunt fallacis Trahaerni fautores, at <u>non potuerunt</u>.[121]

---

[119] For a useful discussion of *clausulae*, see G. Orlandi, 'Clausulae in Gildas' De Excidio Britanniae' in M. Lapidge and D. Dumville (eds), *Gildas* (Woodbridge, 1984), 129–49.

[120] Cf. also §9/1 *tyrannus possideret*, §12/2 *oppressorem depugnarent*, §12/9 *in domino gubernare*, §13/4 *fortunae congratulabantur*, §14/18 *resistere potuerunt*, §16/1 *in Venedotia pullularunt*, §18/11 *decurrisse putarentur*, §18/19 *nec ecclesiis pepercerit*, etc.

[121] It is worth observing that this tricolon came in for some shabby treatment from the scribes. Of the nine manuscripts deriving from Peniarth 434, six of them omit the second sentence of the three (§32/11), and Thelwall's annotations had anyway succeeded in destroying the rhetorical structure, which was then further mangled in *D* by another set of annotations (on *D*, see above, pp. 14–15, and below, p. 40–1); for the significance of this omission for the stemma of the manuscripts of *VGC*, see above, p. 11.

When we turn to other late eleventh- and twelfth-century writers, similar narrative patterns can be identified. A particularly good example is the death of Hugh, earl of Shrewsbury, at the hands of King Magnus, an episode found in *VGC*, the *Brutiau* and related texts, Giraldus Cambrensis, and in various Old Norse sources.[122] The description in Giraldus Cambrensis is fuller and more detailed but it uses the same style of fast moving narrative:

> Et quanquam comes a vertice capitis usque ad talum pedis, praeter oculos suos solum, ferro fideliter esset indutus, tamen dextro percussus in lumine, perforato cerebro, in mare corruit moribundus.[123]

Again, if we turn to Rhigyfarch's life of St David, similar narrative patterns can be discerned; in the following extract from a miracle performed by St Aidan the pattern of present participles and ablative absolutes is particularly striking:

> alio autem tempore dum sanctus Aidanus, eius discipulus, casu quodam ad firmandum doctrine acceptum foris legeret, monasterii affuit prepositus, <u>imperans</u> ei ut ad deportanda de ualle ligna, <u>acceptis duobus bubus</u>, iniret. Erat enim silua in longinquo posita. Discipulus autem Aidanus citius dicto <u>oboediens</u>, nec librum claudendi moram <u>accipiens</u>, siluam petit. <u>Paratis autem lignis, iumentisque impositis, regrediens</u> uiam carpit.[124]

However, the contrast with sixteenth-century writers of Latin from Wales is more striking.[125] The impact of the Renaissance on Wales saw a marked increase in interest in the classical world and in classical texts. Writers of this period tended to seek to emulate classical prose writers, and especially Cicero. The result was a tendency to write long, complex sentences with frequent subordination; ablative absolutes are relatively rare, being replaced by full subordinate clauses. This is well brought out in the long, complex periods of writers such as John Prise; the following example, a single sentence from his *Historiae Brytanicae Defensio* (1573), considers the possibility that Ulysses and other voyagers reached Britain:

> At vt Vlissem sic et alios simili vel errore, vel novas terras indagandi studio ductos, hanc insulam statim a navigij vsu reperto adiisse, nec tam vberem et temperatam, incultam omnino reliquisse verisimile quidem est, nec tam Gallos accolas, tametsi eam in conspectu habuerint, quum locorum amplitudine pro libito, vt credendum est, tum gauderent, quam Graecos, inter quos (vt saepe iam dictum est) navigij vsus primum vigere cepit, huc primum appulisse.[126]

---

[122] *VGC* §28/3–9; *ByT* (Pen. 20), 28a22–29b2 (= *ByT* (Pen. 20 tr.), 20. 33–21. 22); *ByT* (RB), 36. 21–38. 13; *BS*, 88. 30–90. 27; Giraldus Cambrensis, *Itinerarium Kambriae*, II, 7 (p. 129); for the Old Norse sources, see Jesch, 'Norse historical traditions'.

[123] Giraldus Cambrensis, *Itinerarium Kambriae*, II, 7 (p. 129).

[124] *Rhigyfarch's Life of St David*, ch. 35 (p. 15, trans. pp. 38–9).

[125] For a general discussion, see C. Davies, *Latin Writers of the Renaissance* (Cardiff, 1981).

[126] *Historiae Brytanicae Defensio*, 57.

The following passage from the *Commentarioli Britannicae Descriptionis Fragmentum* of Humphrey Lhuyd shows a similar tendency (reflected in the printed text by a need to bracket off the subordinate clauses):

> Quae res olim Britannis a nimis superstitioso monacho Augustino, et nimium hisce frivolis tribuete, Beda maximo vitio dabatur (adeo ut illos eam ob hanc causam haereticos vocare ausus est) nunc (quamvis sub Niceni Concilij anathemate aliter mandatum sit) a pontificibus ipsis et tota ecclesia Europaea contemnitur.[127]

On the other hand, they were perfectly capable of writing simple narrative prose when necessary. The following example could easily come from the pages of *VGC*:

> Maritimam huius tractus partem Richardus Clarensis vir nobilis classe invectus, aedificatis ad ostia Tifii et Ystwyth castellis, sui iuris fecit. Praesidiisque impositis, in Angliam reversus est: cumque accepisset suas a Cambris obsideri, maximis auxilijs fretus terrestri itinere auso satis temerario eis opitulari conatus est, sed apud Coed Grono non procul ab Abergevimi [sic], ab Ierwertho de Caerlleon cum omnibus suis deletus est.[128]

There is a control over the narrative and it has a directness which can sometimes be lost in longer sentences.

Some interesting aspects of sixteenth-century Latinity emerge from a consideration of the fate of one of the fair copies of *VGC*. As has been demonstrated above, manuscript *D* (BL, Additional MS, 19712) was the second fair copy to be made of Peniarth 434.[129] It was then subsequently annotated and a new fair copy made of it, namely *C*, which is in the hand of Sir John Wynn. The changes introduced into *D* are largely stylistic and throw an interesting light on one scholar's view of the Latinity of *D* at the end of the sixteenth century.[130] The annotator of *D* indicates his stylistic preferences from the beginning by replacing the opening *cum*-clause with an ablative absolute, *Regnante in Anglis Edwardo; in Hibernia Therdelacho* (fol. 1r1 = *VGC*, §1/1).[131] He also ends the text as he began: the final paragraph of *VGC* begins with a statement of Gruffudd's age when he died, *cum duos et octoginta annos Griffinus complevisset* (*VGC*, §35/6), which is replaced by an ablative absolute, *tandem duobus et octoginta annis completis* (fol. 10v28). It is clear that the

---

[127] *Commentarioli Britannicae Descriptionis Fragmentum*, 56.

[128] Ibid., 62.

[129] See above, pp. 14–15.

[130] For a brief discussion, see C. Davies, 'Sixteenth-century Latin translation', 161, who thought that the changes had only been made in *C*; cf. also HGC cclxxv–cclxxvi.

[131] The pattern of reference is by folio and line reference to *D* followed by the cross reference to the edited text in *VGC*. The edited text of *VGC* may not correspond exactly to the text quoted above which is the underlying text of *D*, a fair copy which incorporates the annotations of both Edward Thelwall and Thomas Wiliems (see pp. 14–15 above for details).

ablative absolute is the subordinate clause of preference; he uses it to replace, for example, a nominal time phrase: *post hanc pugnam* (*VGC*, §12/8) by *qua victoria parta* (fol. 3r3); a present participle clause: *pecunias suas ac facultates suas secum deducentes* (*VGC*, §15/4) by *rebus suis ac facultatibus una asportatis* (fol. 4v6). He seems particularly keen to eradicate present participle contructions either by ablative absolutes (as above) or by a gerund in the ablative, for example, *exterminans* (*VGC* §29/6) by *exterminando* (fol. 9r27), or by replacing them with finite verbs; for example, *spolia optima domum referrens* (*VGC*, §13/2) is replaced by *spoliaque opima domum reportat* (fol. 3r16), *desaeviens* (*VGC*, §18/18) by *desaevit* (fol. 5v28) added at the end of the clause, *condignas sumens poenas* (*VGC*, §23/14) by *meritas sumpsit poenas* (fol. 7r24–5), *metuentes* (*VGC*, §29/1) by *metuebant* (fol. 9r14), etc. He also displays some lexical preferences; for example, he tends to replace forms of *pugnare* with forms of *dimicare* (e.g. fol. 3r12). He is also keen on *nempe* often in combination with more verbose conjunctions; for example, *quomodo* (*VGC*, §12/8) is replaced by *quemadmodum nempe* (fol. 3r6), *sicut* (*VGC*, §31/7) by *simili nempe modo ac* (fol. 9v16).

The medieval Vita Griffini filii Conani

It has been argued above that the Peniarth 434 version of the life of Gruffudd ap Cynan represents a copy of the original Latin life which was translated into Welsh in the early thirteenth century. This section considers what we can establish about this text and its transmission.

(a) Transmission

The text, as we have it, is unlikely to represent the version which left the author's pen. Several stages of transmission can be detected. At least one stage of copying is presupposed if the suggested emendation of §5/8 is accepted. The text is *ut insula Cycladis inter mare Tyren et Daniam* 'just as island of the Cyclades lies between the Tyrrhenian Sea and Denmark', and is being used as an analogy for how the Hebrides (*insulae Daniae*) lie in a line north of Ireland on the sea route from Scandinavia. Geographically, however, the text makes no sense, and it is suggested in the notes to §5/8 that the text originally read *ut insula Cycladis inter mare Tyren et Ioniam*. The Welsh text, likewise, has *rung mor Tyren a Denmarc* (*HGK*, 4. 3 = *MPW*, 56. 12), and so the error, if that is what it is, must have crept in between the original composition and the version from which the Welsh text was made. A similar instance is §14/11 *in insulam Adron (quae et Focarum insula dicitur)* 'to the island of Adron (which is also called the island of seals)'. It is argued in the notes to this passage that the original has something like *ad Ron insulam .i. focarum insula* where *ron* is the

Old English or Old Irish word for seal, and that this was rewritten at some point as *in insulam Adron*. This would help to explain the gloss, and clarify §23/9 *in quandam insulam (quae Dinieuyt vocatur)* corresponding in the Welsh version to *en ron enys, nyt amgen enys dinewyt e mor* 'in the island of Ron, namely the island of the seals' (*HGK*, 20. 9–10 = *MPW*, 72. 29–30). At §14/11 the changes must have occurred before the translation was made. At §23/9, the original Latin text may have had something like *ad Ron insulam* but this was changed to a vaguer *in quandam insulam*, perhaps through uncertainty as to whether this was the same island as in §14/11, although it is possible here that the original Latin text had *in quandam insulam* and that the Welsh text was adding precision. These examples, then, provide evidence for changes between the original and the Welsh translation and for changes in the subsequent transmission.

The establishment of the original Latin text of the life of Gruffudd ap Cynan also allows us to identify errors in the early transmission of the Welsh text, that is, errors which predate the archetype of all the extant versions. Two instances have already been discussed above.[132] At the battle of Mynydd Carn the *carnedd* in question is identified as *sub quo thesauros absconditos olim opinantur* (§18/17), but the corresponding section of the Welsh text has *a dan er honn y cladwt rysswr* 'under which a hero was buried' (*HGK*, 16. 15 = *MPW*, 69. 2–3). The second is the misreading of *neu* as *nei* (*HGK*, 7. 15 = *VGC*, §10/6 *vel . . . vel*).

Although Simon Evans used the fragmentary version in Peniarth 17 for as much of the text as he could, the Latin text now allows us to identify textual errors in Peniarth 17 in cases where the Latin text agrees with the reading of the other later manuscripts. In §2/1 the Latin text has the name *Esyllt* which is also found in all the other manuscripts except for Peniarth 17 which has *Etill* (*HGK*, 1. 14 = *MPW*, 53. 17). While we cannot rule out the possibility that the name in the Latin text has been modernized, it is just as likely that *Etill* has been imported into Peniarth 17 from another genealogy. At §14/11 the Latin text has *ut ad naves deducat*, but the Peniarth 17 version of the Welsh text contains *o'e anvod* 'against his will' instead of *a'e anvon* of the other versions (*HGK*, 11, n. 3); the Peniarth 17 version is erroneous as *a'e anvon* correctly translates the Latin. At §21/1 the Latin text has *pedites sagittariosque*, while the Peniarth 17 version of the Welsh text has *a phedyt saethydyon* 'archers on foot' (*HGK*, 18. 7 = 70. 24–5) against *a phedyt a saethydyon* of the other manuscripts (*HGK*, 18, n. 1). The other manuscripts preserve a better rendering of the Latin text.

A further point may be made about the original Latin text. Occasional discrepancies between the Latin and Welsh versions might be explicable in terms of the misreading of a manuscript written in an insular script, which was in some instances comprehensible to the Welsh translator but not to the copyist

---

[132] See above, pp. 28–9, 33 respectively.

who was perpetuating the line of transmission of the Latin text.[133] The evidence
is slight but it is worth drawing attention to it. Two examples suggest confusion
of *t* and *c*: at §15/2 *VGC* has *navibus . . . mare profundum saltantibus*, the last
word is corrected by Thelwall to *sulcantibus*, thus matching the Welsh *gan
rwygaw dyvynvoroed* 'cleaving the deep seas' (*HGK*, 12. 9 = *MPW*, 64. 26); the
Latin phrase, literally, 'dancing (over) the sea', is striking but may well be an
error with an original *sulcantibus* in insular script misread as *saltantibus*.
Similarly, the name *Uchdryt* (*HGK*, 23. 28) is preserved in the Latin text as
Vchtrico (§26/3). Another possible instance may account for the confusion
between Homer and Virgil at §23/17, where the Latin refers to *Homerum* and
the Welsh to *Maro vard* (*HGK*, 21. 19–20 = *MPW*, 74. 5). Is it possible that the
original had *Maronem* in insular script and that the capital *M-* was misread as
H- and that there was confusion of *n* and *r*? If so, again the Welsh translator
was correct in his reading. On the other hand, it is perfectly possible that the
error went in the other direction, and that the original had *Homerum*. Or,
thirdly, the Welsh translator simply preferred to refer to Virgil.

(b) Place of composition

Simon Evans tentatively suggested that Clynnog Fawr might be implicated in
some way in the writing of *HGK* and/or its Latin predecessor.[134] Clynnog
certainly figures prominently in *HGK*, as a place of refuge for the sons of Merwydd
(*HGK*, 8. 3–4), as the place where two brothers from Anglesey received their
cyfarws from Gruffudd (*HGK*, 10. 20–2), as a beneficiary of his will (*HGK*, 32. 1),
and with Simeon of Clynnog present at his deathbed (*HGK*, 32. 9–10). All the
references to Clynnog in *HGK* are in the Latin but, insofar as they are
comprehensible, they are slightly different.[135] At §12/2 (which is one of the most
difficult sentences to read in the whole manuscript) the beginning of the
sentence reads *Ex quo loco milites armatos (viz. filios Merwydd) in Kelynnauk
et sanctuarium misit metu hominum Powisiae* 'From here he sent armed soldiers,
namely the sons of Merwydd, to the sanctuary at Clynnog out of fear of the
men of Powys'; it is ambiguous as to whether they were sent into sanctuary or
whether they were sent to the sanctuary to protect it from the men of Powys.
The rest of the sentence is so corrupt it is difficult to make anything of it. At
§34/7 in the list of churches which benefit from his largesse, Clynnog is
apparently promoted in the Welsh text to second from fourth in the Latin: *Ac*

---

[133] For a suggestion that the insular tradition may have survived from the twelfth into the thirteenth
century in areas such as Clynnog Fawr, 'beyond the flood of Norman influence', see Huws,
Medieval Welsh Manuscripts, 38.

[134] *HGK*, p. ccxlix; see also P. Sims-Williams, 'Clas Beuno and the Four Branches of the Mabinogi', in
B. Maier and S. Zimmer (eds), *150 Jahre Mabinogion* (Tübingen, 2001), 111–27.

[135] For further details on what follows, see the relevant notes.

Ecclesiae Caercybi decem solidos ac tantundem Penmonae, Germani, Dinerth, Gelynnawc, Enlli, Meivot, multisque praecipuis aliis ecclesiis. While this might indicate a more favourable attitude towards Clynnog, it is difficult to be certain; the variation in word order may just as easily be a result of scribal error with a scribe omitting some of the names and inserting them later on. At §35/1, in the Latin text the equivalent to the laudatory adjectives (*gwr addfet o oet a doethinap* (*HGK*, 32. 11)) are not used of Simeon, though similar words are used of the prior of the monastery at Chester. The overall impression would be that the references to Clynnog are slightly different, but not sufficiently for us to build anything substantial upon the differences. If, however, all the differences were significant, we might wish to argue that Clynnog may have been more involved in the Welsh translation than in the original Latin version or that these additions reflect further Clynnog reworking at the translation stage of a text already associated with them in some way. The former of these is not unlikely in the light of the general impression that *VGC* is less firmly focused on Gwynedd than is *HGK*.

The evidence for this impression is cumulative and made up of relatively small variations between the text of *VGC* and *HGK*. The absence of the men of Gwynedd from the battle of Mynydd Carn has already been discussed, as has the lack of laudatory adjectives describing Simeon of Clynnog.[136] At §10/2 the action switches from Ireland to Wales and the change of geographical context is marked in the Latin text by *in Cambria*, but this is missing in the Welsh text, which simply moves into the description of the unjust rule of Trahaearn and it is taken for granted that the scene is Gwynedd. The mention at §31/1 of the support of a unnamed bishop of Bangor in establishing Gruffudd's friendship with Henry, *Bangorensis episcopi interventu*, is more firmly dated to before 1109 in the Welsh text by the identification of the bishop as Hervé (*HGK*, 28. 4). At §33/5 in the Latin text Gwynedd simply gleams with churches; in the Welsh text they are *kalcheit* 'lime-washed' (*HGK*, 30. 18), perhaps reinforcing the comparison with shining stars, but adding detail not in the Latin version. Pejorative statements about Gruffudd and men of Gwynedd have been removed in the Welsh version; for example, when Gruffudd is on the run, he is compared with a runaway slave, *quasi erro* (§22/8).[137] On the other hand, interest in Gwynedd seems to be indicated by the observation in both the Latin and Welsh versions that Bangor gets a bigger legacy than anywhere else, though perhaps tellingly we are not told in either text how much it was, simply that it was *etiam amplius* or *a mwy no hynny* (*VGC*, §34/5 = *HGK*, 31. 19), that is, more than the 20 *solidi* given to Dublin, St David's, Chester and Shrewsbury. This is an awkward phrase not only in its vagueness but also because it seems oddly out of place and has the air of an afterthought.

---

[136] See above, p. 34.

[137] The reference to the people of Gwynedd as *imbecilliores* 'weaker, incapacitated' (§25/2), which is omitted from *HGK* could be taken to be pejorative, but does not need to be; see the note on §25/2.

Apart from a cumulative vagueness about Gwynedd, further evidence may be provided by the terminology of nationality in *VGC*. In a wide-ranging discussion of the terminology of nationality in Wales, for example, the use of *Cambri* and *Cambria* beside *Wallenses* and *Wallia*, Huw Pryce has proposed that in the twelfth century the 'Cambrian' terminology was associated with St David's and material emanating from there.[138] When this proposal is tested against *VGC* it is striking that the terminology is overwhelmingly 'Cambrian'. All the references to the Welsh and Wales are to *Cambri* and *Cambria*, except for three instances: neither of the first two, §5/10 (*Wallice*), §22/4 (*Wallia*), occurs in *HGK* and so they are likely to be later introductions into the text of *VGC*. The third instance, *certamine Wallorum* (§23/12), is curious because it uses a form otherwise unattested in Cambro-Latin, namely *Wallorum* implying a singular *Wallus*, rather than *Wallensium* (or *Cambrorum*);[139] that the Welsh are being referred to here is supported by the text of *HGK* which has *emlad e Kemry* (*HGK*, 20. 22). The context is a siege and it is suggested in the notes that the original had *certamine vallorum* and that this was misunderstood as *Wallorum* at an early stage in the transmission before the Welsh translation had been made. The evidence for 'Cambrian' usage in *VGC* could, on the one hand, undermine Pryce's thesis, as it would provide evidence of 'Cambrian' usage in north Wales; on the other hand, if it turns out that the 'Cambrian' terminology is exclusively Menevensian at this period, it would suggest that the original Latin text of *VGC* was composed by someone in St David's or by someone trained in 'Menevensian' Latinity. 'Cambrian' terminology was, however, also the norm in sixteenth-century Latin usage, and it might be objected that the evidence for 'Cambrian' usage in *VGC* is simply a feature of its sixteenth-century origins, or at least that it provides evidence for redaction in the early sixteenth century. But the above discussion has presented a case for the twelfth-century Latinity of *VGC*, and in that context it is more likely that the 'Cambrian' terminology is of that period.[140] Furthermore, the 'Cambrian' terminology is so embedded in the text (and the few examples of 'Wallensian' terminology so easily rejected as secondary) that it is difficult to believe that it could have been replaced so consistently throughout. If so, the relative vagueness of *VGC* in matters of Venedotian detail, discussed in the preceding paragraph, would also be explained by a place of composition outside Gwynedd. One striking feature of *VGC* is that, while the detail about Gwynedd is vaguer than in *HGK*, the detailed passage about St David's is more or less identical; as a result, a Menevensian presence tends to loom larger in *VGC* than it does in *HGK*.

[138] H. Pryce, 'British or Welsh?', *EHR*, 116 (2001), 775–801.
[139] Note, however, *inter Walos et Anglos* in the twelfth-century *Quadripartitus* version of the Dunsaete Ordinance (*Die Gesetze der Angelsachsen*, I.377), from manuscript R, dated by Liebermann to c.1160; see also P. Wormald, *The Making of English Law* (Oxford, 1999), 236–44.
[140] See above, pp. 35–41.

(c) Date of composition

A related issue at this point is the date of composition. It is clear that *VGC* was composed after the death of Gruffudd in 1137, perhaps in the reign of his son, Owain. Beyond that, *VGC* does not offer much that is new. If we assume that the Waterford dating clause about the son of Harald ruling in Waterford until this day, *hyt hediw* (*HGK*, 3. 27), which has been lost from *VGC* due to damage to the corner of the page (§5/7), was originally in the text, then the composition date is probably before 1171.[141] If so, it may be useful to explore when in that period, from 1137 to 1170, links between Gwynedd and St David's might have been closest. Another factor may also be relevant. When Gruffudd lands at St David's and receives a warm welcome, he lands at Porth Clais which is described strikingly as *non longe a sede archiepiscopali* (§17/1; cf. *ker llaw archescopty Mynyv* (*HGK*, 13. 19)).[142] If this phrase is to be given its full weight, then it raises the issue of St David's claims for metropolitan status which came to the fore in this period. More specifically, it was a major issue during the bishopric of Bernard, who died in 1148. Bernard's successors, David fitz Gerald (1148–76) and Peter de Leia (1176–98), were both required to swear an oath not to pursue any claim for metroplitan status.[143] In the context of the life of Gruffudd ap Cynan, the support which Owein Gwynedd gave to St David's is important, not least because of the important role played by Simeon of Clynnog in urging Owain to support Bernard.[144] One possibility, then, and it remains a tentative suggestion only, is that *VGC* was composed in the context of the relationship between St David's and Gwynedd at some point in the latter part of the bishopric of Bernard (after 1137 but before Bernard's death in 1148). Was it perhaps composed as a *quid pro quo*, or simply as a gift, in return for the support of Gwynedd? If so, that might help to account for the Menevensian Latinity of *VGC*, as betrayed by its 'Cambrian' usage of nationality terms, and also for that sense of distance from Gwynedd discussed above. It should be recalled that there were close dynastic links as Gruffudd ap Rhys had married the daughter of Gruffudd ap Cynan, Gwenllian. Furthermore, it may also be significant that from 1136 Owain Gwynedd and his brother Cadwaladr occupied Ceredigion, and it was only in 1150–1 that most of Ceredigion was taken by the sons of Gruffudd ap Rhys of Deheubarth. In other words, a composition date

---

[141] On arguments for a date as late as the thirteenth century, see K. L. Maund, *Ireland, Wales and England in the Eleventh Century* (Woodbridge, 1991), 171–82, and Duffy's review for a rejection of her views.

[142] See *HGK*, 73, n. 13.19, where it is suggested that the original Latin might have had *metropolis* or the like here.

[143] R. R. Davies, *Conquest, Co-existence, and Change* (Oxford and Cardiff, 1987), 191; M. T. Flanagan, *Irish Society, Anglo-Norman Settlers, Angevin Kingship* (Oxford, 1989), 34–5; M. Richter, *Giraldus Cambrensis* (Aberystwyth, 1976), 38–56 (for a calendar of the surviving correspondence on the issue, ibid., 130–2, and the references cited there).

[144] Cf. *HGK*, pp. ccxlviii–ccxlix and p. 107; see also Giraldus Cambrensis, *De invectionibus*, 2, 8–10; *Episcopal Acts*, I, 136, 207, 259–60, 265.

of 1137 × 1148 would coincide with a period of Gwynedd dominance in an important part of the diocese of St David's.

(d) Historical implications

At this point, it may be helpful to draw attention to some of the significant differences between the two versions, some of which have historical implications. These will not be explored in full here, but further discussion can be found both above and in the notes to the text. The main difference has already been mentioned, namely the tendency for the Latin text to be less firmly focused on Gwynedd than the Welsh text. This is discussed further in the preceding section. Other differences include the following.

The genealogies are part of the text and mostly correspond to the genealogies in *HGK*. There are two small gaps in relation to *HGK*, one at least of which is explicable by eye-skip.[145] One reason for drawing attention to this here is that Patrick Sims-Williams had tentatively suggested that the genealogies in *HGK* might not necessarily have been the same as any genealogical information in the original Latin life.[146]

The early sections relating to Ireland and Viking activity are of particular interest to historians. Unfortunately, this is the most damaged part of Peniarth 434, and so some questions cannot be answered; for example, the sentence about Waterford (end of §5/7), which supplies a dating clause implying that *VGC* was composed before 1171, has been lost, though the size of the gap would suggest it had been there originally. Nevertheless, some matters have been clarified. According to the Latin text, Gruffudd's grandfather, Olaf, king of Dublin, came from *Scotia* (§4/1).[147] The section on Alanus is a little clearer: he is the brother of the king of Llychlyn and he is killed by Twr. If Alanus has been correctly identified as St Olaf, the form of his name, *Alanus*, might originally have been *Alauus*, or perhaps *Amlauus* or *Anlauus*.[148] With regard to the lands ruled over by Olaf, the form *Arennae* (§4/2) corresponding to *Renneu* 'Rinns' (*HGK*, 2. 20 = *MPW*, 55. 2) might encourage us to think in terms of the Isle of Arann rather than Galloway.

Later in the text, the men of Gwynedd seem to have been absent from the Battle of Mynydd Carn, as do Meilir ap Rhiwallon and men of Powys (§§17–18). The effect of this in part is to change our overall perception of Gruffudd's relationship with the people of Gwynedd and Anglesey, and it tends to throw into higher relief their inclination to revolt against Gruffudd and to let him down at every available opportunity.

[145] See the notes to §3.
[146] Sims-Williams, 'Historical need', 28: 'and we cannot even be sure that the translator took over the genealogies unchanged from his Latin exemplar'.
[147] See the notes to §4/1–2.
[148] See the notes to §5/1–4.

From a historiographical standpoint, *VGC* follows the convention of medieval historical and biographical texts in that the composer was well versed in the conventions of biographical writing deriving ultimately from Suetonius and in the drawing of copious parallels with classical and biblical figures.[149] Almost all of them are also found in *HGK*, such as the regular analogy between Gruffudd and Iudas Maccabaeus (and therefore between Hugh, earl of Chester, and Antiochus), and between Gruffudd and David, highlighting the themes of freeing a nation from foreign domination, internal betrayal, resistance and resurgence. However, the Latin life also allows us to pursue biblical allusions which have not recognizably survived translation into Welsh. For example, the Maccabaean theme is more deeply embedded in the text than has been realized: at §14/14 (and again with slightly different phrasing at §18/8) Gruffudd is described as 'like a giant or a lion', *ut gygas vel leo*, which is derived from 1 Macc. 3.3–4. Similarly, Gruffudd's building projects in Gwynedd (§33/2–3), and especially his church-building, might be seen in the light of Maccabaeus rebuilding the temple in Jerusalem in 1 Macc. 41–51. Again, the plan to kidnap Gruffudd at §19/3–4 might be compared with the attempted kidnapping of Maccabaeus (1 Macc. 7.28–9). A number of other biblical allusions also come to light. The description of William Rufus leaving 'not even a dog alive pissing against a wall' (§25/1) has been discussed above.[150] At §32/7 Henry plans to destroys the people of Gwynedd at sword point, *in ore gladii*, a common Old Testament phrase.[151] When the Normans fall from their horses like figs from a tree at §28/6, it is likely that Old Testament imagery is intended, though a direct parallel is less easy to track down.[152]

The general impression of the range of Old Testament reference is that it is being used by someone who is at home with the phraseology of the Bible to the extent that he did not check his references. There are a number of instances where the reference makes superficial sense, but does not stand up to detailed scrutiny; for example, at §12/4 the parallel between Anian, the messenger, and the young Amalechite (1 Samuel 31–2 Samuel 1) only extends as far as the delivery of the

---

[149] On the biography in medieval Wales, see J. B. Smith, *The Sense of History in Medieval Wales* (Aberystwyth, 1991), 6–7, 12; see also more generally G. B. Townend, 'Suetonius and his influence', in T. A. Dorey (ed.), *Latin Biography* (London, 1967), 79–111; K. R. Bradley, *Suetonius' Life of Nero* (Brussels, 1978), 15–19; F. Leo, *Die griechische-römische Biographie* (Leipzig, 1901), 1–16, and more generally in the medieval period, W. Berschin, *Biographie und Epochenstil in lateinischen Mittelalter* (Stuttgart, 1986–91). For general discussion of biblical reference, see A. Gransden, *Historical Writing in England* (London, 1996), 95 (William the Conqueror as Samson and Solomon), 192 (heavenly portents of disaster: King David in 1138, Stephen in 1141), 456 (Edward I, Wallace likened to Herod and Nero); see also R. W. Hanning, *The Vision of History in Early Britain* (New York, 1966). On Judas Maccabaeus generally in medieval historiography, see J. Dunbabin, 'The Maccabees as exemplars in the tenth and eleventh centuries', in K. Walsh and D. Wood (eds), *The Bible in the Medieval World* (Oxford, 1985) 31–41; M. Keen, *Chivalry* (New Haven, 1984), 117–22.

[150] See pp. 25–6 above; for the full biblical references, see the notes for §25/1.

[151] See the notes to §32/7 for detailed references.

[152] See the notes to §28/6 for possible parallels.

message; the latter is executed by David, while the former is rewarded by Gruffudd. Similarly, the comparison of Gruffudd with Hezechiah at §34/2 and elsewhere in the latter stages of *VGC* works well, provided we do not recall that Hezechiah was also used as the paradigm of the good king succeeded by a bad son, Manasseh.[153]

All the examples discussed so far are identical in *VGC* and *HGK*, but there are also some instances where the translator seems to have added his own layer of biblical reference, which is largely New Testament in character in contrast to the predominantly Old Testament nature of the frame of reference in *VGC*. At §26/10 the people of Gwynedd escape into the wilds *Francorum aliarumque externarum gentium metu* 'through fear of the French, etc.', but the Welsh text has *rhag ofyn yr Iddewon, nit amgen, y Ffreink a chenedloedd ereill* 'for fear of the Jews, namely the French and other peoples' (*HGK*, 24. 21–2 = *MPW*, 77. 2–3). All the biblical references employed elsewhere in this text would make the men of Gwynedd analogous to the Jews. The allusion is probably New Testament, referring to the presecution of Christ by the Jews; compare, for example, *propter metum Iudaeorum* 'because of fear of the Jews' (John 7.13, etc.). After §26/10 the Welsh translator added an extra sentence about people suffering when they have lost their leader, *Kanys megys y dyweit dwywawl ymadrawdd: 'digwyddaw a orug y bobl hep tywyssawg'* 'For as the Holy Word says: "the people fall without a leader"' (*HGK*, 24. 23–4 = *MPW*, 77. 4–5). This seems to have been carried over as a paraphrase from §19/7 where Matthew 26.31 is quoted directly in the context of Gruffudd's kidnap. There are also indications that the translator himself was so steeped in the Bible that he tended to make biblical allusions more precise; for example, at §21/3, *At populorum clamor ad Deum ascendebat, ipseque illis opportuno tempore subsidium tulit* 'But the cries of the peoples rose to God, and He at an appropriate time brought help to them', the Welsh translator replaced the second clause with *ac enteu a'e guerendewis wy* 'and He listened to them' (*HGK*, 18. 9 = *MPW* 70. 28). The first part of this sentence is biblical (for example, Exod. 2:23, *ascendit clamor eorum ad Deum ab operibus*) and it is likely that it triggered in the Welsh translator the usual biblical continuation, *et (ex)audivit (Deus)*, or the like.[154] There is finally one instance where the translator may be making a Maccabaean allusion more precise (perhaps the composer of the original was working from memory): at §26/1 Hugh of Chester is compared with Antiochus and is described as *malorum omnium architectus*, but in the Welsh translation this phrase has been replaced by *gureid er holl drwc* 'the root of all the evil' (*HGK*, 23. 11 = *MPW*, 75. 27) which has a closer biblical parallel: the first time Antiochus appears in 1 Maccabees, he is described as a *radix peccatrix* 'an evil scion' (1 Macc. 1.11).

---

[153] Cf. also §25/9 (Gruffudd holding back like David), §35/1 (anointment by oil), §35/5 (lamentation on the death of Gruffudd as at the death of Joshua).
[154] Cf. also §28/2 where a similar replacement occurs.

Method of editing

The text edited here is the underlying text of Peniarth MS 434. It is presented with a facing translation. The minimal apparatus under the text indicates only the few cases where the text of the manuscript has been emended. Section (a) of the main apparatus contains all changes made to the text by Edward Thelwall. Subsequent additions and changes made by Thomas Wiliems and others are listed in section (b) of the apparatus. No attempt is made to restore a twelfth-century version of the text, though obvious later features are pointed out in the notes; for example, the arabic numerals are retained when in a twelfth-century text Roman numerals would be expected.

For the first twenty pages of the manuscript the top corner of each page has suffered from rodent damage. It is worst on page 1 and with decreasing severity the whole page is intact by page 20. In order to provide a complete text, where possible the gaps have been filled with the corresponding text from Cotton, Vitellius C.ix, the earliest surviving copy; this text is printed in italics. There are cases, for example, §12/1, where the text of Cotton, Vitellius C.ix is too different to be used to fill the gap; in such instances gaps have been left in the text, indicated by [...] or by [... ...] to indicate large gaps, and the difficulties are indicated in the notes. Similarly, in the few instances where nothing can be made of the underlying text the gap is indicated by [...]; again the difficulties are indicated in the notes. Where the text of Cotton, Vitellius C.ix seems too long to fit in the space, it is bracketed with ( ). The complete text of Cotton, Vitellius C.ix is printed in Appendix 3.

In a few cases, a gap was left by the scribe of the main text, probably where the exemplar was illegible; they are indicated by < >. Some of these gaps were filled by the annotator; these are noted in the apparatus.

In some instances, the text has required emendation to make sense; these are indicated in the apparatus beneath the text and discussed in the notes. Such emendations have been made sparingly and usually in order to restore grammatical sense. In most cases, however, the text of Peniarth 434 has been retained and any emendation suggested and discussed in the notes.

The text is divided into sections which correspond to the section divisions in *HGK* (see the concordance, pp. 210–11). The sections are numbered and within each section the sentences are numbered. Reference to the text is by section and sentence number; thus, for example, §34/2 refers to the second sentence of section 34.

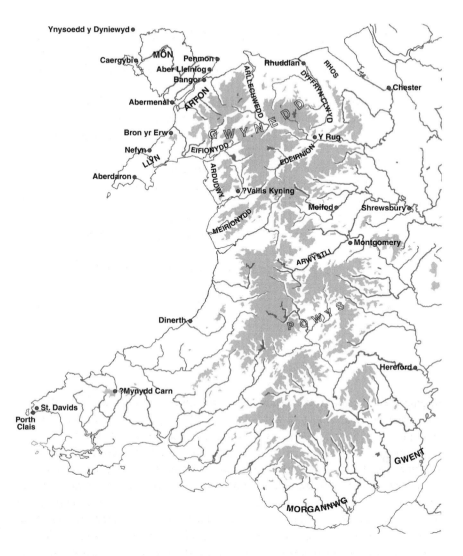

Map of Wales showing places mentioned in *VGC*.

Vita Griffini filii Conani

(NLW, Peniarth MS, 434)

§1

[p. 1][1]*Cum in Anglia regnaret Edwardus dictus Confessor et apud Hybernos Therdelachus rex, nascitur in Hybernia apud civitatem Dublinensem Griffinus rex Venedotiae, nutriturque in loco Comoti Colomkell* dicto Hybernice Swrth *Colomkelle, per tria miliaria distante a domo suorum parentum.*

§2

[1]*Eius pater Cyna*nnus erat rex Venedocie, *mater vero Racvella* filia Avloedi regis Dublinensis *civitatis, ac quintae partis* Hybernie. [2]Prosapia quidem *quam nobili ac regia* oriundus erat Gruffinus cum pater*na tum materna quemad*modum genealogiae recto ordine a pa*rentibus* dedu*ctae* monstrant, quarum series sequitur.

§3

[1]Siquidem Griffinus filius fuit Cynani filii Ja*cobi*, filii Idwali, filii Elissae, filii Meurik, filii Anarauti, filii Rhodri, filii Esyllt, quae fuit filia Cynani de castro Dyndaythwy, filii Idwali Dyre, filii Cadwalederi Benedicti, filii Cadwallawn manus oblongae, filii Einawn Yr*th*, filii Cunedae regis, filii Ederni, filii Paterni vest*is* ceruleae, filii Tageti, filii Jacobi, filii Guid*awc*, [p. 2] *filii Keni, filii Caini, filii Gorgaini, filii Doli, filii Gurdoli, filii Dwvyn, filii Gordwvyn, filii Anwerit, filii Onnet, filii Diawng, filii Brychweni, filii Yweni, filii Avallach, filii Avlech, filii Beli Magni.* [2]At rursum Rhodri fuit fil*ius Mervyn Vrych*, filii Gwriat, filii Elideri, *filii Sandef*, filii Alkwm, filii Tagit, filii *Gwen, filii Dwc*, filii Llywarch senioris, filii *Elidir Llydan*wyn, filii Meirchiawn Gvl, *filii Gorwst Ll*edlwm, filii Keneu, filii Coeli Godebaw*c*, filii Tegwan Cloff, filii Dehewent, filii Vrbani, filii Gradi, filii Rivedeli, filii Rydeyrni, filii Eudeyrni, filii Eudyganti, filii Eudos, filii Eudolei, filii Avallach, filii Aflechi, filii Beli Magni, filii Manogani, filii Eneit, filii Kyrwyt, filii Crydoni, filii Dyvynarthi, filii Prydein, filii Aet Magni, filii Antonii, *f*ilii Seirioel, filii Gurwsti, filii Bruti [p. 3]Ysg*wydwyn, filii Eboraci, filii Membricii, filii Madauci, filii Locrini, filii Bruti ducis Romani, filii Sylvii, filii*

The Life of Gruffudd ap Cynan

Translation

§1

¹When Edward (called the Confessor) was ruling in England and King Toirrdelbach was ruling over the Irish, there was born in Ireland in the city of Dublin, Gruffudd, king of Gwynedd, and he was fostered in a place in the commote of Colum Cille called in Irish Sord Coluim Chille, which lies three miles away from the home of his parents.

§2

¹His father, Cynan, was king of Gwynedd, his mother Ragnell, daughter of Olaf, king of the city of Dublin and of a fifth part of Ireland. ²From how noble and regal a lineage Gruffudd stemmed, both on the paternal and maternal side, the corresponding genealogies, derived from his ancestors in direct line, demonstrate; their sequence follows.

§3

¹Gruffudd was indeed the son of Cynan, son of Iago, son of Idwal, son of Elisedd, son of Meurig, son of Anarawd, son of Rhodri, son of Esyllt, who was the daugher of Cynan from the castle of Dindaethwy, son of Idwal Dyre, son of Cadwaladr Bendigaid, son of Cadwallon of the long hand, son of Einion Yrth, son of King Cunedda, son of Edern, son of Padarn blue-shirt, son of Tegid, son of Iago, son of Gwyddog, son of Cain, son of Gorgain, son of Doli, son of Gwrddoli, son of Dwfn, son of Gwrddwfn, son of Anweryd, son of Onned, son of Diwng, son of Brychwen, son of Ywain, son of Afallach, son of Aflech, son of Beli Mawr. ²And again Rhodri Mawr was the son of Merfyn Frych, son of Gwriad, son of Elidir, son of Sardest, son of Alcwm, son of Tegid, son of Gwain, son of Diwg, son of Llywarch Hen, son of Elidir Llydanwyn, son of Meirchion, son of Gorwst Lledlwm, son of Cenau, son of Coel Godebog, son of Tegfan Cloff, son of Dehewaint, son of Urban, son of Gradd, son of Rhyfeddel, son of Rhideyrn, son of Euddygant, son of Euddos, son of Euddolai, son of Afallach, son of Aflech, son of Beli Mawr, son of Manogan, son of Enaid, son of Cerwyd, son of Cryddon, son of Dyfnarth, son

Ascanii, filii Aeneae Ysgwydwyn, f*ilii Anchisis, filii Capis, filii* Assaraci, filii Trois, filii *Erictonii, filii* Dardani, filii Jovis, filii Satu*rni, filii Coelii* filii Creti, filii Cyprii, filii Ja*van, filii Japhet*, filii Noe hen, filii Lamech, fi*lii Mathusalem*, filii Enoch, filii Jaret, filii Mah*aleel, filii* Cainan, filii Enos, filii Seth, filii. *Adae*, filii Dei.

§4

[1]Nobilitas Griffini ex stirpe materna deducitur sic: Griffinus rex filius Racnell filiae Auloedi Regis Dubliniae, et quintae partis Hybernie, Insulae Mannae, qui e Scotia genus ducebat. [2]Aliarum complurium insularum rex etiam habebatur ut Daniae, Galovidiae, Arennae, Monae et Venedotiae, ubi eius castellum (dictum Castellum Auloed) fossa et muro quam munitissimum construxit, cuius [p. 4] ru*dera apparent, et vocabatur Castellum Auloedi, quamvis Cambrice appelletur Bon y Dom.* [3]*Auloed iste fuit filius Sutrici regis, filii Auloed regis Cirian, filii Sutrici, filii Auloed regis filii Harfageri Regis qui f*ilius fuerat regis *Daniae.*

§5

[1]*Animadversione* hoc dignum est fuisse Haraldum, *Haraldum Harfagyr suo*sque binos fratres filios regis Daniae, *cuius fratrem* Alanum regem et religionis sanctitate *et virtutis gloria* corporis praestantem, Twr quidam *princeps i*nter preliandum interfecit. [2]At dum spolia illi detraheret ac precipue collo torquem aureum ponderis gravissimi (quo ornamenti genere reges nobilesque tunc utebantur) extorqueret, adhaesit manibus torques genuaque defixa ventri iungebantur. [3]Atque hoc fuit primum, quo eum miraculo ornaverat Deus; deinceps vero Dani eum divorum numero adscripserunt, eum honoribus sunt prosequuti non modicis, adeo ut templa ad eius nominis gloriam erigerent, ac per Daniam cultus ei perficerent, maxime vero *nau*tam illum continuo invocabant, sacrificia [p. 5] donaque *alia illi offerentes, si quando inter navigandum in pericula inciderent.* [4]*Caeterum qui illum occidit princeps, post hoc facinus Thurkiawl* est appe*llatus, qui tantae innocentiae regem* peremisset.

[5]Neque hoc praetereundum vid*etur, tres istos* fratres mari longe lateque p*erlustrasse cum* classe regio more instru*ctissima, ac tandem* in Hyberniam pervenisse. [6]Ver*um non multo* antea Haraldus Harfagyr exercitu*m du*cens copiosum eam erat ingressus, totamque Hyberniam pertransierat summa crudelitate incolas mactando fugandoque sic maximam eius partem sibi subiugarat. [7]Ipse vero civitatem Dublinensem aliasque civitates, castella atque

of Prydain, son of Aedd Mawr, son of Antonius, son of Seirioel, son of Gwrwst, son of Brutus Ysgwyddwyn, son of Eboracus, son of Mambricius, son of Madog, son of Locrinus, son of Brutus, the leader of Rome, son of Silvius, son of Ascanius, son of Aeneas Ysgwyddwyn, son of Anchises, son of Capys, son of Assaracus, son of Trois, son of Ericthonius, son of Dardanus, son of Jove, son of Saturn, son of Coelius, son of Cretus, son of Cyprius, son of Iavan, son of Japhet, son of old Noah, son of Lamech, son of Methusalah, son of Enoch, son of Jaret, son of Mahaleel, son of Cainan, son of Enos, son of Seth, son of Adam, son of God.

§4

[1]The noble status of Gruffudd is derived from his mother's line as follows: king Gruffudd, son of Ragnell, daughter of Olaf, king of Dublin and of a fifth part of Ireland, of the Isle of Man, who derived his ancestry from Scotland. [2]He was also considered to be the king of several other islands in as much as he was regarded as king of Denmark, of Galloway, of Arran, of Anglesey and of Gwynedd, where he built his castle (called the castle of Olaf) which is as strong as possible with its ditch and rampart, parts of which are still visible, and it used to be called Castle of Olaf, though in Welsh it is called Bon y Dom. [3]That Olaf was the son of king Sutric, son of Olaf Cirian, son of Sutric, son of king Olaf, son of king Haarfagr who had been the son of the king of Denmark.

§5

[1]It is worth noting that Harald Haarfagr and his two brothers were sons of the king of Denmark, whose brother, king Alan, outstanding in the sanctity of his devotion and in the fame of his courage and of his appearance, was killed in battle by a prince, Twr. [2]But while Twr was removing spoils from him, and in particular was twisting off a golden torc of great weight (a type of ornament used by kings and nobles at that time), the torc stuck to his hands and his knees were locked and joined to his stomach. [3]And this was the first miracle by which God had marked him out; subsequently the Danes numbered him among their gods and bestowed great honours on him to the extent that they raised temples to the glory of his name and throughout Denmark they established a cult to him; and in particular they used to call upon him as a sailor, offering him sacrifices and other gifts, whenever they fell into danger while sailing. [4]However, the prince who killed him was called after this deed Thurkiawl, because he had killed a king of such great innocence.

[5]And this should not seem to be overlooked: that those three brothers travelled far and wide over the sea with their fleet, fitted out very well in the royal manner, and in the end came to Ireland. [6]Not long before Harald Haarfagr at the head of a large army had entered it, and had crossed the whole of Ireland slaughtering and routing the inhabitants with the greatest cruelty, and in this

presidia edificabat, ubi iam in huius regni possessione confirmatus acquieverat, fratremque alterum in una illarum quas [p. 6] condiderat, *urbium praefectum constituit, quae illorum usitato sermone vocatur Porthlarg, cuius posteritas in hodiernum diem eius urbis dominio potitur.* [8]*At ipse Haraldus totam Hyber*niam *insulasque cunctas Daniae* regebat, quae ex *illo latere Hyber*niae adiacent, ut insula *Cycladis inter* mare Tyren et Daniam. [9]*Tertius fra*trum scilicet Rodulphus in Gallias *naves direxit,* ubi fortiter se gessit, variisque praeli*is Gal*los perdomuit, Galliaeque portionem non modicam subiecit, quam hoc tempore Normaniam vocitamus, quod viri Northwegiae ibi sedes fixerant, scilicet genus a Dania originem deducens. [10]Hanc regionem in duodecim partes sunt partiti ad numerum Baronum vel similitudinem ducum, qui in aliam Galliae partem, Britanniam vel Wallice Lydaw dictam, olim advenerant. [11]Hic civitates multas condiderunt ut Rodwn ad Rodwlfi regis primi perpetuam memoriam, ut Roma a [p. 7] Romulo *nomen acceperat, et a Remo Rhemi: necnon alias urbes, castella, locaque presidiis firmata constituit.* [12]Ab hoc *Rodulpho genus deducunt reges Norman*niae qui Anglie *regnum armis sibi acquisiverunt,* scilicet Willhelmus, et filii du*o, qui ei in regno* constant. [13]At Wilhelmus ille, *vel Rufus, Henricus,* neposque Stephanus coaeta*nei regis Griffini* fuerant. [14]Huius< > ergo fu*erat stirpis* Griffini series, quae paternam ma*ternamque nobilitatem* spectat.

§6

[1]Atque ut paulo longius progrediamur, aviae genus non ignobile fuerat: siquidem Ragnel, mater Gruffini, filia erat praenobilis faeminae, Vaelcorcre, filiae Dunlugi, qui natus etiam erat Tethel regis Laginiae, quintae scilicet partis Hyberniae. [2]Preterea Slani mater Auloed regis filia erat Riyeni regis Innen, quae Hyberniae duas partes continebat. [3]Gurmlach etiam mater Sutrilii regis erat. [4]Haec [p. 8] Murchathum *regem Laginiae patrem habuit: cui ferunt tres filios nobilitate insignes fuisse, scilicet Duncathum regem Innen, Sutricum regem Dublinensem, atque Moelchelen regem* Midif: *suscepisse necnon tradunt* Murcathum regem *Laginiae ex hac* regina Maelmordan filium. [5]*Erant Griffino* fratres duo uterini Ultoniae *reges ambo,* scilicet Ranald filii Mathgauyn, *qui tanta for*titudinis gloria precelluerit, ut intra dies quatuordecim Hyberniae binas partes sibi subiugarit. [6]Admirandum quoddam quasi monstrum marinum erat, cui similem vel pedum potestate vel saltandi peritia Hybernia non habuit. [7]Equum aluit multis naturae dotibus ornatum cui ob egregias facultates < >

---

4   Laginiae] Laginiaei MS.

way had subjugated a very large part of it for himself. [7]He indeed began to build the city of Dublin and other cities, and castles and forts where now he had settled confirmed in the possession of this kingdom, and he established one brother in one of the cities which he had founded as governor of the town which in the common speech of those people is called Porthlarg, and his descendants hold the city under their control to this day. [8]But Harald himself used to rule over the whole of Ireland and all the islands of Denmark, which lie off that side of Ireland, just as island of the Cyclades lies between the Tyrrhenian Sea and Denmark. [9]The third brother, namely Rodulphus, directed his ships to Gaul, where he conducted himself bravely, and overcame the Gauls in various battles, and subdued a large part of Gaul, which today we call Normandy because the men of Norway had established their abode there, since they derived their ancestry from Denmark. [10]They divided this region into twelve parts, according to the number of 'barons', or like the leaders who had formerly arrived in another part of Gaul, namely Brittany, or in Welsh Llydaw. [11]Here they founded many cities such as Rouen in the everlasting memory of Rodulfus, their first king, just as Rome had taken its name from Romulus and Rheims from Remus; furthermore he established many other towns, castles and places strengthened by strongholds. [12]From this Rodulphus the kings of Normandy, who acquired for themselves the kingdom of England, derived their origin, namely William and his two sons who succeeded him in the kingship. [13]And that William, or Rufus, and Henry, and his nephew Stephen, were contemporaries of king Gruffudd. [14]Such therefore was the genealogy of Gruffudd which relates to nobility on both his father's and his mother's side.

§6

[1]And to go further, the ancestry of his maternal grandmother had not been ignoble: indeed Ragnell, the mother of Gruffudd, was the daughter of an extremely noble woman, Vailcorcre, daugher of Dunlang, who was also the son of Tethel, king of Leinster, a fifth part of Ireland. [2]Furthermore, Slani, mother of king Olaf, was daugher of Ryen, king of Innen (Munster), which contained two fifths of Ireland. [3]Gurmlach was the mother of king Sutric. [4]Her father was Murchadh, king of Leinster, and they say he had three sons of outstanding nobility: Dunchath, king of Innen (Munster), Sutric, king of Dublin, and Moelchel, king of Mide; furthermore, they say that Murchadh, king of Leinster, produced a son by that queen, namely Maelmorda. [5]Gruffudd has two uterine brothers, both kings of Ulster, namely Ranaldus mac Mathgamna, who excelled in such great glory of bravery, that within fourteen days he subjugated (the) two parts of Ireland for himself. [6]He was something to be admired, like some great sea-monster, the like of which in speed of foot or skill at jumping Ireland did not possess. [7]He bred a horse endowed with many gifts of nature who on account of its outstanding abilities he named Isliniach; the leap of each was

Isliniach nomen indiderat; eiusdem dimensi utriusque saltus aestimabatur.
⁸Comparandus hic quidem erat vel Cinnari Achillis vel Bucephalo Alex[p.
9]andri imperatoris. ⁹*Alter Griffini frater*, Eth*minach Gawyn rex etiam Ultoniae
fuerat.*

§7

¹Quum *huc usque delibauimus generis nobilitatem*, ea quoniam Griff*inum
humano quodam modo et secundum* rerum terrenarum rationem at*tingit, operae
pretium* me facturum spero, si eius quasi *caelestem prosapiam* et divinum genus
exordiar de *quo ut communi etiam* cum aliis hominibus ille psalterii vers*us
testatur*, 'Vos dii estis, et filii excelsi omn*es', ita* ut vere illud affirmetur, fuisse
Griffinum Kynani, Kynanum Adae, Adam vero Dei filium.

§8

¹Quam celebris ergo habenda cum sit Griffini nobilitas cum terrena tum
caelestis, sumamus illud Merlini Britannicorum facile principis oraculum, qui
de Griffino sic prophetasse dicitur:
    ²'Saltus ferinus presagitur venturus de mari,
    insidiaturus, cuius nomen corruptor multosque corrumpet'.
³Charissimi mihi Cambri, quos fraterna [p. 10] dilectione *complector, Griffinum
cernit*is *cum terrena generis nobilitate, cum M*er*lini vaticinio commendatissimum:
festin*andum *itaque videtur, hiis tamen feliciter i*actis *fundamentis, ad ei*us praeclare
res gestas *operaque magni*fica, quae antiquorum more *percurrere su*mus polliciti
non Diana, vel *Apolline, sed* ipso Christo auspice antico ac d[. . .

§9

¹Cum itaque iam Gruffinus moribus esset excultus enutritus tenerrime, et
adolescentiae annos attingeret materna in domo interque cognatos, saepe illi
solebat mater referre qualis, quantus eius pater extiterat, quam ampla < >,
quamque celebre regnum debebatur, atque etiam quam crudelis iam tyrannus
possideret. ²Quibus ille vocibus anxius, multoties [p. 11] animo subtristi m*ulta
secum versabat, tandem vero* in curiam Murch*athi regis profectus*, querelas apud
eum *et reliquos Hyberniae reges* < > deposuit *gravissimas, monstrando* gentem
extraneam in eiu*s paternam heredi*tatem dominari, humiliterque *petendo, ut ei*
auxiliares copias subministr*arent, quibus* eam vel armis recuperaret.
³C*onsensum est* in eius subsidium polliceturque quisque *opportu*no tempore
suppetias ferre. ⁴Quo responso laetus summas gratias Deo illisque egit.

judged to be of the same length. [8]It was to be compared with Cinnaris of Achilles, or with Bucephalus of Alexander the Great. [9]The other brother of Gruffudd had also been a king of Ulster, Aed mac Mathgamna.

§7

[1]So far we have presented the nobility of his race, and that since it refers to Gruffudd in a human way and according to the reasoning of earthly matters, I hope that I shall be doing something worthwhile, if I shall set out his, as it were, heavenly pedigree and divine lineage, about whom in common with other men that verse of the psalter testifies: 'you are gods, and sons of the most high are you all'; thus let it be truly affirmed that Gruffudd was the son of Cynan, Cynan the son of Adam, and Adam the son of God.

§8

[1]Since it is being considered how fine the nobility of Gruffudd is, both earthly and heavenly, let us take that well-known prophecy of Merlin, easily the chief of the British poets, who is said to have prophesied about Gruffudd:
[2]'A fierce attacker is prophesied who will come from over the sea
intent on onslaught; his name is despoiler and he will despoil many.'
[3]Welshmen most dear to me, whom I embrace with fraternal affection, you see Gruffudd with an earthly nobility of race, most commended by the prophecy of Merlin; and so it seems we should hasten forward, now that these basic facts have been happily set out, to his famous achievements and magnificent deeds, which in the custom of the ancients we have undertaken to recount under the guidance not of Diana or Apollo, but of Christ himself the ancient [...].

§9

[1]And so when Gruffudd was already cultivated in his habits, brought up most gently, he was spending the years of his youth in his mother's home and among his relatives, his mother would often recount to him what kind of man his father had been, and how great he had been, how rich his realm, and how famous a kingdom was owed to him, and also how cruel a tyrant now held it. [2]Upset by these words, he would often turn these things over sadly in his mind, and in the end he set out to the court of king Murchadh, and set his most serious complaints before him and the other kings of Ireland, showing that a foreign people were ruling over his paternal inheritance, and seeking humbly that they should help him in providing auxiliary forces by which he might regain it even by force of arms. [3]It was agreed to help him, and each promised to provide help at the appropriate time. [4]Overjoyed at this response he gave great thanks to God and to them.

§10

[1]Et quum expectatum tempus advenerat, naves extructas conscendit, vela dat ventis, mareque Cambriam versus s< >, appulitque in portum dictum Abermeney. [2]Atque in Cambria tunc principatum gerebant iniuste ac indebite Trahaearn filius Caradoci et Kynwric filius Rhiwallon rex Powisiae in totam [p. 12] Venedociam, *quam inter se su*nt partiti. [3]*Ex hoc loco Griffinus nuntio*s misit ad homines *Insulae Monae, et Arvoniae*, et tres filios Merwyd *in Llino, scilicet Asserum*, Meiriawn, et Gwrganum*, aliosque viros*, ut qua poterant celeritate, *ei occurrerent*. [4]Isti postposita omni cunctatione v*eniunt, s*alutant, adventus causas querunt. [5]Quibus cum expossuisset vehementius ab illis contendebat, ut eum adiuvarent in hereditate paterna vindicanda (siquidem ad illum iure spectabat in illos dominari) atque ut arma secum caperent adversus eos, qui in eius possessiones iniuste dominarentur, ex aliis locis quasi adventitios.

[6]Ab hac congressione sic finita, concilioque hoc secreto absoluto, Griffinus rursum per mare iter arripit vel versus castrum Rudlan versus Robertum Baronem nobilem et potentem, vel ad [p. 13] Hugonem Comit*em Cestriae, ut auxilia vel precibus* impetraret adu*ersus hostes grassantes in avitas* ditiones. [7]Postquam v*ero cognovit Robertus quis* esset, cuius causa ad*ventasset, et quid ab e*o contenderet, pollicitus *est se ei adiutorem futurum*.

---

[4]   adventus] advensus MS

§11

[1]Dum istis consultaverat, accessit *ad Griffinum mulier* sapiens Tangwystyl appellata, *eius cognata*, et uxor Lywarchi Olbiwch, ut eum *(suum cognatum existentem)* salutaret, et omine quodam prediceret illi regnum. [2]Itaque dono illi obtulit camisiam perpulchram et quam < > optimam ex < > Griffini ap Lln. ap Seisill quondam regis contextam. [3]Siquidem Lywarch eius maritus in hoc castro magna aestimatione habebatur, et a thesauris fuerat Griffino ap Lln.

§12

[1]Hinc tandem conscensa navi Gruffinus in Aber Meney revertitur. [2]Ex quo loco milites armatos (scilicet filios Merwydd) in Kelynauc et sanctuarium misit metu hominum [p. 14] Powisiae [... ...]liorumque potentium cum [... ...]aginta probatos quos [... ...] Tegeinglia elegerat et [... ...]si in cantredum Llyen, ut *Kynwricum oppress*orem depugnarent. [3]Isti animose pro*fecti, et in eum impro*viso securum et nihil expectantem p[...] impetum fecerunt, eumque et suorum maximam partem occiderunt. [4]In statione apud Abermeney consederat Gruffinus hoc tempore, rei eventum expectando, et illis faelicia comprecando, cum ecce precurrens iuvenis quidam Arvonensis, Anianus nomine, ut primus nuntium laetum portaret, scilicet occubuisse depopulatorem, praemiumque quasi

§10

[1]And when the awaited time arrived, he prepared the ships and boarded them, set sail, and ploughed a furrow through the sea to Wales, and put in at a port called Abermenai. [2]In Wales at that time Trahaearn son of Caradog and Cynwrig son of Rhiwallon, king of Powys, were holding power unjustly and undeservedly over the whole of Gwynedd which they had divided between themselves. [3]From this place Gruffudd sent out messengers to the men of the island of Angelsey and of Arfon and to the three sons of Merwyd in Lleyn, namely Asser, Meirion and Gwrgan, and to other men that they might come to meet him as quickly as they could. [4]They set aside all delay and came and greeted him and asked why he had come. [5]When had explained to them, he sought more urgently from them that they might help him to regain his paternal inheritance (certainly it was right for him to rule over them) and that they should take up arms with him against those who were ruling over his territory unjustly, as if newly arrived from other parts.

[6]When he had finished this meeting, and this secret council was dispersed, Gruffudd set off by sea again either to the castle of Rhuddlan to the noble and powerful Baron Robert, or to Hugh, Count of Chester, to beg for help against the enemies ravaging his ancestral possessions. [7]After [Robert] had found out who he was and why he had come and what he was asking of him, he amicably promised to help him.

§11

[1]While he had been consulting these people, there came to Gruffudd a wise woman called Tangwystl, his kinswoman, and wife of Llywarch Olbiwch, to greet him as a kinsman and to predict by a certain omen that the kingdom would be his. [2]And so she offered as a gift to him a very fine shirt, the best she had, and < > which had once belonged to Gruffudd, son of Llywelyn, son of Seisill, who had once been king. [3]Indeed Llywarch, her husband, was held in high regard in this castle and had been in charge of the treasury for Gruffudd ap Llywelyn.

§12

[1]From here Gruffudd finally boarded ship and returned to the port of Abermenai. [2]From here he sent armed soldiers, namely the sons of Merwyd, to the sanctuary at Clynnog out of fear of the men of Powys and other powerful men with [...] chosen whom [...] had chosen from Tegeingl and [...] into the cantred of Lleyn in order to defeat the oppressor Cynwrig. [3]Those men keenly set out and attacked him unexpectedly when he was free from worries and expecting nothing [...] and killed him and a very large part of his men. [4]At this time Gruffudd had settled in camp at Abermenai awaiting the outcome of the venture and praying for their success, when behold a young man of Arfon, called Anian, came running ahead to be the first to deliver the good news,

omen reciperet, scilicet mulierem speciosam, Dylad vocatam, quae concubina prius fuerat Bleddyni regis, quemadmodum olim iuvenis quidam Amalechita ex bello Philistino in montibus [p. 15] Gelboae ad David *cucurrit, portans armillam et sceptrum Saulis regis cui David do*navit laetus et < >.

⁵Iam reversi milites in exp*editionem superiorem* victoria missi ovantes, persuade*nt Griffino, ut ex* hoc omine progrederetur ad re*cuperandam Monam,* Arvoniam, Lleynam, et Angliae con*terminos ut po*puli sui submissionem acceptaret, totamque Venedociam illi haereditario iure debitam circuiret, quam misericors illi Deus iam obtulerat lustrare.

⁶Hiis gestis exercitum copiosum in cantredum Meirioneth ducit ubi Trahaern male possessorum alter habitabat pugnaque commissa est in loco vallis Kyning, Cambrice dicta Gwaeterv, vel ager sanguinis, in hunc usque diem. ⁷Deus illi victoriam concessit eo tempore de inimicis suis decideruntque multi ex parte Trahaerni; [p. 16] qui *et ipse cum paucis vix elapsus* aufugit incol[...] *(conservatus) ex bello: quem Gruffinus* cum exercitu per deserta *et montes usque ad fines* patriae suae persequutus est. ⁸*Post hanc pugnam Gri*ffini nomen percrebuit: rex *Venedotiae publice* salutabatur, qui quasi gigas *ad currendam* viam < > afferens summa laetitia *circumfusus est,* quod Venedotiam ab iniquis et paganis dominis oppressam posset liberare: quomodo Iudas Maccabaeus terram Israel a dominatione regum infidelium et gentibus conterminis liberasset, in eos irruendo saepissime. 9Itaque rebus ad hunc modum peractis, caepit regnum iure regere, populum pacificare, uniuersaque virga ferrea attamen in domino gubernare.

⁶ Gwaeterv] gwaeter MS.
⁸ percrebuit] percrebruit MS

§13

¹Tempore iam modico elapso, proborum hominum suasu, exercitum recollegit numerosum perrexitque versus castrum Rudlan, ut cum Roberto castri custode et aliis Francis pugnaret, qui modo illuc ex [p. 17] Anglia deducti in conf*inia Venedotiae ad habitandum* commigrarent. ²Cum ver*o signo dato exercitum e* castris eduxerat, cun*cta vastat, ac incendit, spo*lia quam opima domum referens. ³*Equites illi loricati gale*atique < > complures, lapsi ex *equis in illa* pugna ceciderunt, multi etiam p*editum: ac vix pauci G*allorum in Turrim salvi sese receperunt *incol*ume*s*. ⁴Postquam reges, barones, cognatique Griffini in Hybernia res ab eo prosperime gestas accepissent, ut qui apud eos natus et enutritus fuerat, eius fortunae congratulabantur.

namely that the ravager had fallen, and to claim his reward as a boon, namely a beautiful woman, called Dylad, who had previously been the concubine of king Bleddyn, just as once a young Amalechite ran to David from a battle with the Philistines in the mountains of Gilboa carrying the armband and sceptre of king Saul, and David gladly gave him and < >.

[5]Now the soldiers who had been sent on the aforesaid mission returned proclaiming their victory and they persuaded Gruffudd that he should move forward from this good omen to recover Anglesey, Arfon, Lleyn and those territories on the border with England, that he should accept the submission of his people, and that he should make a circuit of the whole of Gwynedd owed to him by hereditary right, which God in his mercy towards him had now offered to him to purge.

[6]With this done he led his large army into the cantred of Meirionydd where Trahaearn, the other of the usurpers, lived, and a battle was fought in the valley of Kyning, called in Welsh Gwaederw, or bloody field, to this day. [7]God granted him victory at that time over his enemies, and many on Trahaearn's side fell; he himself saved from the battle [...] scarcely escaped with a few men, and Gruffudd pursued him with his army through deserts and mountains right up to the boundaries of his country. [8]After this battle the name of Gruffudd grew in fame: he was publicly hailed as king of Gwynedd, like a champion running a race and he was surrounded by great rejoicing because he had been able to free Gwynedd which had been oppressed by cruel and pagan lords; just as Judas Machabaeus had freed the land of Israel from the domination of unbelieving kings and from neighbouring tribes by attacking them incessantly. [9]And so when matters were completed in this way, he began to rule the kingdom by right, to bring peace to the people, and to govern everything in the Lord yet even so with a rod of iron.

§13

[1]When some time has elapsed, by the persuasion of the nobles, he regathered his large army and marched towards the castle of Rhuddlan to fight with Robert, the warden of the castle, and the other French, who at some time had been brought there from England and were migrating to live within the boundaries of Gwynedd. [2]When the signal was given and he led his army out from the camp, laid waste and burnt everything taking home extremely rich spoils. [3]Many of their armoured and helmeted cavalry fell from their horses and perished in the battle, and many of the infantry too; and barely a few of the Gauls safely retreated to the tower unharmed. [4]After the kings, barons, and Gruffudd's kinsmen in Ireland heard that matters had turned out very well for him, they welcomed his good fortune as one who had been born and reared among them.

§14

[1]At tres illi filii Merwydd, virique Lleyn universi, in Griffinum dominum suum legitimum insurrexerunt, et nocte quadam intempesta, ex equitibus Hybernis et familia Gruffini, qui apud eos diversabantur, quinquaginta duos occiderunt. [2]Cum huius discordiae inter Griffinum ac suos subditos fama ad Trahaern pervenisset, statim ille [p. 18] Powisiae *incolas adiit roga*tque ut secum adversus *Venedotiam in ultionem mortis Kyn*wrici consanguinei sui cum *expeditis militibus proficis*cerentur. [3]Hinc Gwrgeneus *filius Caecilii et regulus Pow*isiae eiusque cohors una cum Tra*haerno eiusque co*horte ad subiugandum Griffini regnum *veniunt.* [4]*Quod u*bi tres filii Merwydd, virique Llyen et Eviony*th au*divissent, ut periuri, foedifragi et hostium fautores, prodere Griffinum dominum suum meditantur hostiumque ductores fiunt. [5]Simili se flagitio inquinarunt duo fratres de Mona, Theodorus scilicet et Gollwynus, accepto tamen prius a Griffino Kellinawc vawr. [6]Proditione hac cognita hostiumque adventu, Griffinus de Mona Arvonia, una cum Danmarcis et Hybernis quos potuit, deducit secum in hostes. [7]Fit bellum crudele et atrox; utrimque decertatum est acerrime. [8]At de exercitu Gruffini interfecti complures iacebant, captique in praelio nonnulli. [9]Scilicet, Keritus, nutritius, Varudri princeps Hybernorum [p. 19] et dominus Cruc Brendan (mons ille est excelsus divi Brendani heremitae, novem cantredos circumiacentes habens) et de optimatibus Monae septuaginta occubuerunt. [10]Adhuc tamen Griffinus equo insidens inter confertissimos hostes gladio mortifero quasi metere proditores ac inimicos videtur, non aliter atque Agamemnnon rex Frigiae olim proeliabatur. [11]Tandem cum Theodorus Monensis proditorum caput stricto gladio visus sit Griffinum ex posteriori ephippii parte interficere, Gwyneus Baro etiam Monensis eum e proelio aufert ut ad naves deducat, quae in portu Abermeney erant a quo in Insulam Adron (quae et focarum insula dicitur) abierunt: indeque in Llwchgarmawn in Hyberniam pertransierunt. [12]Illa vero insulae pars (in quo depugnatum) usque ad hunc Bron yr Erw, vel Erw yr Allt, vocitatur.

[13]Nemo miretur has humanarum rerum vicis[p. 20]situdines, ut interdum vincere, interdum fugere sit necesse: proditio siquidem cum primis causa est. [14]Sic enim in manus Demetrii regis infidelis populus Israeliticus Iudam Maccabeum regem ac principem suum tradiderunt: verum Bellator hic Dei, ut gygas vel leo seipsum ultus est in utrosque. [15]Iulius Caesar qui continuis bellis orbem terrarum sibi subiugarat, a senatoribus Romanis in ipso Capitolio Romano proditione ac pugionibus confoditur. [16]Arthurus etiam regum totius Britanniae rex praenobilis et fama nunquam intermoritura dignus duodecim bella contra Saxones ac Pictos gessit. [17]In quorum primo fusus fugatusque erat ex proditione in civitate Llwyd Coet quae et Llwyn Llwyt dicitur. [18]At in

[6]   adventu] adventus MS.
[11] Llwchgarmawn] Llwchgarmaw MS (suspension mark omitted).

§14

[1]But the three sons of Merwydd and all the men of Lleyn rose up against their legitimate ruler, Gruffudd, and in the middle of one night they killed fifty-two of the Irish cavalry and warband of Gruffudd who were lodged among them. [2]When news of this discord which had arisen between Gruffudd and his own people reached Trahaearn, he immediately approached the men of Powys and asked that they gather their soldiers and set out with him to Gwynedd to avenge the death of Cynwrig their kinsman. [3]From there, Gwrgenau, son of Caecilius, and a sub-king of Powys and his warband came with Trahaearn and his warband to subjugate the kingdom of Grufudd. [4]When the three sons of Merwydd and the men of Lleyn and Eifionydd heard this, like perjurers, treaty-breakers and helpers of the enemy, they plotted the fall of their master Gruffudd and became guides for the enemy. [5]Two brothers from Anglesey, namely Tudur and Gollwyn, likewise joined the plot even though they had received Clynnog Fawr from Gruffudd. [6]When Gruffudd realized their treachery and that the enemy was coming, he brought with him men from that part of Anglesey facing Arfon together with as many Danes and Irish as he could against the enemy. [7]There was a bloody and fierce battle and it was fought out very fiercely on both sides. [8]But out of Gruffudd's army many lay killed and some were captured in battle. [9]Ceryd, his foster-father, mac Ruaidrí, prince of the Irish and lord of Cruc Brendan (that is the lofty mountain of St Brendan the hermit, which is surrounded by nine cantreds), and seventy nobles of Anglesey fell. [10]Gruffudd, however, was still sitting on his horse among the tightly packed enemy and looked as if he was harvesting traitors and enemies with his death-dealing sword, just like Agamemnon, the king of Phrygia, once used to fight. [11]Finally when Tewdwr of Anglesey, the chief traitor, drew his sword and seemed to kill Gruffudd from the rear part of his saddle, Gwyncu, also a lord of Anglesey, carried him from the battle to lead him off to the ships which were in the port of Abermenai from where they went away to the island of Adron (which is also called the island of seals); and from there they crossed to Wexford in Ireland. [12]That unfortunate place (where they were defeated) is called to this day Bron yr Erw or Erw yr Allt.

[13]No one should be surprised at the changes in human fortunes that sometimes it is necessary to win and sometimes to flee: indeed usually the cause is treachery. [14]For in this way the unfaithful people of Israel delivered Judas Macabaeus, their king and leader, into the hands of Demetrius, the king; Judas, however, this warrior of God, like a giant or a lion avenged himself on both.

[15]Julius Caesar who had subjugated the whole world by continuous warfare was assassinated by treachery and daggers by the senators of Rome on the Capitolium itself. [16]Even Arthur, the outstandingly noble king of the kings of the whole of Britain, worthy of undying fame, waged twelve wars against the Saxons and the Picts. [17]In the first of these he had been totally routed by

reliquis de Saxonibus < > subditorum suorum oppressoribus poenas dignas sumpsit, cui ne seni quidem resistere potuerunt.

§15

[p. 21] ¹At Griffinus in Hyberniam appulsus de proditoribus oppressoribusque acerbissime conquestus est coram regibus principibusque qui tanta indignitate commoti persuadere conantur, ut statim in patriam iam reparatus rebusque necessariis instructis reverteretur. ²Quorum vocibus acquiescens cum triginta navibus Hybernorum Danorumque militibus plenis mare profundum sulcantibus in patrium solum vehitur, portumque Abermeney occupat, ubi Trahaern dominantem reperit. ³Qui audito classis regiae adventu, cepit tristitia affici, suspiria alta ducere, timore et tremore contabescere. ⁴Qui itaque illi in Llyen et Ardudwy favebant, pecunias suas secum deducentes transmigrare fecit in cantredum Meirionyth quem eorum opere aequificerat, cum ex adverso eiusque exercitus Griffinus partem reliquam in Llyen et Arvonia in Monam transportat, ut securi in eius tutela acquiescerent. ⁵At indignati cives domesticique eius, quod promissa illis non sint persoluta, maximam Monae partem [p. 22] depopulati sunt, ac in patriam reverti navibus spoliis onustis tentant; ipsumque invito secum auferunt. ⁶Nec fuit haec civium suorum ad Griffinum opprimendum proditio remissior, quam illa prius Cambrorum.

² sulcantibus] sultantibus MS.
⁵ depopulati] de ... v ... MS

§16

¹Hinc mala innumera in Venedotia pullularunt.

²Ad has miserias accessit: paulo post Hugo Comes Cestrie, aliique < > ductoribus, scilicet Robertus Rutlandiae, Gwarinus Salopiae, Gwalterus Herefordiae comites, exercitum amplissimum equitum peditumque collegerunt, comitantibus etiam Gwrgenev ap Seisill, virisque Powisiae, et per montium iuga in Llyen usque pervenerint. ³In quo cantredo ubi castra per hebdomadam posuissent, omnia longe lateque depopulantur, fundunt, fugant, et plena cadaveribus relinquunt, adeo ut octo annorum spacio pro deserto regio illa haberetur; populusque tanta clade relictus miseria hac coactus quasi in alienas terras dispersus, cuius maxima pars durissimam servientur servitutem alibi, et vix quisquam in patriam vnquam reversus est. [p. 23] ⁴Fuerat prima clades a Normannis illata, primusque eorum in Venedotiam ingressus, postquam in Angliam advenerint.

³ haberetur] habebaretur MS

treachery in the country of Llwyd Coed, which is also called Llwyn Llwyd. [18]But in the remaining battles he took worthy vengeance against the Saxons and the Picts, the oppressors of his own subjects, and they could not resist him even as an old man.

§15

[1]But after Gruffudd had been driven to Ireland he complained most bitterly about his betrayers and oppressors before the kings and leaders, and they upset by such a great injustice tried to persuade him to arrange all the necessary resources and, then restored, to return immediately to his land. [2]Agreeing with their views, with thirty ships full of Irish and Viking soldiers ploughing a furrow across the deep sea he returned to his native soil, and he seized the port of Abermenai, where he found Trahaearn ruling. [3]When Trahaearn heard of the arrival of the royal fleet, he began to be overcome by sadness, to give out deep sighs, and to waste away in fear and trembling. [4]Those who supported him in Lleyn and Ardudwy he made them move bringing their wealth with them into the cantred of Meirionydd which by their labours he had laid low, while Gruffudd transported the remaining part of his army in Lleyn and Arfon across from the opposite side to Anglesey so that they might remain secure under his protection. [5]But the companions and his servants became angry that his promises to them had not been fulfilled and plundered most of Anglesey and attempted to return to their country with their ships laden with spoils, and they took him with them, even though he was unwilling to go. [6]And this betrayal by his own companions was no more easy to bear for the oppressed Gruffudd than that betrayal previously by the Welsh.

§16

[1]Then, countless evils arose in Gwynedd.

[2]To these misfortunes was added the following: a little afterwards, Hugh, earl of Chester and other war leaders, namely Robert of Rhuddlan, Guarin of Shrewsbury and Walter of Hereford, collected a very large army of cavalry and infantry, and accompanied also by Gwrgenau ap Seisill, and the men of Powys, came through the mountain passes to reach Lleyn. [3]They placed their camp in that cantred for a week, and then plundered, routed and put to flight everything far and wide and left everywhere full of corpses to the extent that for the following eight years that region was regarded as a desert; and the populace abandoned after such a great disaster was forced by this misfortune as if scattered in a foreign land and most of them served out their harshest slavery elsewhere and scarcely any of them ever returned to their native land. [4]That was the first disaster inflicted by the Normans and their first entry into Gwynedd after they arrived in England.

§17

[1]Cum iam annis nonnullis in Hybernia Griffinus trivisset curiam < > apud Diermit regem et alios viros illustres, classem in portu Porthlarc rebus instruxit ad iter necessariis, quam dono regis acceptam civibus Hybernis ac Britannis onustam duxit prosperrimo per mare cursu, adspirantibus etiam secundis ventis in portum dictum Porth Cleis non longe a sede archiepiscopali Menevensi. [2]Ad cuius adventum Rysus ap Theodvr, rex australium Cambrorum, Menevensis episcopus, doctores, chorus universus Sancti Davidis, clericique omnes Menevenses, in portum sunt profecti Rysusque Griffinum sic est allocutus: [3]'Salve, Cambrorum regum rex, ad te confugio; tibi genua flecto supplex auxilium suppetiasque petens'. [4]Tum Griffinus, 'Quis es tu et cuius huc advenisti causa?' [5]Rysus inquit, 'Sum filius Theodori huius modicae ditionis dominus: [p. 24] nunc vero oppressus, profugus, et interritus, in sacro hoc delitesco loco'. [6]'Quis', ait Griffinus, 'te in hoc fugere coegit?' [7]'Domine', inquit ille, 'tres Cambriae reges praecipui, cum exercitibus suis in hunc principatum delati, cives assidue opes exhauriunt'. [8]'At quinam', ait Griffinus, 'tam potentes reges, qui hanc pervagantur dominationem tanta multitudine constipati?'. [9]'Caradocus', inquit ille, 'filius Griffini de Guenta vch coet et is coet, cum asseclis suis, incolae Morgannvc, una cum Normannis, et Trahaearn rex cum habitantibus Arwystli'. [10]Auditis vero nominibus oppressorum, ira indignationeque aestuans Griffinus quaerit quodnam illi laboris praemium constitueret, si hostes eius oppugnaret. [11]'Dimidium', inquit, 'ditionis meae tibi dabo, homagiumque tibi praestabo'. [12]Conditionem accepit Griffinus. [13]Aedemque Divi Davidi sacram ambo petunt, cum orandi tum foederis gratia.

[13] Divi] D. *MS*

§18

[1]Quo confirmato [p. 25] benedictioneque ab episcopo accepta, statim Griffinus iter accepit sequentibus eum Danis, Hybernis, amicisque aliis ad numerum centum sexaginta, agmen primum ductante Kyndelw filius < > Monensis. [2]Resus etiam cum perpaucis australibus laetus simul proficiscitur, perbelle secum actum cogitans, quod tam opportunum auxilium est nactus.

[3]Longo iam itinere dimenso ad vesperam in montes perveniunt, ubi castra posuissent praedicti reges. [4]Tum Resus Griffinum sic est allocutus: 'Domine, differamus bellum in crastinum, quod iam advesperascit'. [5]'Differ', inquit Griffinus, 'quousque tibi placuerit, ego vero cum ea, quam paratam manum habeo, in eos impetum faciam'. [6]Quod, ut dixerat, praestabat. [7]Terrore ingenti continentur reges, stupentque dum copias Griffini faeroces, constipata militum agmina, splendentia vexilla, Danos bipennibus armatos, Hybernos iacula ferreis cuspidibus ferentes conspiciunt. [p. 26] [8]Ipse vero Griffinus proelium primus irruit, non secus ac gigas vel leo cuncto gladio inimicos prosternens,

§17

¹When for some years Gruffudd had spent time < > at the court of king Diarmait and other nobles, he drew up a fleet in the port of Porthlarg with the equipment necessary for a voyage, and he led this fleet, which he had accepted as a gift from the king, laden with Irishmen and Britons on a very prosperous sea voyage; with favourable winds he put into the port called Porth Clais not far from the seat of the archbishop of St Davids. ²Upon his arrival Rhys ap Tewdwr, king of the southern Welsh, the bishop of St David's, scholars and the whole choir of St David's, and all the clerics of St David's, set out to the port, and Rhys addressed Gruffudd as follows. ³'Hail, king of the kings of Wales, I take refuge with you; I bend my knee as a suppliant to you seeking your help and support.' ⁴And Gruffudd replied, 'Who are you and for whose sake have you come here?' ⁵I am the son of Tewdwr, lord of this small realm; now indeed oppressed, in exile, and fearful, and I am lying hidden in this holy place.' ⁶'Who', said Gruffudd, 'has forced you to flee here?' ⁷'Lord', he said, 'three kings of Wales in particular who come into this realm with their armies and their companions drain our resources endlessly.' ⁸'But who', asked Gruffudd, 'are these so powerful kings who wander about this kingdom accompanied by such a crowd?' ⁹'Caradog, son of Gruffudd, of Upper and Lower Gwent with his followers, the inhabitants of Morgannwg, together with the Normans, and king Trahaearn with the people of Arwystli.' ¹⁰When he heard the names of the oppressors, seething with anger and rage Gruffudd asked what reward he would offer for his efforts, if he were to attack his enemies. ¹¹'I shall give you,' he said, 'half of my kingdom, and I shall offer you homage'. ¹²Gruffudd accepted the arrangements. ¹³Both made for the church sacred to St David and prayed for their agreement.

§18

¹When this was confirmed and a blessing received from the bishop, Gruffudd immediately set off accompanied by Danes, Irish and other friends to the number of one hundred and sixty, the head of the column led by Cynddelw, <son of Conws>, of Anglesey. ²Rhys also with a few southerners joyfully set off at the same time, thinking to himself that this was a fine undertaking because he had gained such timely help.

³After a long journey near evening they reached the mountains where the above mentioned kings had placed their camp. ⁴Then Rhys said to Gruffudd, 'Lord, let us put off the battle until tomorrow as it is now getting dark.' ⁵'Put it off', replied Gruffudd, 'for as long you like, but I shall attack with the force I have ready.' ⁶And he did so, just as he said. ⁷The kings were overcome with great terror and were stunned as they saw the fierce forces of Gruffudd, the dense columns of soldiers, the gleaming standards, the Danes armed with two-headed axes, and the Irish carrying iron-tipped spears. ⁸Gruffudd himself was

milites suos animose in hostes provocans, et ne terga adversariis darent exhortans. [9]Fit bellum atrox et cruentum in quo ne filius quidem patri pepercit. [10]Clamor militum in caelum usque ascendit: resonare visa est terra fremitu equorum ac peditum: pugnaces voces longe lateque exaudiuntur, strepitus armorum ingens fuit. [11]Tanta strages facta est, dum Griffini exercitus hostes suos subiugarent, ut sudoris et sanguinis flumina decurrisse putarentur. [12]Tandem Trahaern effusis visceribus transfoditur, et in terram pronus deiectus, quasi herbas viventibus carpere dentibus ex armis visus est. [13]Cuius cadaver ut carnem suillam in lardum Gucharki Hybernus sale conduerat; hoc in loco ceciderunt de familia eius equites 25 quasi eum stipantes, alii vero primo agmine [p. 27] multa praeterea millia interficiuntur, reliquorum nonnulli terga verterunt, in fugam se precipitarunt. [14]Griffinus ex consueta vincendi experientia eos per sylvas, valles, paludes, et montes tota nocte, lucente luna, persequitur ut ex tanto numero vix unus aliquis in patriam sit reversus.

[15]Ab hoc bello terribili fortiter per Griffinum confecto, Resus subduxit sese a tutela et societate uni tam illustris nec in eius conspectum se postea < >. [16]Qua perfidia commotus Griffinus eius ditionem depopulari constituit, quod et factum est. [17]Montes autem in quibus hoc bellum gestum est, incolae montes Carn appellant, quod ibi lapidum ingens cumulus congestus sit, sub quo thesauros absconditos olim opinantur. [18]Postquam vero hanc regionem maxima clade depopulationeque funditus devastasset, in Arwistlensem pagum copias duxit, in quo cede et flamma desaeviens, uxoribus virginibusque eorum in captivitatem [p. 28] tractis Trahaerni iniurias rursum in illarum capita persolvit. [19]Postremo in Powisiam se contulit, ubi summa crudelitate in hostes usus est, adeo ut nec ecclesiis pepercerit. [20]Ita tandem inimicis omnibus fusis < > terraque eorum in solitudinem redacta, in paternam hereditatem honorifice susceptus < > regebat Venedotiaque summa tranquillitate ad aliquod spacium gavisa est.

[10] fremitu] fremitum *MS*

§19

[1]Dum ad hunc modum Griffinus regni sui deliciis frueretur, Meiriawnus Rufus Baro illi fidelitate obstrictus, eum coram Hugone comite Cestriae maliciose non solum accusavit, sed prodidit sic. [2]Duos Francos Hugonem scilicet prius nominatum, et Hugonem Salopiae filium Rogeri de castro Baldwini persuasit ut equites peditesque secum usque locum Rvc dictum in Edeirnyon ducerent. [3]Tum proditor hiis adulatoriis verbis eum decepit: 'Salutant te', inquit, 'princeps magnifice, comites duo illustres, qui tibi vicini [p. 29] in terminis regni

the first to rush into battle, just like a giant or a lion laying low enemies with every blow of his sword, furiously calling forward his soldiers against the enemy and urging then not to turn their backs to the enemy. [9]It was a savage and fierce battle in which not even a son spared his father. [10]The shouting of the soldiers rose to the heavens; the earth seemed to resound with the thunder of horses and infantry; violent cries were heard far and wide and the crashing of weapons was terrible to hear. [11]So great a slaughter occurred, while the army of Gruffudd was defeating his enemy, that rivers of sweat and blood was thought to have flowed down. [12]In the end Trahaearn was pierced through spilling his entrails, lying face down on the ground and seemed as if disarmed he were eating the grass with his living teeth. [13]Gwcharki the Irishman had preserved his body in salt like pork being turned into bacon; in this place there fell of his household twenty-five horsemen as if accompanying him and others in the front rank; many thousands in addition were killed, and of the remainder some turned and plunged into headlong flight. [14]Gruffudd, as was his usual habit in victory, pursued them through forests, valleys, marshes and mountains throughout the night by the light of the moon so that out of such a great number scarcely one returned to his own country.

[15]After this terrible battle so bravely fought by Gruffudd, Rhys withdrew himself from the protection and company of one so illustrious and was afterwards not seen by him. [16]Gruffudd upset by his treachery decided to ravage his land, and that is also what happened. [17]The mountains where this battle was fought are called by the locals the mountains of Carn, because a huge pile of stones was heaped up there under which they believe that treasure had once been buried. [18]After he had completely devastated this region with the greatest plundering and ravaging, he led his forces into the territory of Arwystli where, raging with slaughter and fire, he dragged their wives and daughters off into captivity and again avenged the wrongs done by Trahaearn with their lives. [19]Finally, he himself went off into Powys where he employed the greatest cruelty against his enemies to the extent that he did not even spare the churches. [20]And so with all his enemies finally routed, and their lands reduced totally to desert, he was received with honour into his paternal inheritance and began to rule, and Gruffudd enjoyed the greatest tranquillity for some time.

§19

[1]While Gruffudd was enjoying the delights of his kingdom in this way, the baron Meirion Goch though bound by loyalty towards him not only brought a malicious accusation against him before Hugh, earl of Chester, but also betrayed him in the following way. [2]He persuaded the two earls, the afore-mentioned Hugh and Hugh of Shrewsbury, son of Roger of Baldwin's Castle, to bring cavalry and infantry with them in great numbers to the place called Y Rug in Edeirnion. [3]Then the traitor deceived him with these flattering words: 'Two

habitant. ⁴Hii summo a te contendunt, ut apud Ruc in Edeirnion ad colloquendum venire digneris, interposita sponsione eundi redeundique salve'. ⁵Huius vocibus fidem adhibens Griffinus, in illum sui principatus locum profectus, ut in conspectum comitum venerat, comprehendi eum mandarunt, et in publica foetentique custodia Cestriae ferreis catenis devinctum annis duodecim tenuerunt. ⁶Famulos vero eius tum etiam captos, amputatis singulorum pollicibus dextris, inhumanius afflictos, liberos dimiserunt. ⁷Alii audito tanto facinore, in varias regiones sunt dispersi, non aliter atque illud divinum oraculum habeat: 'Percutiam pastorem, et dispergentur oves gregis'.

§20

¹Coaetanei Griffini retulerunt eum fuisse staturae mediocris, capillis flavis, capite calido, facie rotunda, et formosi coloris, oculis decenter latis, superciliis perpulchris, barba decora, collo subrotundo, carne candida, membris robustis, digitis longis, [p. 30] tibiis rectis, et speciosis pedibus; doctrinae fuerat perpolitus et externarum linguarum excellens; in milites clementem et munificum, in hostes magnanimum, in proeliis fortissimum.

§21

¹Interim Hugo Comes Cestriae in ditionem eius copias ducens non postposuit, castella aliaque praesidia diversis in locis edificari curavit, Francorum more, quo et terrae illi dominaretur. ²Hoc tempore castellum in Mona constituit, aliud in Arvon in antiqua urbe Constantini imperatoris filii Constantii Magni, aliud apud Bangor, aliudque in Meirionyth: in quibus ad < > equites, pedites, sagittariosque posuit tantaque crudelitate usus est, quantam nulla unquam aetas viderat. ³At populorum clamor ad Deum ascendebat, ipseque illis opportuno tempore subsidium tulit.

§22

¹Siquidem post sedecim annorum spacium e carcere Griffinus liberatus est, idque evenit sic: iuvenis quidam Eiderniensis Kynwricus Hir nomine una cum sodalico modico Cestriam veniens [p. 31] ad necessaria coemenda, conspicit forte in palatio civitatis vinctum suum regem, quem in amplexibus abreptum clam e civitate subduxit, iterque in patriam vespere conatur, civibus iam caenantibus, atque domi apud se tacitus diebus nonnullis aluit. ²Quibus elapsis valetudineque recuperata, latenter noctu Griffinum in Monam deduxit, ubi Sandef ap Ayre clanculum defensit < >. ³Verum non multo post, conscensa navi, in Hyberniam transfretare tentavit. ⁴At ventus adversus eum in portum Hodni in australibus partibus Walliae coegit. ⁵Inde pedestri itinere pergens novem sibi familiarissimis comitatus (quorum nonus ibi occubuit), tribus

noble earls greet you, magnificent prince, who live as your neighbours on the borders of your kingdom. [4]In short, they beg you to think it right to come to speak with them at Y Rug in Edeirnion, with a guarantee of safe passage in both directions.' [5]Gruffudd, putting his trust in these words set out for that place in his kingdom, and when he came into the view of the earls, they ordered that he be arrested and they held him bound in iron chains in a foul public prison in Chester for twelve years. [6]As for his servants who were captured with him, they were sent away free after being treated inhumanely in that they had the thumbs of their right hands chopped off. [7]When others heard of this great deed, they scattered in various directions, just like the divine oracle had it: 'I shall strike the shepherd and the sheep of the flock shall be scattered.'

§20

[1]Contemporaries of Gruffudd reported that he was a man of moderate stature, with fair hair, a clever head, a round face, of good colour, eyes properly borne, fine eyebrows and a good beard, a round neck, fair skin, strong limbs, long fingers, straight legs, and comely feet; he was very polished in his education and outstanding at foreign languages; towards his soldiers he was kind and generous, towards his enemies spirited, and very brave in battle.

§21

[1]Meanwhile, Hugh, earl of Chester, did not delay in leading forces into his lands, and had castles and other garrisons built in various places in the French custom so that he might control that land. [2]At this time he established a castle on Anglesey, another in Arfon in the ancient city of the emperor Constantine, son of Constantine the Great, and another at Bangor, and another in Meirionydd; to < > he placed in them cavalry, infantry and archers and he employed such cruelty as no age had ever seen. [3]But the cries of the peoples rose to God, and to them He at an appropriate time brought help.

§22

[1]Then after a period of sixteen years Gruffudd was freed from prison, and it came about in the following way. A certain young man of Edeirnion, called Cynwrig Hir, came to Chester with a small group of companions to buy supplies, and by chance he caught sight of his king in chains in the palace of the city, and he grabbed him in his arms and secretly smuggled him from the city, and by night he attempted the journey to his own country while the citizens were having dinner, and then for some days he tended to him at home without telling anyone. [2]After a few days had elapsed and he had recovered his strength, he took Gruffudd to Anglesey secretly by night, where Sandef ap Ayre looked after him in hiding. [3]Then not long after, he boarded a ship and attempted to cross over to Ireland. [4]But a contrary wind forced him into the

vicibus uno eodemque die cum praesidiariis militibus illius regionis pugnavit, terque eos superavit, quum octo tantum illi superessent comites unumque ipse ex adversariis generis nobilitate praestantem interfecit, sicque ex illorum manibus evasit.

[6]Iter hoc in Ardudwy usque confirmavit, incertus [p. 32] quo pergeret, ne proderet Francus. [7]Tandem filii Collwini, Eginir, Gellan, Merwyd, Edenyved eum ad se receperunt, rebusque necessariis in solitudinis latibulis sustentarunt. [8]At diebus mensibusque transeuntibus cum sexaginta viris illi adhaerentibus, per Venedociam quasi erro quidam diversa loca circumiuit damna inferenda non modica quousque Hugo Comes vixit: ut olim David filius Isai Bethlaeemita in terra Iudaea tempore Saulis regis.

[9]Cum vero Franci, qui in castellis morabantur, eum tanta mala machinantem senserant, ipsi milites in defensionem patriae relicti, eum per sylvas, perque agros, ut canes venatici cervum indagare et persequi student. [10]Itaque sublata omni spe evadendi, navem canonicorum Aberdaron conscendit, in qua remigum importunis laboribus in Hyberniam tandem pervenit. [11]Inde infra mensem reversus in eadem puppi, in flumine a quo solvebat [p. 33] stationem reperit.

§23

[1]A qua in insulas Daniae maturiori capto consilio ad Gothreum regem familiarem suum adnavigavit, ut ab eo naves aliaque ad res suas necessaria impetraret. [2]Quoque primis suis temporibus ad eum confugerat, confisus se subsidia accepturum. [3]Cuius adventum contristatus rex compati atque condolere crebris eius miseriis coepit. [4]Ad extremum Griffinus cum classe sexaginta navium Monam appulit, ut cum Francis castella tutantibus ipse, quique cum eo ex insulis devenerant, proeliatur. [5]At incolae summo illi impedimento fuere. [6]Bellum gestum est saevum et crudele ab aurora usque ad vesperam, multique utrinque caeciderunt, quique animo forti praestabant in primo impetu. [7]Tum Griffinus in confertissimos hostes prorupit, seque in primum agmen dat, ut Francos loricatos, galeatos bipennibusque armatos prosterneret, ut David rex inter Philisthaeos. [8]Nox proelium diremit, navesque in insulas sunt [p. 34] profectae. [9]At ipse in quandam insulam (quae Dinieuyt vocatur) cum una solummodo navi secessit, ex qua navem e Cestrensi portu vectam occisis nautis depraedatus est ac postero die Lleyn versus vela dans, in portum Nevin salvus cum suis omnibus intravit. [10]Quod ubi ad cantredorum incolas fama detulisset, convolarunt statim ex singulis regni partibus, qui ad principis sui obsequia obstricti tenebantur, homines de Lleyn, Evyonyd, Ardydwy, Arvon, Ros, ac Dyffryn Clwyt. [11]Collecto sic ingenti exercitu confirmatus Griffinus, perlegente

port of Hoddni in south Wales. [5]From there travelling on foot accompanied by nine of his closest companions (one of which perished there), he fought with the military garrisons of that area three times in one and the same day, and three times he defeated them, and when there were only those eight companions left, he himself killed one of the enemy of high, noble birth, and thus he escaped from their hands.

[6]He continued on this journey as far as Ardudwy, though uncertain as to where he might go lest a Frenchman might betray him. [7]Finally the sons of Collwyn, Eginir, Gellan, Merwyd and Ednyfed took him in and supported him in deserted hiding places with the necessary supplies. [8]After some days and months sixty men joined him and he travelled through various parts of Gwynedd like a runaway slave inflicting serious losses as long as earl Hugh lived, just like David, son of Jesse of Bethlehem, in the land of Judaea in the time of King Saul.

[9]But when the French, who were staying within their castles, realized that he was plotting great misfortune, the soldiers themselves left to defend the land sought and pursued him keenly through woods and fields like hunting dogs pursuing a stag. [10]And so giving up all hope of evading them, he boarded a ship belonging to the canons of Aberdaron in which after a huge effort of rowing he finally reached Ireland. [11]From there within a month he returned in the same ship and found a landing at the river from which he had set sail.

§23

[1]From there after adopting a more thoughtful plan he sailed to the islands of Denmark to his friend, king Godfrey, to get from him ships and other things necessary for his affairs. [2]In his youth he had also taken refuge with him and he was confident that he would get support. [3]The king saddened by his arrival began to sympathize and condole with his many sufferings. [4]Finally, Gruffudd came to Anglesey with a fleet of sixty ships so that he himself and those who had come with him from the islands might wage war against the French garrisoning the castles. [5]But the inhabitants proved a very great obstacle for him. [6]A battle was fought savage and cruel from dawn till dusk and many fell on both sides and especially in the first clash those who were outstanding in bravery. [7]Then Gruffudd rushed forward into the most densely packed part of the enemy and placed himself in the front line, so that he might lay low the French in their armour, their helmets and armed with two-headed axes, like King David among the Philistines. [8]Night halted the battle and the ships set off for the islands. [9]But he himself took himself off separately in only one ship to a certain island (which is called Dinewyd) from where he plundered a ship sailing from the port of Chester and killed the sailors, and on the next day sailing for Lleyn he safely entered the port of Nefyn with all his men. [10]When the news of this reached the inhabitants of the cantreds, they immediately rushed to him

eum Deo optimo maximo, copias duxit adversus castellum quod superius diximus in Mona exaedificatum, quod ad aliquot dies expugnavit. [12]At Franci obsessi e muris, praesidiis, et turribus in eos iacula torserunt, sagittas emiserunt, saxa deiecerunt, aliisque sese instrumentis defensitarunt: donec tandem quotidi[p. 35]ano et assiduo oppugnationis certamine Wallorum cedere sint coacti, ceciditque eorum dux, vel senescallus, cuius erat hoc castellum, aliique sexaginta quattuor cum eo. [13]Hoc castello flammis consumpto hostibusque expugnatis, tanto successu laetus Griffinus adversus reliqua in eius regno castella pergit: quae pugnando caepit, diruit ac incendit, populumque in ipsis universum gladio occidit. [14]Ad hunc modum adversariis omnibus devinctis Venedotiam a castellis vacuam reddidit, et paternam haereditatem adeptus est Venedotiaque per biennium pace ac tranquillitate est usa. [15]Nec praetereundum videtur, quod postquam Griffinus apud Aber Lliennawc in Mona pugnasset missis sexaginta militum iuvenibusque strenuis quatuordecim ad incendia et predas agendas, multosque ex castellanis excidisset penitusque omnia devastasset, ad aliam Monae regionem proficiscitur, [p. 36] ubi naves eius tres in anchoris starent, subito alii castellani una cum inhabitantibus Monam, eum adoriuntur, toto illo die persequuntur, eiusque postremum agmen sepius ad prelia provocant: attamen, ut antea, Griffinus caeptum iter aggreditur, spolia aufert, Francos ac Saxones vinctos secum et captivos deducit, insidiatorum horum continuata pugna quam plurimos interfecit. [16]In hoc proelio cadit Gellan cytharaedus, penkerd, iuxta naves ex parte Griffini.

[17]Quanta scientiarum varietate, quanto eloquentiae splendore perpolitum esse oporteret qui Griffini egregia facinora, res praeclare gestas in Cambria, Hibernia, insulis Daniae subiectis, aliisque diversis nationibus enarrare posset; ingenue fateor deesse mihi facultatem, immo nec tanto oneri posse esse parem, si vel soluta oratione Tullii eloquentia pollerem, vel adstricta < > Homerum vincerem.

§24

[1][p. 37] Dum variis fortunae fluctibus iactaretur Griffinus, modo prosperis, modo adversis, in uxorem accepit Angharat filiam Ywein ap Edwin, quam huius principatus prudentiores referre soliti sunt, sapientem fuisse nobilem, modestam, capillis candidis, oculis ac < > corpore accipitrino. [2]Singulas etiam corporis partes habuisse ad proportionem compositas quam aptissime, tibias rectas, pedes concinnos, digitos longos, ungues tenerrimos; affabilem praeterea fuisse tradiderunt, sermone elegantem, habita ac gesta quam decoram,

from every single part of the kingdom, the men of Lleyn, Eifionydd, Ardudwy, Arfon, Rhos and Dyffryn Clwyd, who were held bound by their loyalty to their lord. [11]Gruffudd, strengthened by this great army which had gathered in this way, with God the best and greatest supporting him, he led his forces against the castle which we said above had been built in Anglesey and took it by storm over a period of some days. [12]But the French under siege hurled spears and fired arrows and threw down stones from the walls, strongholds and towers, and defended themselves in all other ways, until finally they were forced by the continuous daily contest of the siege of the Welsh to yield, and their leader fell, the seneschal, who was in charge of the castle, and another sixty-four with him. [13]After this castle had been burnt down and the enemy taken by storm, overjoyed by such a success Gruffudd went against the remaining castles in his realm, and by warfare he captured them, destroyed them, and burnt them down, and slew all the people in them. [14]In this way with all his enemies cast into chains he rendered Gwynedd free of castles, and acquired his paternal inheritance, and for two years Gwynedd enjoyed peace and tranquillity. [15]And it should not be passed over that after Gruffudd had fought at Aber Lliennog in Anglesey with sixty soldiers and fourteen strong youths sent off to burn and plunder, and he had killed many of the people in the castle and had completely laid waste everything, he went off to the other side of Anglesey where three of his ships were standing at anchor, and suddenly the other men of the castle together with the men of Anglesey attacked him, and pursued him for the whole day, and kept provoking his rearguard into battle; nevertheless, as before, Gruffudd undertook the journey he had begun, carried off plunder, and brought with him French and Saxon captives in chains, and killed as many as he could of the ambushers in prolonged battle. [16]In this battle fell Gellan, the harpist, the *pencerdd*, near the ships on Gruffudd's side. [17]With what variety of knowledge, with what splendour of eloquence should he have been, he who could narrate the famous deeds of Gruffudd and his achievements in Wales, Ireland, and the subject isles of Denmark, and among various other peoples; I freely admit that I do not have that ability, nor indeed would I be equal to such a great task even if I had the power of the eloquence of Tullius in oratory or I could defeat Homer <in verse>.

§24

[1]While Gruffudd was being tossed about by the variable waves of fate, sometimes favourable, sometimes unfavourable, he took as his wife Angharad, daughter of Owain, ab Edwin; the wise men of his realm used to report that she was wise, noble, modest, fair-haired, with eyes < > and a hawk-like body. [2]Each single part of her body suited her as fittingly as possible, straight legs, elegant feet, long fingers, very slender nails; they said furthermore that she was genial and elegant of speech, in habit and gesture how decorous, sensible, and cautious,

perspicacem, cautam, in consiliis prudentem, in familiares clementem, in egenos liberalem, et ad res praeclaras omnes instructissimam. ³Ex hac octo suscepit liberos, filios tres, scilicet Kadwallon, Ywein ac Kadwaladyr, filias vero 5, scilicet Gwenllian, Margret, Ranillt, Susannam, Annest: fuere illi ex concubinis liberi aliquot.

§25

¹At ubi Willelmus ensis longi rex Angliae bellicas [p. 38] expeditiones, fortitudinem et saevitiam Griffini in Francos accepisset, aegerrime tulit, ac totius regni vires in eum commovit, et in Venedotiam equitum peditumque varias turmas duxit, quibus incolas omnes funditus destruere et < > pessundare proposuit, ut ne canem mingentem ad parietem relinqueret. ²Aggressus est sylvas ac lucos scindere et evertere, ut ne vel umbra quidem, qua se imbecilliores tutarentur, superesset. ³Hic primus omnium tabernacula ac castra intra castella muris cincta posuit. ⁴Atque huius expeditionis Cambrorum nonnulli et auctores et ductores erant. ⁵Audito tanto belli apparatu < > in occursum Griffinus copias totius principatus collegit, < > in angustiis viarum insidias collocans, in quas subito incideret a montibus descendens exercitus. ⁶Has Anglus reformidans per intestina terrae Cestriam pervenit: ex hoc eius itinere nec incolae damnis, quae minatus, affici[p. 39]ebantur, nec perfidi ductores laborum fructus, quos sperabant, perceperunt, nisi forte unica sit quisque vacca donatus. ⁷At Anglus equitum maximam partem, currus, famulos, equosque quam plurimos amisit. ⁸Ita Francorum iactantia concidit, ad nihilumque devenit: copiae Griffini modo anticipare, modo subsequi, modo a dextris, modo a sinistris illis esse solebant, ne eius subditis nocerent. ⁹Quod si Griffinus suos, dum abditos lucos pertransirent, in eos immisisset, postremum illum diem Anglus ac Franci sensissent; verum cohibuit suorum faerociam Griffinus, ut olim David se gessit erga Saulem.

⁸ iactantia] iactantiam MS

§26

¹Rebus ad hunc modum non succedentibus, Hugo comes Cestriae (de quo supra) malorum omnium architectus, ut anteactis temporibus Antiochus, classem onustam parat, ut quem caeperat intimum doloris sensum ex praesidiorum suorum trucidatione, dirutis funditus castellis et equitibus mala morte multatis, iam saltem in Cambros [p. 40] vlcisceretur. ²Ad hanc rem paratum habuit Hugonem alterum comitem scilicet Salopiae vna cum sua cohorte, ut simul

sensible in advice, kind to friends, generous to the poor and most well-informed in all important matters. [3]He had eight children by her: three sons, Cadwallon, Owain, and Cadwaladr, and five daughters, Gwenllian, Margret, Ranallt, Susanna, and Annest; he also had some children by concubines.

§25

[1]But when William of the long sword, king of England, received news of the hostile expeditions and the bravery and savagery of Gruffudd against the French, he found it intolerable, and he roused the strength of his whole kingdom against him, and led into Gwynedd various squadrons of cavalry and infantry with which he planned to destroy and < > exterminate the natives so that he might not leave even a dog pissing against a wall. [2]He also embarked upon a scheme of cutting down and destroying the forests and groves so that not even, as it were, a shadow might be left by which the weaker might protect themselves. [3]First of all he placed his tents and camps within castles surrounded by walls. [4]Some Welshmen were his leaders and guides. [5]When Gruffudd heard of this great preparation for war < >, he gathered the forces of the whole realm to go and meet them and he placed ambushes in the narrow passes on the roads so that as the army was coming down out of the mountains it would suddenly fall into them. [6]Fearing such tactics the Englishman returned to Chester through the centre of the land; and from this expedition of his neither did the natives suffer any damage with which he had threatened them, not did the treacherous guides gain the rewards of their labours for which they had hoped, except that each might by chance be presented with a single cow. [7]But the Englishman lost a very large part of his army, and wagons and servants and a very large number of horses. [8]In this way the presumption of the French collapsed and came to nothing: the forces of Gruffudd were accustomed sometimes to engage them from the front, sometimes to pursue them from the rear, sometimes from the right, sometimes from the left so that they should not do damage to his subjects. [9]And if Gruffudd had sent his men against them, as they were crossing through the pathless forests, the Englishman and the French would have seen their final day, but he restrained the ferocity of his men, just as once David behaved towards Saul.

§26

[1]While matters were proceeding unsuccessfully in this way, the above mentioned Hugh, earl of Chester, architect of all misfortunes, like Antiochus of old, since he held a deep sense of grievance at the murder of his own garrisons, with his castles totally destroyed and cavalry slaughtered, prepared a heavily laden fleet and now would be avenging himself at once upon the Welsh. [2]In this venture he had another Hugh, earl of Shrewsbury, with his own army,

proficiscentes multimodas iniurias a Griffino illatas, innumeraque accepta incommoda illi reponerent. [3]Itaque tandem phalanges suas in terras Griffini ducunt, preeuntibus cum suis asseclis Yweino ap Etwin, et Vthtrico fratre suo. [4]Res haec ubi patefacta fuerat, Venedotiae Powisiaeque incolas quasi e somno excitavit, ut fortius illis abiecto quamvis obediendi vel ore resisterent. [5]Cuius rei causa Powisiae principes, scilicet Kadwgan et Meredith eius frater traduxerunt suos omnes in patriam Griffini: maturoque capto consilio, sese ambo in Monam receperunt quo in loco, quasi in firmissima civitate altissimo pelago undique cincta, conquieverunt: idque maxime quod naves longae sexdecim de Hybernia in subsidium Griffini mittebantur, quibus adversus comitum classem maritimo bello decertarent. [p. 41] [6]Comites huius rei certiores facti, nuntios clam ad classis praefectos destinant, ut amplissimis muneribus promissis rogarent, quatenus Griffinum in eius summis periculis maximisque angustiis fallerent auxilioque omni destitutum relinquerent, quod effectum praestiterunt. [7]Siquidem Francorum dolis delusi, totam insulam (fracta fide Griffino data) vacuam praesidiis in direptionem hostibus tradiderunt. [8]Hac Francorum fallacia Griffinus in summam animi aegritudinem coniectus, consilii dubius fuit, quid adversus vel vim Francorum vel classis defectionem opus esset facto. [9]Itaque re prius cum suis deliberata, arrepta quadam navicula, una cum Cadwgan ap Bleddyn in Hyberniam transfretavit, populum eiusque bona Dei voluntati ac protectioni commendans, qui subvenire cunctis cum angustiis premuntur promisit. [10]At plebs multis modis miserabilis, eius absentiam sentiens, fuga sibi salutem quaesiuit, ut in specibus subterraneis, locis palustribus, sylvis, lucis, agris [p. 42] incultis, cisternis, paludibus, ruderibus, ac rupibus locisque aliis absconderent, latitabant ac sese occultabant, Francorum aliarumque externarum gentium metu, qui in eorum perniciem advapulabant. [11]Non fuit difficile iam comitibus eorumque exercitui per totam insulam longe lateque eodem illo die pervagari, populum concidere, aliquorum bona diripere, aliorum membra detruncare, donec nox eos a persequendo retardaret.

[2] Griffino] Griffinus MS.
[5] Kadwgan] Kadwallawn MS

§27

[1]Verum ecce postero die inexpectato singulari Dei providentia, regia classis appropinquans sese in conspectum obtulit, qua a Francis animadversa (siquidem iam dominasset Danos foedifragos qui Griffinum deceperant) ad consuetas sibi fallendi artes se contulerunt. [2]Atque ex Cambris confoederatis emiserunt quosdam ad insulanos, qui eos ad concordiam hortarentur persuaderentque statim firmare pacem quibus possent rationibus optime. [3]Nam timebant ne ex utraque parte simul urgerentur, scilicet ne eodem tempore et

so that setting out at the same time they might avenge those many injuries perpetrated by Gruffudd and the countless losses caused by him. [3]And so finally they led their troops into the lands of Gruffudd with Owain ab Edwin and his brother Uchtryd and their followers ahead of them. [4]When the situation became known, it roused the natives of Gwynedd and Powys as if from sleep so that they might resist them more bravely casting aside even the appearance of obedience. [5]Because of this, the princes of Powys, namely Cadwgan and Maredudd, his brother, brought out all their people into the land of Gruffudd; and after taking proper counsel together they both withdrew to Anglesey where, as if in a very strong city surrounded on all sides by the deepest sea, they settled themselves; and this principally because sixteen long ships were being sent from Ireland to help Gruffudd with which they might fight against the fleet of the earls in naval battle. [6]When the earls discovered this, they secretly sent messengers to the commanders of the fleet promising them very great rewards and asking them to fail Gruffudd when he was in the greatest danger and in dire straits, and to leave him deprived of all support; and this is what they did. [7]Indeed deceived by the trickery of the French and with their promise to Gruffudd broken, they handed the whole island over to the enemy empty of guards to be plundered. [8]Gruffudd was cast into the deepest agony of indecision by the deception of the French, uncertain in his plans as to whether he should act against the force of the French or the defection of the fleet. [9]And so after he had thought the matter over with his people, he seized a small boat and with Cadwgan ap Bleddyn he sailed across to Ireland, commending his people and his property to the good will and protection of God who promised to help all whenever they are oppressed by troubles. [10]But the people to be pitied in so many ways, when they realized that he had gone, sought safety for themselves in flight and went off to lie hidden and to conceal themselves in underground caves, marshes, forests, groves, uncultivated fields, water tanks, bogs, ruins, cliffs and other places, through fear of the French and other foreigners who were driving them to destruction. [11]It was not difficult for the earls and their army to wander the length and breadth of the whole island on that same day, to slaughter people, to plunder the property of some, to chop the limbs off others, until night brought a halt to their pursuit.

§27

[1]But behold on the next day unexpectedly by the singular providence of God, an approaching royal fleet came into view, and when it was spotted by the French (indeed now it would have overcome the treaty-breaking Danes who had deceived Gruffudd), they turned to their well practised arts of deception. [2]And they sent to the islanders some of the Welshmen who were in league with them to urge them to make a pact and to persuade them immediately to establish a peace on whatever terms they could best achieve. [3]For they were afraid that

cum Cambris profugis ex una et cum hac regia classe ex altera [p. 43] parte dimicandum foret. [4]Hac ratione fallaces Franci miserrimum populum huius insulae gravissima servitute oppressum v[...]da spe in fraudem pellexerunt, ne aetas sequens maiorum suorum tantas clades olim recordaretur.

[4]   pellexerunt] pellexit MS

§28

[1]Veruntamen classem, quam superius inopinato conspectam diximus, ad regem Llychlyn spectantem, divini numinis singularis anima in Monam dirigere est dignata, ut plebem suam miseriis involutam tandem liberaret. [2]Siquidem ad dominum suum ex infinitis praessuris et anxietatibus clamavit, et Deus eam salvam fecit.

[3]Cum vero regi, qui huic classi praefuit, per interpretes monstraretur, quae haec esset insula, quis eius princeps, quantae ibi caedes fierent, quam dira persequutio, quique essent tam cruentae stragis autores, condolere coepit ac fremere: itaque naves tres ad littus tendere praecepit. [4]Quod cum Franci perceperunt, quamvis timidiores mulierculis, loricati, et pro more suo in equis sedentes ad pugnandum cum rege [p. 44] quique in terram e navibus erant expositi procedunt. [5]Rex vero eiusque nautae fortiter ex adverso cum eis dimicarunt. [6]Cadunt Franci ex equis, ut ficus de arboribus, alii mortui, alii vulnerati crebris ictibus Danorum. [7]At rex e puppi sagittam < > Hugonis Comitis Salopiae oculum perfodit, qui in terram exanimatus licet armatus prosternitur diutiusque cum ferro luctatur. [8]Franci vero ex hoc fortuito eventu in fugam versi Danis terga ostendunt. [9]Rex autem classem inde statim subduxit quae ad perscrutandas insulas Britanniae ac Hyberniae, quae totius orbis ultimae habentur, cum ingenti militum manu iter hoc suscepisset.

§29

[1]At Hugo Comes aliique Franci < > laetitia perfusi praedas quas egerunt omnes < > loca cantredorum Monae deduxerunt, metu etiam Griffini quem singulis momentis expectarent; quo etiam in loco omnium inhabitantium frumenta bovesque [p. 45] sunt partiti, quorum dimidiam partem secum Cestriam transportaverunt.

[2]Tum aderant Dani illi periuri proditores qui Griffinum fefellerant quia Hugo illis prolixe promiserat virorum, mulierum, servorum, virginum portionem amplissimum perfidiae praemium. [3]Persolvebat ille quidem illis ut fidelis infidelibus, ut illud divinum confirmaret. [4]Nam postquam ex singulis partibus collegisset cunctas amiculas edentulas, incurvas, claudas, monoculas, obeses et

they might be pressured on two fronts at the same time, namely, lest at the same time they would be forced to fight with the Welsh fugitives on one side, and with this royal fleet on the other. [4]In this way the deceitful French ensnared in deceit the wretched people of this island oppressed by the heaviest slavery into treachery with a [...] hope, so that subsequent generations might not remember such a disaster.

§28

[1]However, the singular spirit of a divine mind thought it right to steer that fleet, which we have said had been unexpectedly spotted and which belonged to the king of Llychlyn, to Anglesey in order at last to free his people beset by misfortunes. [2]Indeed, they called upon their Lord out of their unending burdens and anxieties, and God made them safe.

[3]When the king in command of this fleet was told through guides what island this was, who was its king, how great the slaughter was happening there, how terrible was the persecution, and who the perpetrators of such a cruel massacre were, he began to share their grief and become angry; and so he sent three ships to go to the shore. [4]When the French saw this, though more fearful than little women, in full armour and, as was their custom, mounted on horseback they went into battle with the king and those who had landed from the ships. [5]But the king and his sailors fought bravely against them. [6]The French fell from their horses, like figs from a tree, some dead, others wounded by the unceasing blows of the Danes. [7]But the king < > an arrow from the prow of his ship and it struck Hugh, earl of Shrewsbury, in the eye and he was laid low on the ground lifeless, though he was in full armour, and for a while struggled with the weapon. [8]The French were put to flight by this chance occurrence and showed their backs to the Danes. [9]The king, however, immediately withdrew his fleet because he had undertaken this journey with a huge band of soldiers to look at the islands of Britain and Ireland which are regarded as the furthest of the whole world.

§29

[1]But earl Hugh and the other Frenchmen overcome with joy took their plunder which they had gathered together with them into the safer places of the cantreds of Anglesey through fear of Gruffudd whom they were expecting at any moment; there they also divided the corn and cattle of the inhabitants, half of which they took with them to Chester.

[2]Then, the Danes appeared, those lying traitors who had deceived Gruffudd because Hugh had lavishly promised them a very generous share of the men, women, slaves and girls, a fine reward for treachery. [3]He then paid them like a faithful man to the unfaithful, as the divine word confirmed. [4]For after he had gathered from every part all the toothless hags, the hump-backed, lame, one-eyed,

imbecillas, obtulit has Danis in mercedem proditionis. ⁵Quam mancipiorum squalentem catervam ubi vidissent, sublatis anchoris, altum petierunt Hyberniam versus. ⁶At qui tunc temporis ibi praeerat poenas de illis sumpsit gravissimas, alios morte, alios membrorum ascissione, aliosque in exilio perpetuo mulctando ex toto suo regno exterminans.

¹ metu] metum *MS*

§30

¹Atque ecce eodem tempore Griffinus antiqua sua [p. 46] consuetudine de Hybernia reversus, universam patriam in solitudinem redactam, subditosque in alia loca traductos invenit. ²Itaque legatos ad Hugonem comitem mittit, quorum opera effectum est ut in pacis conditiones inter eos sit conclusum. ³Inde in illo cantredo concessae sunt illi villae tres. ⁴Ab hoc tempore per annos complures Griffinus vitam tenuem duxit, curisque variis distentam, spe tamen meliori ac divina providentia se consolando.

§31

¹Transacto tot annorum spacio, in curiam Henrici Regis Angliae qui fratri successit se contulit a quo Bangorensis episcopi interventu, vitam, favorem, familiaritatem, multarum rerum cognitionem adeptus est. ²Cui etiam rex summa cum pace ac gratia concessit cantredos Lleyn, Eivionyd, Ardydwy, et Arllechwed una cum incolis eorum < >. ³Ut vero in patriam est reversus Griffinus a curia regis, in illorum terrarum possessionem intrat, Deo [p. 47] gratias agens, qui deponit potentes de firmis suis sedibus, exaltat humilem, qui debitorem creditoremque facit, qui hominem humiliat, eundem ad honores evehit. ⁴Deinceps omnia Griffino prospere creverunt, quia in Domino spem fixam habuerat. ⁵Delabuntur < > ad eum quotidie reliqui de Ros cum muneribus, non expectata vel petita Comitis Hugonis licentia, sicque populorum multitudinem abundabat.

⁶Anno sequenti in Monam ipse cum suis profectus ibi gubernando habitabat; inde in alios commotos se contulit. ⁷Hoc modo in Venedocia potentiam ac pristinum statum recuperavit, ut Maccabaeus filius Mattathiae olim in Israel. ⁸Subditos etiam gravissimo servitutis iugo, qui propter crebras bellorum necessitates expressi fuerant, liberavit, totamque Venedotiam gaudio replevit, ut Israelitae e captivitate reversi Babylonica.

fat and weak, he offered them to the Danes in payment for their treachery. [5]When they saw this wretched band of prisoners, they raised anchor and took to the open sea and made for Ireland. [6]And he who was ruler at that time punished them severely, some with death, others by the chopping off of limbs, and driving others from every part of his kingdom into perpetual exile as a punishment.

§30

[1]And behold Gruffudd at the same time following his old custom returned from Ireland and found his country completely reduced to a desert and his subjects carried off elsewhere. [2]And so he sent ambassadors to earl Hugh, and by their efforts it came about that conditions of peace were concluded between them. [3]As a result three vills in that cantred were conceded to him. [4]From this time on for several years Gruffudd led a humble life spent in various cares, consoling himself with hope of better things and divine providence.

§31

[1]After some years had gone by, he travelled to the court of Henry, king of England, who had succeeded his brother, and with the intervention of the bishop of Bangor he gained from him a living, favour, friendship, and recognition of his many possessions. [2]The king even granted him in peace and good-will the cantreds of Lleyn, Eifionydd, Ardudwy, and Arllechwedd along with their inhabitants and possessions. [3]When Gruffudd returned to his land from the king's court, he entered into the possession of these lands, thanking God who deposes the powerful from their strongholds and raises the humble, who makes one person a debtor and another a creditor, who humbles a man and then raises that same man to high honour. [4]Then everything developed favourably for Gruffudd because he had held his hopes fixed upon God. [5]Other people daily drifted to him from Rhos with their possessions without waiting for or asking for the permission of the earl Hugh, and thus he he began to increase the number of his people.
[6]In the following year, he himself with his men set out for Anglesey and there he lived and ruled, and from there he travelled to the other commotes. [7]In this way he regained his previous power and standing in Gwynedd, just like Maccabaeus, son of Mattathias once in Israel. [8]He also freed from the heavy yoke of slavery his subjects who had been oppressed on account of the interminable necessities of war, and he filled the whole of Gwynedd with rejoicing, like the Israelites returning from captivity in Babylon.

§32

[1]At Comes moleste tulit, quia se invito possessiones haereditarias vel perquiserit vel evicerit, immo [p. 48] rex Angliae eius hoc facinus admiratur. [2]Itaque thesaurum exfodit maximos sumptus erogando et in regem Scotiae, Scotos Australesque Cambros. [3]Has copias in Griffini principatum ducit, positis castris intra murata castella. [4]Ipse vero Griffinus bellorum necessitates sepius expertus, ex adverso castra metatur in nivosi montis Eryri quasi bracchiis. [5]Quibus ex locis legati utrimque sepius sunt missi, atque tandem post inducias, in pacis formam est consensum. [6]Sicque Henricus in Angliam revertitur, ac Griffinus in propriam ditionem redit.

[7]At rursum Henricus Rex transacto temporis perbrevi spacio, exercitum praeclarum ductans venit, castraque in eodem loco (quo prius) posuit in ipsis scilicet montibus ut iam tandem Griffini principatum funditus eradicaret subditosque eius in ore [p. 49] (ut dicam) gladii perderet, mactaret, et funditus perimeret. [8]Verum Griffinus suos recollegit, et ut in more illi erat, in eius occursum dirigebat, transmissis tamen prius praeciosis quibuscumque una cum uxoribus ac liberis in solitudines montium Eryri, ubi extra omnem periculi metum forent. [9]Quibus rebus evenit ut rex metuens ne in manus Griffini incideret, cum in valles a montium cacuminibus discenderet, in Angliam pace facta reciperet.

[10]O Deus bone, quoties Griffinum subvertere conati sunt Comites, ac non potuerunt. [11]Quoties tentarunt Powisiae incolae, at non potuerunt. [12]Quoties aggressi sunt fallacis Trahaerni fautores, at non potuerunt.

[9]   reciperet] receperet MS

§33

[1]Post tantos exantlatos labores, Griffinus per annos complures divitiis affluens, tranquilla placidaque pace gaudens regnabat, regumque vicinorum familiaritate cum summa concordia est usus, scilicet Henrici [p. 50] Regis Angliae, Murchathi Regis Hyberniae, regumque qui insulis Daniae praeerant fuitque percelebre eius nomen, non solum in regnis adiacentibus, verum etiam in remotissimis terris.
[2]Iam per Venedociam coeperunt bonarum omnium rerum incrementa fieri; iam coepit populus ecclesias fundare, glandes seminare, arbores plantare, pomaria, hortos ac stagnis fossis et sepibus munire, aedificia extruere, frumenta ac fructus Romanorum more in usum colligere. [3]Basilicas vero erexit Griffinus iuxta palatia sua, quae maximis sumptibus magnifice exedificasset et sustentasset. [4]Quid vero efflueret? [5]Venedocia cum ecclesiis < > iam firmamento ac stellis cum dedicationibus; populum suum virga ferrea gubernabat, etiam concordiam ac pacem cum regnis vicinis aluit, filios adhuc iuvenes in extre[p. 51]mis regni cantredis praepositos coll[. . .]velit ut essent quasi < > cum extraneis nationibus

§32

[1]But the earl was angry that Gruffudd against his will had seized or conquered his own hereditary territories; moreover, the king of England was surprised at this deed of his. [2]And so, he dug into his treasury and paid massive sums to the king of Scotland, the Scots and the Southern Welsh. [3]He led these forces into the kingdom of Gruffudd and placed his camps within walled castles. [4]But Gruffudd himself, having very frequent experience of the demands of wars, set his camp opposite him on the arms, as it were, of snowy Eryri. [5]From their positions ambassadors were sent regularly from both sides and finally after a truce there was an agreement on a form of peace. [6]Thus Henry returned to England and Gruffudd returned to his own realm.

[7]But after a short period of time, Henry returned with a fine army, and placed his camp in the same place as before, namely in the very mountains themselves, so that he might at last root out the realm of Gruffudd and destroy his subjects at sword-point (as it were), slaughter them, and completely wipe them out. [8]But Gruffudd gathered his people and, as was his custom, directed them to meet Henry, after sending his valuables with the wives and children across into the deserted areas of the mountains of Snowdon where they would be out of any fear of danger. [9]It turned out, however, that the king, fearing that he might fall into the hands of Gruffudd as he descended out of the mountain tops into the valleys, made peace and withdrew to England.

[10]Kind God, how many times the earls tried to overturn Gruffudd, and could not! [11]How many times the inhabitants of Powys made an attempt upon him, and could not! [12]How many times the accomplices of the traitor Trahaearn attacked him, and could not!

§33

[1]After enduring such great labours, Gruffudd ruled for many years, affluent with wealth and rejoicing in a calm and unbroken peace, and was on the friendliest terms and greatest concord with neighbouring kings, namely, Henry, king of England, Murchadh, king of Ireland, and the kings who ruled the islands of Denmark, and his name was famous not only in the adjacent kingdoms but even in the furthest lands.

[2]Now throughout Gwynedd all kinds of good things began to increase; now the people began to found churches, sow acorns, plant trees, and build orchards and gardens and surround them with pools, ditches and fences, to construct buildings, and to gather for use the produce and fruits in the manner of the Romans. [3]Gruffudd also built large churches next to his palaces which he built and established beautifully sparing no expense. [4]What then was the result? [5]Gwynedd < > with churches and dedications like the heaven with stars; he governed his people with an iron rod but also encouraged peace and concord with kingdoms neighbouring him, and he placed his sons, while still young, in

oppositio cum hiis qui rebus novis studere vellent. [6]Reguli minores eius curiam sepius petebant interdum auxilii impetrandi, interdum consolationis ac consilii causa, quoties eos alienorum iniuriae urgebant.

§34

[1]Ad extremum iam longa senectute confectus, et oculorum lumine amisso, operibus se misericordiae totum dedit, apud se cogitans quamvis ex rebus militiae gestis memoriam esset relicturus perpetuam, in secretiorem quendam locum secedere, ut divinarum rerum contemplationi intentius vacaret, ac vitae sanctius ducendae incumberet, dominationibus terrenis penitus contemptis. [2]Atque ubi iam vitae terminum appropinquare intellexit, liberos convocari praecepit, ut quae a morte sua fieri et observari vellet illis exponeret, quemadmodum aliquando Ezechias [p. 52] rex fecerat. [3]Itaque substantiam suam omnem < > in partes divisit, cuius iustitia in aeternum permanebit. [4]Ecclesiae Christi Dublinorum viginti solidos donavit, quo in loco et natus et nutritus fuerat, singulisque cathedralibus ecclesiis Hyberniae necnon Ecclesiae Menevensi, abbatiis Cestriae et Salopiae tantundem. [5]Etiam amplius quod ecclesiae Bangorensi legavit. [6]Ac Ecclesiae Caercybi decem solidos ac tantundem Penmonae, Sancti Germani, Dinerth, Gelynnawc, Enlli, et Meivot, multisque praecipuis aliis ecclesiis. [7]Haec episcopis, archidiaconis, praesbyteris, clericis, doctoribus, Christianisque indigentibus concessit ut Sancti Spiritus protectione defensitaretur, qui omnia scrutatur et cognoscit.

§35

[1]Ad eum iam in extremis agentem vitaeque finem expectantem accesserunt ex omni eius principatu viri celebres et prudentissimi, scilicet David episcopus Bangor, Simeon archidiaconus, prior Monasterii Cestriae [p. 53], homo et doctrina et sapientia insignis, compluresque alii presbyteri et discipuli, ut oleo consecrato eius corpus inungerent, iuxta praeceptum Iacobi Apostoli.

[2]Erant una eius filii, quibus ille benedicendo praedixit quae illis olim eventura essent, ad similitudinem Iacobi patriarchae, qui filiis suis in Aegypto benedixisset: atque in mandatis dedit, ut fortiter se gererent, inimicisque magno animo resisterent, ut ille postremis suis temporibus egerat.

[3]Aderat etiam eodem tempore regina Angharat eius uxor cui dimidiam omnium bonorum suorum partem, duas terrae portiones cum porticibus Abermeney legavit.

[4]Necnon filie eius praesentes erant, et filiorum nonnulli, atque horum singulis partes assignavit ad [p. 54] comodius post [...] discessum vivendum. [5]Cambri, Hyberni ac Dani Griffini mortem flebilibus vocibus sunt prosequuti, non secus atque Iudei Iosue filium Nun olim lugebant.

charge of the most distant cantreds of his kingdom so that they might be, as if
< > with foreign peoples, as opposition to those who might wish to rise up against
him. [6]Minor kings would often make for his court sometimes to seek help,
sometimes for consolation and counsel, whenever foreigners were causing them
trouble.

§34

[1]In the end, now worn down by old age and having lost the sight of his eyes, he
gave himself over to tasks of mercy, thinking to himself what perpetual memorial
he might leave of his military achievements, and he withdrew to a more remote
place to give himself time for a more intense contemplation of divine matters
and to lead a more godly life, completely despising worldly powers. [2]And when
he realized that the end of his life was near, he ordered his children to be
summoned so that he might set out for them what he wished to happen and to
be carried out, just as the king Ezechias once did. [3]And so he divided his
possessions, the justice of which will remain for ever. [4]To the church of Christ
in Dublin, where he was born and fostered, he gave twenty pieces of silver, and
to each cathedral church of Ireland and the church of St David's, the
monasteries of Chester and of Shrewsbury the same amount. [5]Even more did
he bequeath to the church of Bangor. [6]And to the church of Holyhead he gave
ten pieces of silver, and the same amount to Penmon, Llanarmon, Dinerth,
Clynnog, Enlli and Meifod, and to many other major churches. [7]These he
granted to the bishops, archdeacons, priests, clerics, doctors and needy
Christians so that they might be defended by the protection of the Holy Spirit
who sees and knows all things.

§35

[1]And now as he was reaching the end, and waiting for the end of his life, there
came to him from the whole of his realm famous and wise men, namely, David,
bishop of Bangor, Simeon, the archdeacon, the prior of the monastery of
Chester, a man outstanding in learning and wisdom, and many other priests
and scholars so that they might anoint his body with consecrated oil according
to the precept of the apostle James.

[2]His sons were with him, and he blessed them and predicted what would
eventually happen to them, like the patriarch Jacob who blessed his sons in
Egypt; and he gave them instructions to conduct themselves bravely and to
resist their enemies fiercely as he had done in his latter years.

[3]The queen Angharad, his wife, was also present at the same time and he
bequeathed her half of his possessions and two portions of land together with
the harbour dues of Abermenai.

[4]His daughters were present, and some of their sons, and to each he assigned
shares so that they might live more comfortably after his death. [5]Welshmen,

[6]Cum duos et octoginta annos Griffinus complevisset, ex hac vita discessit. [7]Sepultusque est in ecclesia Bangor, splendido erecto monumento ad sinistram altaris magni partem. [8]Praecemurque ut eius anima cum aliorum praeclarorum regum animabus in Domino conquiescat. [9]Amen.

Irishmen, and Danes lamented the death of Gruffudd, just like the Jews once mourned Joshua, son of Nun.

[6]Gruffudd was eighty-two years old when he departed this life. [7]He was buried in the church at Bangor with a gleaming monument erected to the left of the high altar. [8]Let us pray that his soul may rest in peace in the Lord with the souls of other famous kings. [9]Amen.

Apparatus

This apparatus is in two parts. Part (a) contains all the changes and annotation associated with Thelwall. Part (b) contains all the later annotation in the manuscript.

(a) Thelwall annotation

§1

[1]Swrth] *a word partially lost and now illegible was added above and then deleted.*

§2

[1]*Cyna*nnus] nnus *deleted.* Avloedi] v *changed to* u. Dublinensis] ensis *deleted and* civi[... *added above.* [2]Gruffinus] inus *added above*

§3

[1]Meurik] Mauricii *added above.* Rhodri] e *added above with insert mark between* d *and* r; magni *added above with insert mark after* Rhodri. Esyllt] *deleted and* Essildis *added above.* Dyre] .i. Capriae *added above with insert mark after* Dyre. Cadwallawn] awn *deleted and* ani *added above; in comparison with HGK* filii Catmani, filii Iacobi, filii Beli, filii Runi, filii Maglocuni, filii Caswallani *missing here (text in this note restored from interlinear gloss in manuscript D (BL Additional 19712) and also found in C and Ch, but not in Cotton Vitellius C.ix).* manus oblongae] *deleted and* longimani *added above.* Einawn] *deleted and* Eniani *added above.* Yrth] th *lost at damaged edge.* Guidawc] awc *lost but* auci *added above; catchword lost.*

[2]Rhodri] e *added above with insert mark between* d *and* r; cus *added above with insertion mark after* Rhodri; m[*added above with insertion mark after* Rhodri, *probably for* magni. *Vrych]* ...]is *added above with insertion mark after* Vrych, *possibly for* .i. versicoloris. *Llydan*wyn] ...]didi *(probably for* .i. lati candidi) *added above with insertion mark after* Llydanwyn. Meirchiawn] wn *deleted and*

ni *added above.* Gvl] *deleted and* macri *added above with insertion mark after* Meirchiawn. *Ll*edlwm] .i. Subnudi *added above with insertion mark after* Lledlwm. Tegwan Cloff] wan *deleted and* vani *added above;* Cloff *deleted and* Claudi *added above.* Dehewent] ent *changed to* eint. Prydein] in *deleted and* ni *added above.* Gwrwsti] *in comparison with HGK and Cotton Vitellius C.ix* filii Riwalloni, filii Regatae, filiae Lyri, filii Rudi, filii Bladudi, filii Llywelit *missing.* Bruti] *deleted and* Riwallani *added above.* Y*sgwydwyn*] Ysg *confirmed by catchword which was subsequently deleted and* filii R... *added after; for the full words, cf. Cotton Vitellius C.ix which has* ysgwdwy *crossed through.* Aeneae Ysgwydwyn] .i. humeri candidi *added above with insertion mark after* Ysgwydwyn. Noe hen] N *corrected from* M; hen *deleted.*

§4

[1]materna] sic *added above with an insertion mark after* materna. sic] *deleted.* Racnell] ll *deleted and* llae *added above after* Racnell. Hyberniae] ac *added above with insertion mark after* Hyberniae. Insulae Mannae] Mevaniae uel *added above.* qui e Scotia] olim *added above.* aliarum] et rex nuncupabatur *added above with insertion mark before* aliarum.

[2]rex etiam habebatur] *deleted and* et provinciarum *added above;* provinciarum *then deleted and* regionum *added.* Arennae] *deleted and* Arran insularum in mari occidentali Hiberniae *added above;* mari *then deleted and* hyberniae mari *added at end.* eius] *deleted.* rudera] ru *visible in catchword.*

§5

[1]*suo*sque] *deleted and* [e]t suos *added above.* Daniae] *deleted and* Noruegiae *added above.* corporis] *deleted and* inter Danos *added above.* iungebantur] iun *deleted and* iu *added above.*

[3]eum honoribus] eum *deleted and* et *added in right margin.* nautam] am *deleted and* ae *added above.* donaque] *confirmed by catchword.*

[7]presidia] *deleted and* expugnacula oppida *added above; these words were then deleted and* munitiones *added after.* condiderat] *confirmed by catchword.*

[8]*Hyber*niae] *deleted and* [Sco]tiae *added above.* Mare Tyren] *underlined.*

[9]modicam] sibi *added above with insertion mark after* modicam. Northwegiae ibi] *capital N emphasized;* th *deleted.* ex Septentrionalibus regionibus genus deducentes *added above with insertion mark after* Northwegiae; genus *then deleted and* originem *added above.* quorum . . . deducens] *deleted.*

[10]partes] *deleted and* provincias *added above.* vel] citeriorem *added above with insertion mark before* vel.

[11]Rodwn] id est, Rothomagum *added above.* primi] conditoris *added above with insertion mark after* primi. Romulo] *confirmed by catchword.* Willhelmus] Normannus re[x, et eius] *added above with insertion mark after* Willhelmus. constant] *deleted and* successerunt *added above.*

[13]At] *deleted.* ille] *deleted and* long[...] *added above.* neposque] *eius added above with insertion mark after* neposque. Stephanus] qui *added above with insertion mark after* Stephanus. fuerant] ant *changed to* unt.

[14]Huius < >] modi *inserted in gap.*

§6

[1]aviae] maternae *added above with insertion mark after* aviae. Ragnel] gnel *deleted and* cuella *added above.* natus etiam] *deleted and* filius *added above.* Tethel] i *added at end of word.*

[2]Slani] S *changed to* A. Riyeni] R *deleted and* V *added above.*

[3]Gurmlach] lach *added under* Gurm *at end of line.* Sutrilii] li *deleted and* c *added above.* Midif] if *deleted and* iviae *added above.*

[5]Ranald] i *added at end.* quatuordecim] *deleted and* quadraginta *added above.*

[6]pedum potestate, vel] *deleted and* virium robustum uel *added above; the* ustum *of* robustum *then deleted and* ore *added above.*

[7]ornatum cui ob egregias facultates] *deleted and* ac velocitatis gloria celebrem cui *added above.* < >] cui *added in gap.* indiderat] derat *deleted and* tum erat *added above.* eiusdem dimensi utriusque saltus aestimabatur] *deleted and* neque ei saltandi agilitate inferior erat Rinaldus *added above.*

[8]quidem] equus *added above with insertion mark after* quidem. Cinnari] equo *added above with insertion mark after* Cinnari. Bucephalo] equo *added above with insertion mark after* Bucephalo.

§7

[1]Quum] um *deleted and* an[do] *added above.* quoniam] *abbreviation deleted and* quoniam *added above.*

§8

[1]Britannicorum] bardorum *added above with insertion mark after* Britannicorum.

[2]corruptor] quia *added above with insertion mark after* corruptor. multosque] que *deleted*.

[3]more] *deleted and* authoritate *added above*. antico ac d[...] *deleted and end of last word lost in edge of page*.

§9

[1]Gruffinus] Gruff. *MS and* inus *added above*. moribus esset excultus enutritus tenerrime] *The base text is very unclear as it has been deleted and variously glossed and reglossed*: puer *above* moribus; studiis praeclaris praesul esset *above* moribus esset excultus; studiis *then deleted and* moribus *added above,* ibus *was then deleted and* um *added above*; praeclaris praesul esset *was also deleted and* probitate cultus *added above*; ac strenissime *above* enutritus *which was then deleted and* magnae [...] *added above*; educatus ac petulanter enutritus *above* tenerrime; educatus *was then deleted*. quam ampla < >] ditio *added in gap*; haereditas *added in right margin and then deleted*. regnum] ei iure haereditario *added above with insertion mark* after regnum.

[2]< > deposuit] *gap in MS before* deposuit; *deleted and* effudit *added above gap*. in] *deleted*. dominari] *deleted and* occupare *added above*.

[3]suppetias] ei *added above with insertion mark before* suppetias.

§10

[1]s<ulcat>] *gap filled in later hand*.

[2]Atque] tunc tum *added above with insertion mark before* Atque. in] ea parte *added above with insertion mark after* in. Cambria] *changed to* Cambriae; quae Venedotia vocabat[ur] *added above with insertion mark after* Cambriae. gerebant] *deleted*. indebite] *deleted and* tyrannice gerebant *added above*. Trahearn] us *added above end of word*. rex] *deleted and* regulus *added above*.

[3]homines] *deleted and* inhabitantes *added above, which was then deleted and* incolas *added above*. Merwyd] i *added to end of word*. Meiriawn] wn *deleted and* num *added above*. ut qua] [s]uperiores *added above with insertion mark after* viros.

[4]adventus] advensus *MS*; sus *deleted and* tus *added above*. querunt] *cedilla added under* e.

⁵vindicanda] *changed to* vendicanda.

⁶Griffinus] inus *added above.* arripit vel] vel *deleted.* castrum] de *added above with insertion mark after* castrum. Rudlan] *deleted and* Rudlanum *added in margin.* versus Robertum] versus *deleted and* ad *added above.* vel ad Hugonem] *deleted and* nepotem *added above*; Hugonem *changed to* Hugonis. comitem] *deleted and* comit[is] *added above.*

⁷cuius] *deleted and* quam ob *added above.* causa] m *added above end of word.* pollicitus] amice *added above with insertion mark before* pollicitus.

§11
¹his consultaverat] *deleted and* de hiis inter se colloquerentur *added above.* sapiens Tangwystl] *deleted and* prudens Tanguistela *added above.* omine] bono quodam *added above with insertion mark before* omine. quodam praedicaret] *deleted.* regnum] praesagiret *added above with insertion mark after* regnum.

²et, quam] et *deleted.* < >] *gap filled by* habuit. optimam] et tunicam *added above with insertion mark after* optimam. ex < >] *gap in manuscript after* ex; *gloss added above* yskin id est pelle. ap Lln.] *deleted and* filii Leolini regis *added above.* ap Seisill] *deleted and* filii Caecilii *added above.* regis] Cambriae *added above with insertion mark after* regis. contextam] *altered to* confectam.

³Llywarch] us *added above end of word.* in hoc castro magna aestimatione habebatur et a thesauris fuerat Griffino ap Llu.] *deleted*; castri praefectus fuit et quaestor fuit apud regem illum Griffinum filium Leolini *added above*; fuit *then deleted*; magnae existimationis et fidei *added above gloss with insertion mark before* apud.

§12
¹Gruffinus] inus *added above.* Aber Meney] portum de *added above with insertion mark before* Aber Meney. revertitur] remigium uiribus fretus *added above with insertion mark before* revertitur.

²(scilicet filios Merwydd) ... hominum] *deleted and* filiorum Merwydi, qui in asylum de Celynnawk propter metum et minas Powisianorum, aliorumque suorum cognatorum confugerant, necnon sexaginta alio[*added above.* Powisiae] *confirmed by catchword.* ...]liorumque potentium] *deleted and* ... berti praedicti *added above.* Tegeinglia] einglia *deleted and* enia *added above;* in auxilium *added above.* elegerat] *deleted and* miserat *added above.* ...]si] *deleted.* Lleyn] *deleted and* de Lleyn *added above.*

³nihil] tale *added above with insertion mark after* nihil. expectantem] *the following word beginning with* p ... *deleted.* fecerunt, eumque] *deleted and* facientes eum *added above.*

⁴Gruffinus] inus *added above.* depopulatorem] *deleted and* tyrannum et inimicum suum *added above.* scilicet] *abbreviation deleted and* scilicet *added above.* mulierem] quandam *added above with insertion mark after* mulierem. Dylad] *deleted and* Deladam *added above.* Bleddyni] ddyni *deleted and* thyni *added above.* regis] Cambriae *added above with insertion mark after* regis. ex bello Philistino] *deleted and* usque ad Philistim ex bello quod gestum fuerat *added above.* et sceptrum] et *added in left margin by original hand.* donavit laetus et ...] *deleted and* in praemium ta[*added above.*

⁵missi] *deleted.* omine] faelici *added above with insertion mark before* omine. Angliae] alios suos [...] *added above above with insertion mark before* Angliae. populi] sui *added above with insertion mark after* populi. acceptaret] et indigenarum homagium *added above.* misericors] iam *added above with insertion mark after* misericors; iam] *deleted and* in suas manus *added above.* lustrare] *deleted.*

⁶cantredum] um *deleted and* um *added above*; de *added above with insertion mark after* cantredum. Trahaern] us *added above the end of the word.* male possessorum alter habitabat] *deleted and* tyrannorum alter morabatur *added above.* Cambrice dicta] qui *added above with insertion mark before* Cambrice; est *added above with insertion mark after* dicta. Gwaeterv] gwaeter *MS*; ter *deleted and* terw *added above.*

⁷Deus] Ac *added before* Deus. multi] *deleted and* plus quam mille *added above.* qui] *guaranteed by catchword.* aufugit] ...]onia *added above with insertion mark before* aufugit. incol[...] *deleted and end of word difficult to read.*

⁸percrebuit] percrebruit *MS*; *third* r *deleted.* afferens] *deleted and* exultans *added above over gap.* letitia] circumfusus est *added above.* paganis] *deleted and* alienigenis *added above.* posset liberare] *deleted and* tam feliciter liberasset *added above*; sset *then deleted and* liberam fecisset *added above.* Iudas] ille *added above with insertion mark after* Iudas. Maccabaeus] olim *added above with insertion mark after* Maccabaeus.

⁹peractis] *deleted and* compositis *added above.* regere] *deleted and* disponere *added above.* virga ferrea] in *added above* virga *with insertion mark before* virga. attamen] *deleted and* gloriose *added above.*

§13

[1]elapso] *deleted and* interiecto *added above.* suasu] *deleted and* consilio *added above.* recollegit] *deleted and* coegit *added above.* castrum] de *added above with insertion mark after* castrum. custode] *deleted and* praefecto *added above.* et aliis] et *added in left margin by main hand;* equitibus *added with insertion mark before* aliis. Francis] et Normannis *added above with insertion mark after* Francis. in] inde *added above.* commigrarent] nt *deleted and* se receperunt *added above.*

[2]*e* castris] e *is restored (text before* castris *is missing);* is *deleted and* um *added above.* cuncta] usque [... *added above with insertion mark before* cuncta; *text following* usque *has been lost.*

[3]complures < >] illis viris Francis *added above gap;* illis viris *then deleted and* e *added above.* Gallorum] G *lost;* allorum *deleted.* salvi] *deleted.* sese] magna cum [...] *added above with insertion mark after* sese; *text after* cum *has been lost.* prosperime] tam *added above with insertion mark before* prosperime; ime *underlined and* e *added above.*

§14

[1]Merwydd] dd *deleted and* di *added above.* in] *deleted and* adversus *added above with insertion mark before* Griffinum. insurrexerunt] latenter *added above with insertion mark before* insurrexerunt. familia] *deleted and* satellitibus *added above.* Gruffini] ini *added above.* apud eos] *deleted and* in illa regione *added above.*

[2]Griffinum] inum *added above.* Trahaern] um *added above.* pervenisset, statim] magnopere laetabatur, et tametsi iam victus esset, et fuga salutem quaeritans *added above and in right margin.* Powisiae] *confirmed by catchword.*

[3]Gwrgeneus] us *deleted and* us *added above. Caecilii] in Cotton Vitellius C.ix* mab Ithael mab Gwerystan etc. *added in right margin in later hand.*

[4]Merwydd] *final* d *deleted.* Llyen] *deleted and* Lleyni *added above.* fautores] deleted *and* adiutores *added above.*

[5]Kellinawc] ...]ens ideo . . . *(dots after* ideo *in text) added above, then deleted and* suo stipendio apud *added between deletion and main text.*

[6]adventu] adventus *MS;* us *deleted and* u *added above.* Danmarcis] *deleted and* Danis *added above.*

⁹nutricius] suus ac *added above with insertion mark after* nutricius. Varudri] us *added above.* Brendan] d *deleted.* mons ille] *deleted and* qui locus *added above.* heremitae] admirabilis *added above with insertion mark after* heremitae.

¹⁰Adhuc tamen] Adhuc *deleted and* At *added above beginning of* tamen. Griffinus] inus *added above.* mortifero] *deleted and* suo rapido *added above.* quasi] vibrat *added above.* videtur] *deleted and* videbatur *added above.* Frigiae] *deleted and* Phrigiae *added above which was then deleted and* Graecorum *added above.* proeliabatur] in bello Troiano *added above next line with insertion mark before* Tandem.

¹¹Tandem cum] Tandem *deleted and* At *added above* cum. visus sit] *deleted and* adcurrens *added above.* interficere] *deleted and* perfossuturus erat *added above;* turus *then deleted and* rus *added above.* Gwyneus] eus *deleted and* us *added above;* vero *added above with insertion mark after* Gwyneus. etiam] *deleted.* Monensis] id conspicatus, adcurrens *added above with insertion mark after* Monensis. ut] *changed to* et, *then deleted and* et *added above.* deducat] *attempt made to change it to* deduxit. erant] *deleted and* in statione erant *added above.* a quo] *deleted and* et inde *added at beginning of next line.* focarum] *deleted and* Phocarum *added above.*

¹²insulae pars] *deleted and* pugna loci nomine *added above.* depugnatum] est *added above with insertion mark after* depugnatum. usque ad] celebratur *added above.* hunc] diem *added above.* vocitatur] *deleted and* appellatur *added above.*

¹³cum primis causa est] *deleted and* regnat ab initio *added above.*

¹⁵ac] *deleted and* ac *added above.*

¹⁶dignus] nus *added in later hand at beginning of line.*

¹⁷dicitur] hodie Lincolnia *added above.*

¹⁸Saxonibus < >] Pictisque *added in gap.* sumpsit] *added above by main hand and required by sense.*

§15
¹principibusque] ibidem *added above.* iam] navibus *added above with insertion mark before* iam. reparatus] u *changed to* i.

²sulcantibus] sultantibus *MS;* tantibus *deleted and* cantibus *written above.* Trahaern] um *added above end of word.*

⁴qui] ac omnes suos *added above.* itaque] *deleted.* Llyen et Ardudwy] *deleted and* Lleyno et Ardudio *added above.* suas] ac facultates *added above.* transmigrare] subito *added above with insertion mark before* transmigrare. fecit] ad se *added above with insertion mark after* fecit. Meirionyth] de *added above with insertion mark before* Meirionyth. quem eorum opere aequificerat] *deleted.* adverso] Gruphynus *inserted after* adverso. Griffinus] *deleted.* in Llyen] *deleted and* Lleyni *added above.* Arvonia] *changed to* Arvoniae. transportat] facultatem *added above and then deleted.* securi] *deleted and* ibi incolumes *added above.*

⁵cives domesticique eius] *deleted and* auxiliarii Dani suique satellites praetorii *added above.* promissa] stipendia *added above.* depopulati] de ...v... *MS; overwritten by* depopulati *in darker ink.* tentant] *deleted and* festinant *added above.*

⁶civium] *deleted and* domesticorum *added above.*

§16
¹pullularunt] exorta sunt *added above and then deleted.*

²paulo] quod *added above.* < > ductoribus] ductoribus *deleted and* belli duces *added above.* Rutlandiae] de *added above with insertion mark before* Rutlandiae; diae *then deleted.* Salopiae] de *added above with insertion mark before* Salopiae; e *of* Salopiae *deleted.* comites] *deleted and* comes *added above.* Gwrgeneu ap Seisill] *changed to* Gwrganeo filio Caecilii. in Llyen] *deleted and* Leynum *added above.*

³pro deserto] *deleted and* desolata et inculta *added above.* haberetur] habebaretur *MS; deleted and* remansit *added above.* tanta] a *added above with insertion mark before* tanta. quasi] fuit *inserted above with insertion mark before* quasi; *both words then deleted.* terras] mendicantes *added above and then deleted.* dispersus] *deleted* and perfugatus est *added above.* servient] vient *deleted and* viebant *added above.* alibi] *deleted and* in exilio per multos annos *added above.*

⁴prima] haec *added above.*

§17
¹trivisset curiam < > apud Diermit] *heavily deleted and difficult to read; the manuscript has a gap after* curiam; apud Diermit *expanded from* adiermit; hospitio exceptus esset apud Diermit *added above.* illustres] *deleted and* nobiles *added above.* classem] insignem *added above.* Porthlarg] de *added above with insertion mark after* Porthlarg. civibus] *deleted and* Danis *added above.*

[2]Rysus ap Theodvr] *deleted and* Rhesus filius Theodori *added above.* Menevensis] et *added above with insertion mark before* Menevensis. chorus] ac *added above with insertion mark before* chorus. Menevenses] *deleted and* ecclesiae Menevensis *added above.* Rhysusque] *deleted and* Rhesusque primus *added above.*

[4]tu] inquit Griffinus *added above with insertion mark after* tu. Rysus] *deleted and* Rhesus *added above.*

[5]modicae ditionis] *deleted and* nuper regionis *added above.* et interritus] *deleted and* ac pene obrutus *added above.*

[7]reges] *deleted and* reguli *added above.* delati] sunt *added above with insertion mark after* delati. cives] *deleted and* eius opes *added above.* opes] *deleted.* exhauriunt] unt *deleted and* entes *added above.*

[9]Guenta vch coet et is coet] *deleted and* Gwenta quae supra, et infra sylvam sita est *added above.* asseclis suis] *deleted and* satellitibus suis *added above.* incolae] ae *changed to* is. Morgannvc] de *added above with insertion mark before* Morgannvc; vc *overwritten by* wc. una cum] *deleted and* cum plurimis aliis balistariis et *added above.* et Trahaearn rex cum habitantibus Arwystli] *deleted and* Meiliricus filius Riwallani cum suis Powisianis, et Trahaernus Rex cum suis etiam Arustlianis *added above; in* Arwystli wy *deleted and* u *added above, and* anis *added to the end.*

[10]oppressorum] *deleted and* eorum, qui Rhesi patriam tanta clade affecerunt *added above.* aestuans] ex *added above the beginning of the word.* quaerit] ab eo *added above.* hostes eius oppugnaret] *deleted and* contra illos eius hostes secum bellum gereret *added above.*

[11]inquit] *deleted and* (inquit Rhesus) *added above.* foederis] ineundi *added above.*

§18

[1]Quo confirmato] iureiurando *added above.* ab episcopo accepta] *deleted and* interposita *added above.* accepit] acce *deleted and* arri *added above.* amicisque aliis] *deleted and* plurimisque Venedot[..] *added above (end of word lost at edge of page).* centum sexaginta] et *added above with insertion mark after* centum. agmen primum ductante Kyndelw filius < > Monensis] Kyndelw *changed to* Kyndeluo; *gap in manuscript between* filius *and* Monensis; *whole phrase deleted and* duce Cyndelo filio Conusi Monensis *added above.*

[2]Resus] h *inserted after* R. quod] *MS has* qd *which was deleted and* quod *added above*. est nactus] est *deleted*; esset *added above* nactus.

[4]bellum] *deleted and* proelium *added above*. advesperascit] et lux defectura est *added with insertion mark*.

[5]manum] *deleted*. habeo in eos] manu *added above and then deleted and* cohorte *added above*.

[7]continentur] tinentur *deleted and* turbantur *added above*. cuspidibus ferentes] cultellata *added above*. conspiciunt] et hastatos scutatosque Venedotos contra pervenire *added above*; se *then added above* contra.

[8]leo] indefessus *added above*. provocans] *deleted and* excitans *added above and changed to* incitans. exhortans] magnanime *added above and then deleted and* alacriter *added above*.

[9]atrox] x *deleted and* cissimum *added above*. cruentum] um *then changed to* us. in quo ne filius quidem patri pepercit] *deleted and* cuius famam post parentum mortem longe celebrabunt filii *added above*; parentum *then deleted and* patrum *added above*; celebrabunt *then deleted and* exaudient *added above*.

[10]militum] *deleted and* proeliantium *added above*. fremitu] fremitum *MS*; m *deleted*; tu *added above*. ac] *added above by main hand*. pugnaces] dimicantium *added above*.

[11]exercitus] *deleted and* copiae *added above*. subiugarent] *deleted and* pugnarent sibique cedere compellerent *added above*; pugnarent *then deleted and* delerent *added below*.

[12]Trahaern] us *added above end of word*. viventibus] *changed to* viventes. carpere] *changed to* carpendo. ex armis] *deleted and* et super arma palpare *added above*.

[13]Gucharki] u *overwritten with* w; us *added above end of word*. conduerat] uerat *deleted and* idit *added above*. hoc] *deleted and* eodem *added above*. familia eius] *deleted and* stipatoribus eius *added above*. quasi eum stipantes] *deleted*. alii vero] eorum *added above with insertion mark after* vero. agmine] deleti sunt *added above and then deleted, and* deleti *added above*. praeterea] *deleted and* suorum *added above*. in fugam] que *added to* in.

[14]ex consueta vincendi experientia] *deleted and* vero victor more suo consueto *added above*. tota nocte] illa *added above*. persequitur] *deleted and* et per totum

diem posterum adeo acriter persecutus est *added above*. ex] vix *deleted and* ex *added above probably by original hand*.

[15]ab hoc bello terribili] *changed to* post hoc bellum terribile. confecto] o *deleted and* um *added above*. Rhesus subduxit] ne periculum proditionis a Griffino sibi intenderetur *added above*; periculum *deleted*; proditionis *changed to* proditio; sibi *deleted at end of line*. a tutela et societate uni tam illustris] *deleted and* sub crepusculum ab amicitia et consortio illius *added above*. < >] *gap filled by* dedit *in later hand*.

[16]eius] *deleted and* suos *added above*. ditionem] Rhesi *added above with insertion mark after* ditionem. constituit] *deleted and* iussit *added above*.

[17]Montes] tes *deleted and* s *added above*. quibus] ibus *deleted and* o *added*. montes] s *deleted and* m *added above*. ibi lapidum cumulus] Garnedd, i. e. *added above*. thesauros absconditos olim opinantur] *deleted and* heroem aliquem multis antea seculis sepeliri ferunt *added above*; sepeliri *then deleted and* sepultum esse *added above*.

[18]devastasset] Gruphinus *added above with insertion mark after* devastasset. tractis] *deleted and* abductis sicque *added above*. illarum] *deleted and* suorum *added above*. ubi summa] victoria potitus *added above*.

[20]fusis] *gap in manuscript after* fusis. solitudinem] penitus *added above with insertion mark after* solitudinem. < > regebat] *gap before* regebat, *then deleted and* reversus est ut eam quietam et pace felicem redderet ac gubernaret *added above*. Venedotiaque] que *deleted and* sic *added in front*. summa] *deleted and* magna *added above*. spacium] *deleted and* tempus *added above*.

§19
[1]illi fidelitate obstrictus] *deleted and* suus diabolico incitatus telo *added above*.

[2]Duos] comites *added in right margin*. de castro Baldwini] *deleted and* de Montegomerico *added above*. persuasit] *deleted and* iussit *added above*. ut] *added above but required by sense*. peditesque] magno numero *added above with insertion mark after* pedites.

[3]in terminis] *deleted and* ad confinia tui *added above*.

[4]summo] pere *added above end of word*. ad colloquendum venire] cum tuis auxiliariis, et hospitibus *added above*. salve] *deleted and* sine periclo *added in right margin*.

[5]eum mandarunt] statim *added above with insertion mark after* eum.

[6]famulos] sectatores *added above and then deleted and* hospites *added after deletion.*

[7]Alii] *deleted and* caeteri *added above.*

§20

[1]Coaetanei] *deleted and* amici ac domestici *added above.* staturae] ae *changed to* a. mediocris] s *deleted.* capite] *underlined and* cerebro *added above.* formosi] i *deleted and overwritten with* a. coloris] *deleted.* decenter latis] *deleted and* cum decore grandioribus *added above.* doctrinae fuerat perpolitus] perpolitus *changed to* perpolitum; *whole phrase then deleted and* expertum *added above;* expertum *then deleted and* peritum *added above.* linguarum] scientia *added above.* excellens] s *deleted and* tem *added above.* in proeliis] et *added above* in.

§21

[1]ducens non postposuit] ad *added before* ducens; *whole phrase then deleted and* ingentes adduxit *added above.* castella] ac *added above beginning of word.* dominaretur] *deleted and* facilius imperaret *added above.* Arvon] ia *added above end of word.*

[2]Constantii] *ending changed to* is. ad < >] *gap in main text filled by* eorum defensionem. posuit] *deleted and* collocavit. Qui *added above.* tantaque] que *deleted.* usus est] *deleted and* tantisque malis patriae incolas affecerunt *added above and extending over next line.* unquam aetas] antea *added above.*

[3]At] Et *added above.*

§22

[1]sic] *deleted and added above* evenit *with insertion mark before* evenit. Hir] *deleted and* Longus *added above.* sodalico modico] *deleted and* paucis sodalibus *added above.* vinctum] *deleted.* regem] vinculis astrictum *added above.* amplexibus] *deleted and* dorso *added above.* conatur] *deleted and* cum sociis conficit *added above.* tacitus] us *deleted and* e *added above.*
[2]Sandef] f *deleted and* vus *added above.* ap Ayre] *deleted and* filius Ayrei *added above.* defensit < >] *gap in manuscript after* defensit; ei necessaria subministravit *added above.*

[5]sibi familiarissimis] *deleted and* electissimis amicis tantummodo *added above.* nobilitate praestantem] in illa regione *added above.*

⁶confirmavit] *deleted and* confecit *added above.* pergeret] ob metum *added above and then deleted.* proderet] ur *added above.* Francus] *deleted and* a Francis *added above.*

⁷Egimir, Gellan, Merwyd, Edenyved] us *added to the end of each name*; ac *added before* Edenyved. ad se receperunt] compassione moti *added above.* solitudinis] *deleted and* desertis *added above.*

⁸At diebus mensibusque transeuntibus cum] *deleted and* post aliquot menses *added above.* viris] i *deleted and* o *added above.* illi adhaerentibus] *deleted and* ad illum coegerunt *added above.* per] ac *added above with insertion mark before* per. quasi erro quidam] *deleted and* de loco in locum palantes *added above.* circumiuit] umiuit *deleted and* umeunt *added above*; *the whole word then deleted and* peragrant *added above.* inferenda] da *deleted and* tes *added above.* quamdiu] *deleted and* dumquoad *added above*; *this then deleted and* dum *added above.*

⁹castellis] *deleted and* praesidiis *added above.* machinantem] *deleted and* operantem *added above.* cervum] defessum *added above.* navem] em *deleted and* iculam *added above.* Aberdaron] de *added above with insertion mark before* Aberdaron. puppi] *deleted and* navicula *added above.* solvebat] flumine *miscopied after* solvebat *and deleted.* reperit] et inde mox in Hiberniam reversus est *added after.*

§23
¹aliaque] *second a deleted and* as *added above*; *this then deleted and* aliaque *added above.* ad] *not in MS but required by sense.*

²quoque] d *added above*; primis suis temporibus] *deleted and* tunc primum *added above.* accepturum] *text has* accepturus *corrected to* accepturum.

³adventum] m *deleted.*

⁴cum] inde *added above with insertion mark before* cum. navium Monam] sibi in subsidium concessa *added above.* proeliatur] *changed to* proeliaretur.

⁷galeatos] et *added above with insertion mark before* galeatos. bipennibusque] *deleted and* sua bipenni *added above.* armatos] o *changed to* u.

⁸navesque] auxiliariae *added above.* Dinieuyt] *deleted and* Phocarum vel vitulorum marinorum insula *added above and in right and left margin.*

⁹Lleyn] *deleted and* Leynum *added above.*

[10]qui ad principis ... tenebantur] *deleted and* scilicet *added above.* Lleyn] *deleted and* Leyno *added above.* Arvon] ia *added at end of word.* Ros] *deleted and* Rossia *added above.* ac Dyffryn Clwyt] *deleted and* et Dyffrynclwyt, i.e. valle Cluydana qui ad sui legitimi principis obsequia exequenda fidem suam tradunt *added above and below.*

[11]perlegente] *deleted and* adiuvante *added above.* optimo maximo] *MS has* opt. max. exaedificatum] esse *added above.* expugnavit] ex *deleted and* op *added above.*

[12]praesidiis] *deleted and* propugnaculis *added above.* saxa deiecerunt] balistis fundis *added above.* instrumentis] bellicis *added above with insertion mark after* instrumentis. quotidiano] *final* o *changed to* ae. assiduo] *changed to* assiduae. oppugnationis] *changed to* oppugnatione; Cambrorum *added above*; certamine Wallorum] *deleted.*

[13]caepit] ae *deleted and* e *added above.*

[14]devinctis] *sic for* devictis; inctis *deleted and* ictis *added above.* vacuam] *deleted and* liberam *added above.* paternam haereditatem adeptus est] *deleted and* suum principatum denuo recepit de suis hostibus condignas sumens poenas. ac sic *added above.* Venedotiaque] que *deleted.* est usa] est *deleted and* est *added after* usa.

[15]postquam] quam *deleted and* ac *added above*; *then* postac *deleted and* cum *added above.* pugnasset] ss *deleted and* r *added above.* missis sexaginta] *deleted and* centum viginti *added above.* militum] um *deleted and* ibus *added above.* ad incendia et predas agendas] *deleted and* comitatus ac castellum incenderat ac penitus devastasset *added above*; rat *deleted and* sset *added above*; omnia *added above with insertion mark before* penitus. excidisset] excid *deleted and* perven *added above.* penitusque omnia devastasset] *deleted.* aliam] a *changed to* u; m *deleted and* d *added above.* regionem] *deleted and* latus *added above.* alii] *deleted.* coeptum] ad *added above with insertion mark before* coeptum. aggreditur] *deleted and* progreditur *added above.* continuata] *deleted and* renovata *added above.*

[16]Gellan] us *added above end of word.* Cytharedus] .i. archimusicus *added above.*

[17]Quanta] *deleted and* Paternus fortasse qua *added above.* quanto] *deleted and* ac quo *added above.* perpolitum esse oporteret qui] eum *added above with insertion mark before* qui; *whole phrase then deleted and* excelluit *added above.* facinora] ac *added above with insertion mark after* facinora. ingenue] ego *added above with insertion mark before* ingenue. esse] me *added above with insertion mark before* esse. < >] *filled with* numeris. Homerum] *deleted and* poesi Maronem *added above.*

§24

[1]Angharat] am *added above end of word.* Ywein ap Edwin] *deleted and* Oweni filii Edwini principis Tegeniae, nunc Englefeld *added above.* principatus] *deleted and* provinciae *added above.* sapientem fuisse] *deleted and* feminam *added above.* modestam] *deleted and* fuisse ingenuae staturae *added above.* oculis ac < > corpore accipitrino] subgrandioribus *in right margin; gap before* corpore *(into which* splendentibus *was inserted)*; accipitrino *deleted*; accipitrino, vel erecto *added above whole phrase.*

[2]sermone] ac *added above with insertion mark before* sermone. gestaque decoram] *deleted*; que *then deleted and* ac *added above, then added before* gesta; cibi et potus largitione liberalem *added above.*

[3]Cadwallon, Ywein ac Kadwaladyr] *deleted and* Cadwallanum, Owenum, et Cadwalladerum *added above.* Gwenllian] am *added above end of word.* Margret] aretam *added above end of word*; Marretam *added above.* Ranillt] *deleted and* Raynildem *added above.* Annest] *deleted and* et Agnetam *added above.* fuere] etiam *added above.*

§25

[1]ensis longi] *deleted and* longa spatha *added above.* mingentem ad parietem] *deleted and* quidem ullum vivum *added above.*

[2]scindere] *deleted and* omnes succidere *added above.* imbecilliores] *deleted*; Gwindyt, .i. Venedoti *added above.* tutarentur] deinceps *added above and then deleted.* superesset] deinceps *added above.*

[3]primus] s *deleted and suspension mark for* m *added above.* omnium tabernacula ac] *deleted.* intra] *deleted and* ad locum vocatum *added above.* castella] a *deleted and* um *added above.* muris cincta] *deleted and* muratum *added above.*

[5]< > in occursum] *gap in MS before* in; in occursum *deleted.* totius principatus] sui *added above.* collegit] ac adversus regem Gulielmum eduxit *added above with insertion mark after* collegit. exercitus] regis *added above.*

[6]intestina terrae] *deleted and* regionem mediterraneam *added above.* pervenit] *deleted and* exercitum reduxit *added above.* ex hoc] *deleted and* in quo *added above.* minatus] esset *added above with insertion mark after* minatus.

[7]Anglus] *deleted.* currus] *deleted and* armigeros *added above.*

[8]copiae] quum interim *added above with insertion mark before* copiae. nocerent] nimium *added at end of line.*

§26

[1]classem onustam] militibus *added above.* caeperunt] ae *deleted and* e *added above.* vlcisceretur] *catchword* vlcisseretur.

[2]Ad hanc rem ... Salopiae] *deleted probably by Wiliems (see Apparatus (b)).* Griffino] Griffinus *MS*; us *deleted and* o *added above.*

[3]ducunt] navibus *added above and then deleted*; classe *added under deletion.* Yweino ap Etwin] *deleted and* ac copiis Oweno filio Edwini *added above.* Vthtrico] *deleted and* Ughtredo *added above.*

[4]Res haec] omnis *added above.* Venedotiae] ae *deleted.* Powisiae] e *deleted and* ni *added above.* incolas quasi e somno excitavit] *deleted and* in unum convenerunt *added above.* fortius] *deleted.* abiecto quamvis obediendi vel ore] *deleted*; vel ore *uncertain*; totis viribus ne subiugarentur *added above.*

[5]Kadwgan] Kadwallawn *MS*; wn *deleted and* nus *added above*; *then completely deleted and* Caduganus *added above.* Meredith] *deleted and* Maredithus *added above*; filii Blethyni filii Cynuyn *added in left margin.* suos] *changed to* suas *and* res *added above.* capto] ibi *added above.* Monam receperunt] cum Griffino *added above.*

[6]classis] Hybernicae *added above.* promissis] *deleted and* pollicitis *added above.* Griffinum] um *changed to* o; a *added before* Griffino. fallerent] *deleted and* deficerent *added above.*

[8]animi] mi *added above.* classis] suae auxiliariae *added above with insertion mark after* classis.

[9]Cadwgan] o *added at end of word.* ap Bleddyn] *deleted and* filio Blethini suo genero *added above.* eiusque] eius *deleted and* sua *added above.* premuntur] maximo *added above.* promisit] *deleted and* clementiae, et bonitatis suae non oblitus consueverit *added above and continued into next line.*

[10]quaesiuit] vit *added above.* ut] *deleted and* ac *added above.* specibus] i *overwritten with* u. locis palustribus] *deleted and* alnetis *added above.* agris incultis, cisternis, paludibus, ruderibus] *deleted and* filicetis montium iugis locisque praecipitibus paludibus et incultis *added above*; dibus *then deleted and* stribus *added above.* aliis] inaccessis *added above with insertion mark after* aliis. absconderent]

suspension mark for second n *deleted.* latitabant] n *deleted;* quo se *added above with insertion mark before* latitabat. occultabant] *suspension mark for* n *deleted.* Francorum] Iudaicorum scilicet *added above with insertion mark before* Francorum. aliarum] *changed to* aliorum. externarum gentium] *deleted and* barbarorum *added above.* advapulabant] vapulabant *deleted and* venerant *added above;* Quoniam (ut divinum dicit eloquium) cecidit populus sine duce *added after* advapulabant.

[11]comitibus] et mora non fuit *added above.*

§27

[1]regia] ia *deleted and* alis quaedam *added above.* a Francis] *deleted.* (siquidem iam dominasset Danos foedifragos] *deleted and* contristati sunt Franci ac foedifragi illi Dani *added above.* Griffinum] a *added before* Griffinum; um *deleted and* o *added above.* deceperant] *overwritten by* defecerant. ad consuetas] ac Franci vero *added above with insertion mark before* ad.

[2]firmare] *deleted and* securitatem ac *added above.* pacem] accipere *added above with insertion mark after* pacem. rationibus] optime *added above with insertion mark before* rationibus. optime] *deleted.*

[3]timebant] Franci *added above with insertion mark after* timebant. parte] simul *added above with insertion mark after* parte. foret] quod ut sperabant effectum est *added after* foret.

[4]miserrimum] um *deleted and* os *added above.* populum] *deleted and* Cambros *added above.* gravissima servitute oppressum v[...]da spe] *deleted and partially illegible;* carceribus circumsessos *added over* gravissima servitute. pellexerunt] pellexit *MS;* it *deleted and* erunt *added above.* ne aetas sequens maiorum suorum tantas clades olim recordaretur] *deleted and* post tantam tamque immanem cladem perpessos quantam ne posteri quidem aetates post multas maiorum aetates oblivioni tradere non possent *added above and below; then,* post *deleted; first* aetates *deleted;* non possent *deleted and* poterint *added above.*

§28

[1]Llychlyn] *deleted and* Llychlinii, uel Noruegiae *added above.* singularis anima] *reading uncertain but seems to be* singulari anima; *deleted and* misericordia singularis *added above.*

[2]praessuris] *deleted and partially illegible;* suis calamitatibus *added above.* anxietatibus] *difficult to read; deleted and* malis *added above.* Deus eam salvam fecit] *deleted and* exaudivit eam Deus *added above.*

[4]quique in terram e navibus erant expositi] *deleted and partially illegible*; cum suis classicis pugnabant *added above*; pugnabant *then deleted and* pugnatoribus *added above*.

[6]arboribus] ficiferis *added above*. Danorum] *deleted and* Noruegensium Lychlynensium *added above*.

[7]rex] autem ipse magnanimus *added above*. sagittam] *followed by gap in manuscript filled by* torquens. Hugonis] is *changed to* em. exanimatus] atus *deleted and* is *added above*. licet armatus prosternitur diutiusque cum ferro luctatur] *deleted and* ex equo suo armato cadit ac super arma aliquamdiu luctatur moribundus *added above*.

[8]fortuito] *deleted*; luctabili *added above and then deleted*. Danis] *deleted and* Lichlinensium ictibus *added above*.

[9]subduxit] quia cum ingenti militum manu iter hoc suscepisset *added above with insertion mark after* subduxit. totius orbis ultimae] *deleted and* extra orbis terminos *added above*. cum ingenti militum manu iter hoc suscepisset] *deleted and* ut Ferillus dixit: Britannos a toto orbe penitus esse discretos ex alienis *added above*; discretos *then deleted and* separatos *added above*; separatos *then deleted and* diuisos *added above*.

§29

[1]Comes] Cestriae *added above with insertion mark after* Comes. Franci < >] *large gap in manuscript after* Franci *filled by* ob discessum Magni regis Noruegensium. perfusi] captivos Venedotos, et suas *added above with insertion mark after* perfusi. quas egerunt secum] *deleted*. < >] *filled by* in tutiora. cantredorum] orum *deleted and* i *added above*; de Rhossia *added above and then deleted*. Monae] *deleted*. metu etiam Griffini quem singulis momentis expectarent] metum *MS*; *whole phrase deleted and* Griffini adventum de hora in horam metuentes *added above*. quo etiam in loco] etiam *deleted*. inhabitantium frumenta bovesque] *deleted and* cuiusque animalia capta *added above*; reliquasque praedas *added at end of line*. sunt partiti] omnes numerabant ac in duas partes *added above with insertion mark before* sunt. transportarunt] runt *deleted and* uit *added above*; Comes *added at end of sentence*.

[2]aderant] etiam *added above with insertion mark after* aderant. fefellerant] *deleted and* prodiderant *added above*. quia] *deleted and* quam *added above*. virginum] captarum *added above*. amplissimum perfi] *deleted and* in suae perfi *added above*. premium] accepturi *added above*.

[4]obeses] *deleted and* inutiles *added above.* imbecillas] becillas *deleted and* potentes *added above.*

[5]altum petierunt] in *added before* altum; petierunt *deleted and* soluerunt *added above.*

[6]praeerat] *deleted and* imperabat *added above.* alios morte] mulctando *added above with insertion mark after* alios. ascissione] b *added after* a *with insertion mark.* exilio perpetuo] *endings changed to* um. mulctando] *deleted.*

<h3 style="text-align:center">§30</h3>

[1]subditosque] suos *added above.*

[2]comitem] Cestriae *added above with insertion mark after* comitem.

[3]cantredo] de Rossia *added above with insertion mark after* cantredo.

<h3 style="text-align:center">§31</h3>

[1]tot] *deleted and* tandem *added above.* annorum spacio] aliquot *added above.* Bangorensis] Eruynii *added above in left margin with insertion mark before* Bangorensis. vitam, favorem, familiaritatem] *deleted and* salutem, amorem *added above.* multarum rerum cognitionem adeptus] *deleted and* intellegendi et sermonis gratiam *added above*; intellegendi *then deleted.*

[2]Lleyn] de *added in front with insertion mark.* incolis] ac *written after* incolis *in error and then deleted.* < >] ac praedis *added in gap*; spoliis universis *added above.*

[3]in illorum] suos subditos *added above*; o *of* illorum *deleted and* a *added above.* possessionem intrat] *the final* m *of* possessionem *deleted*; intrat *deleted and* adduxit *added above.* potentes] *deleted and* divites superbos *added above.* exaltat humiles] humiles *deleted and* et humiles in eorum locos *added above with insertion mark before* exaltat; egenum *added above.* facit] potentem *added above in right margin with insertion mark after* facit. qui hominem] et *added before* qui.

[4]prospere] e *deleted and overwritten by* rime; paulatim succedunt *added above.* quia] *abbreviation expanded above.*

[5]Delabuntur] *deleted and* confugiunt *added above*; gap in MS *after* delabuntur. Ros] *deleted and* Rossia *added above.* muneribus] *deleted*; rebus suis *added above.* Hugonis] *deleted and* Cestriae *added above.* multitudinem] inem *deleted and* o *added above.* abundabat] *deleted and* augere coepit *added at end of line.*

⁶ibi gubernando habitabat;] *deleted and* imperabat *added above.* inde] que *added.*

⁷Venedocia] c *changed to* t. potentiam] *deleted and* suis viribus imperium *added above.*

⁸etiam] singulos *added above with insertion mark after* etiam. crebras] *deleted and* superiores *added above.* expressi] *deleted and* in servitium adacti *added above;* servitium *deleted and* exilium *added above.* gaudio] opibus ac *added above with insertion mark before* gaudio. reversi] *deleted and added after* Babylonica.

§32

¹quia] *changed to* quod *by addition of* d *above.* possessiones ... evicerit] *deleted and* ditionem suam occupaverat Gruphinus *added above;* sic *then added above* occupaverat *with insertion mark after* suam; occupaverat *changed to* occupaverit.

²thesaurum exfodit maximos sumptus erogando et in] *MS reads* erogand; *reading unclear in places; a phrase was added above* exfodit maximas *with insertion mark after* exfodit, *then deleted and now illegible;* in magnam exponit ac uiaticum liberale equitibus ac peditibus domo dedit *added above and then deleted;* aerarium suum recondit, sumptusque ingentes in equites ac pedites fecit *added above* Itaque *running along the top of the page;* aerarium suum recondit *virtually illegible in the damage at the top of the page but restored from the later copies.* regem] etiam *added above with insertion mark after* regem. Australesque] que *deleted and* ac *inserted in front.* Cambros] secum adduxit *added above with insertion mark after* Cambros.

³Has copias] cum *added above with insertion mark before* has; has copias *changed to* hiis copiis. ducit] *deleted and* ingressus est *added above.* intra murata castella] *deleted and* apud Murcastell *added above.*

⁴Ipse] *something, now illegible, deleted above* Ipse. necessitates] *deleted and* stratagemata ac pericula *added above.* quasi] *deleted.*

⁷praeclarum] *deleted and* magnum *added above.* posuit] *deleted.* scilicet] *deleted.* ut] *deleted and* posuit hoc consilio ut *added above.* eradicaret] *deleted and* everteret *added above.* eius] omnes *added above with insertion mark after* eius. funditus perimeret] *deleted and* ad extremam internecionem redigeret *added above.*

⁸Verum] *deleted and* Hoc audito *added above.* suos] in aciem *added above with insertion mark after* suos. recollegit] re *deleted.* praeciosis quibuscumque] *deleted and* familiis suis *added above; this then deleted and* domesticis suis ac colonis *added above.*

[9]reciperet] *MS has* receperet *with* se *added above*; peret *then deleted and* pit *added above.*

[10]Comites] Cestriae *added above with insertion mark after* Comites.

[12]fautores] *deleted and* viri *added above.* non] *deleted and* non *added above.* at non poterant] insidiae suae omnino perficere *added at beginning of next line*; insidiae suae *changed to* insidiosa sua *and* proposita *added above with insertion mark after* sua.

§33

[1]tantos] hosce *added above with insertion mark after* tantos. regumque] aliorum *added in left margin*; the whole phrase *deleted and* regisque *added after it.* Murchathi] ur *lost in tear at top of page; spelling taken from Cotton Vitellius C.ix.* praeerant] nt *deleted and* t *added above.* percelebre] per *deleted.*

[2]pomaria] ac *added above with insertion mark after* pomaria. hortos] colere *added above with insertion mark after* hortos. stagnis] *deleted and* agnis *added above, then deleted.* edificia] murataque *added above with insertion mark in front of* edificia; murata *added after* aedificia *and then deleted.* fructus] terrae *added above with insertion mark before* fructus. usum colligere] *deleted and* alimenti usum convertere *added above.*

[3]magnifice exedificasset et sustentasset] *deleted and* construxerat, ac honorifica conviviorum liberalitate assidue sustentaret *added above*; construxerat *then changed to* construxit; sustentaret *then deleted and* celebrabat *added above.*

[4]vero efflueret] *deleted and* referam amplius *added above.*

[5]Venedocia] c *changed to* t. cum] *deleted and* iam dealbatis *added above*; iam *then deleted and* tunc *added above.* < >] splendere *added in gap and then overwritten to make* splendescebat; *gap left in manuscript after* splendere. iam] *deleted and* non aliter quam *added above.* firmamento] o *changed to* um. ac] *deleted.* cum] *deleted.* dedicationibus] *reading uncertain; manuscript seems to have* didioeibus. etiam] *deleted.* Regnis] sibi added *in right margin.* vicinis aluit] *deleted and* finitimis conservans *added above.* in] *deleted.* praepositos] *end of word lost in tear in page.* coll[...]velit] *deleted and difficult to read*; ut regere discerent *added above and only partially legible due to tear in edge of page.* essent] quasi moenia immobilia *added above.* quasi] *deleted*; adversus *added in space after* quasi. cum] *deleted.* extraneis nationibus] *changed to* extraneas nationes. oppositio cum hiis qui] *deleted and* illosque barbaros *added above.* rebus novis studere vellent] *deleted and* nova contra se molirentur *added above.*

[6]Reguli] vero *added above with insertion mark after* reguli. eius] ad *added above with insertion mark before* eius. curiam] ac patrocinium *added above with insertion mark after* curiam. petebant] *deleted and* confugiebant *added above.* interdum] *deleted.* impetrandi, interdum consolationis ac] *deleted;* ac *then added above.* consilii causa] sui impetrandi *added above with insertion mark between* consilii *and* causa. urgebant] bant *deleted and* rent *added above.*

§34

[1]misericordiae] *deleted and* misericordiae ac pietatis *added above.* apud se cogitans] *deleted and* animo secum versans uersus *added above (reading unclear); then* versans versus *deleted and* reuoluens *added above.* quam eius] *deleted and* quod *added above.* esset relicturus] *deleted and* iam reliquisset *added above.* in secretiorem] propositum etiam habuit *added above with insertion mark before* in; ac solitarium *added above with insertion mark after* secretiorem. contemptis] ac abiectis *added above with insertion mark after* contemptis.

[2]rex] *insertion mark after* rex; *addition lost, but Cotton Vitellius C.ix has* olim. in partes divisit] *deleted and* distribuit *added above* partes.

[4]Dublinorum] *MS reads* Dublinum; apud *added above with insertion mark in front.* abbatiis] tiis *deleted and* thiis *added above.*

[5]Etiam amplius quod] *deleted.* legavit] plus *added above with insertion mark in front of* legavit.

[6]Penmonae] ecclesiis *added above with insertion mark before* Penmonae. Sancti Germani, Dinerth] *deleted.* multisque] Sancti Germani, ac Dinerthi tantundem *added above.* et] *deleted.* praecipuis] *deleted.* ecclesiis] principalibus *added above.*

[7]Haec] *deleted;* bona illa *added at end of line.* episcopis, archidiacanis] *changed to* episcopo, archidiacano; quae dedit *added above and in left margin with insertion mark in front of* episcopis. indigentibus concessit ut] *deleted and* egenis dedit ego *added above.* protectione] *final* e *changed to* i. defensitaretur] *deleted and* commendabo *added above.*

§35

[1]eum] ad *deleted after* eum. archidiaconus] vir aetate ac prudentia maturus *added above.* homo et doctrina et sapientia insignis] *deleted; catchword on previous page is* homo et doctrina *but omitted at the top of next page and added above by main hand.* compluresque alii] esque alii *lost in tear in page but restored from Cotton Vitellius C.ix.* discipuli] *deleted and* scholastici *added above.*

²quae illis olim] *deleted and* quales viri postea *added above*. eventura] a *changed to* i. patriarchae] e *deleted*.

³duas terrae portiones] *underlined and* duo mesuagia uel patrimonia *added above*; terrae *changed to* terrarum. porticibus] *deleted and* porthmiis *added above*. Abermeney] de *added above with insertion mark in front of* Abermeney; portoriis *added above but referring to* porticibus *and* porthmiis.

⁴et filiorum] *deleted and* ac nepotum *added above*. partes assignavit ad comodius post [...] discessum vivendum] *deleted and difficult to read due to damage to the corner of the page*; partem rerum suarum tribuit, [p. 54] qua co*modius post eius* mortem ducere vitam possent *added above (text in italics from Cotton Vitellius C.ix)*. mortem flebilibus vocibus sunt] *deleted and* obitum magno maerore ac luctu *added above*. persequuti] sunt *added above with insertion mark after* persequuti. Iudeei] olim *written in error after* Iudeei *and deleted*.

⁷Bangor] ensi *added above end of word*. splendido erecto monumento] splendido *deleted and* splendida *added above*; erecto *changed to* erecta; monumento *deleted and* tumba *added above*.

⁸ut] nos *added in left margin with insertion mark before* ut. praeclarorum] bonorum ac *added above with insertion mark before* praeclarorum.

(b) Other annotation in Peniarth MS 434

The annotations of Edward Thelwall are noted in Apparatus (a) above. Most of the other annotation is by Thomas Wiliems, but there are also further notes by others. For Wiliems, see the Introduction, p. 5. Wiliems's annotations are usually easy to identify as they are indicated in the margin by a characteristic flower symbol and written in a dense black ink in sharp contrast to the brown inks of the rest of the manuscript (see, for example, Plate 1, 1. 11, Plate 3, 11. 2–11); many of his annotations are in the margins and he indicates the word or phrase in the text to which it refers by underlining. The most systematic annotation is a series of numbers in pencil on every other page usually in the middle of the page (see, for example, Plates 1 and 3); this is Horwood's foliation of the manuscript (James Horwood was a nineteenth-century owner of the manuscript; see the Introduction, p. 6).

In what follows, the annotation in the manuscript is listed in textual order. The annotation is by Thomas Wiliems unless marked by *. It should be noted that not all of the annotation refers to the main text; some of it changes or modifies Thelwall's annotations. The order of an entry is as follows: the text of the note, page reference in manuscript: location in text including an indication of whether it refers to the main text or to Thelwall's annotations (indicated by *(Th)*), and its location in the edited text of *VGC* by paragraph and sentence number. For the first nine pages of the manuscript where the top of the page is badly damaged, line numbers are counted from the bottom of the page; this is indicated by a minus sign after the line number. Much of the annotation is interlinear; since most of the annotation has been placed above the word or phrase to which it refers, the line references refer to the line beneath the annotation. *Insert* means that the word has been added above, with an insertion mark showing where it is to be understood.

[...]	1.14-: *above* Swrth (§1/1)
*1	1.7-: *foliation (s. xix)* (§1/3)
purpur	1.1-: *above* ceruleae (§3/1)
*2	3.9-: *foliation (s. xix)* (§4/1)
*3	5.7-: *foliation (s. xix)* (§5/6)
*munitiones	5.3-: *left margin*, oppugnacula *(Th)* (§5/7)
deletion	6.4-: citeriorem *deleted*.
continentis vel minorem	6.4-: *above* Wallice Lydaw (§5/10)
contemporanei	7.13-: *left margin*, coaetanei (§5/13)
ad	7.11-: *insert after* quae (§5/14)
*4	7.9-: *foliation (s. xix)* (§6/1)
Ego dixi	9.11-: *above* vos, dii ((§7/1)
*5	9.9-: *foliation (s. xix)* (§7/1)
presagire	9.15-: *left margin*, prophetasse (§8/1)
delicate	10.11: *above* annos (§9/1)
precipue	11.3: *left margin (end of l. 3 missing)* (§9/2)
instanter	11.6: *left margin*, humiliter (§9/2)
vna[nimi]	11.8: *insert before* Consensum (§6/8)
	(*cf. 40.3 below*)
*6	11.10: *foliation (s. xix)* (§9/3)
*ulcat	11.14: *added in gap* (§10/1)
tunc temporis	11.15: (§10/2)
Venedotiae	11.16: *above deleted* gerebant (§10/2)
us	11.17: *added to* Kynwric (§10/2)
illis impertiebam	12.6: *above* Isti (§10/4)
Illi autem	12.6: *above* Isti (§10/4)
dicentes venisti exoptate	12.7: *above* salutant (§10/4)
recuperanda	12.10: *left margin*, vindicanda (§10/5)
strenue	12.12: *left margin before* secum (§10/5)
Rudlanum	12.18: *insert after* Robertum (§10/6)
*7	13.10: *foliation (s. xix)* (§11/2)

paludamentum	13.11: *left margin*, tunicam *(Th)* (§11/2)
diploidem	13.11: *above* yskin *(Th)* (§11/2)
consutum	13.12: *above* contextam (§11/2)
nobilium	13.18: *insert before* suorum *(Th)* (§12/2)
ex cognatione sua	13.18: *above* cognatorum *(Th)* (§12/2)
cum industria	14.5: *above* Isti animosi (§12/3)
portum interdictum	14.9: *above* Abermeney consederat (§12/4)
liberalis	14.11: *left margin*, iuvenis (§12/4)
*Reg. 1	14.16: *left margin (biblical reference)* (§12/4)
centurias	15.7: *left margin (part of l. 7 missing)* (§12/5)
*8	15.8: *foliation (s. xix)* (§12/5)
illorum hortatu	15.11: *insert before* exercitum *(*§12/6)
permagnum	15.11: *above* copiosum (§12/6)
conduxit	15.12: *above* ducit (§12/6)
angustae	15.14: *left margin*, Kyning (§12/6)
multa milia	15.17: *left margin*, plus quam mille *(Th)* (§12/7)
optimatum	16.15: *left margin*, proborum hominum (§13/1)
rex	17.8: *above* reges (§13/4)
que	17.8: *added to* Barones (§13/4)
et	17.8: *insert before* cognati (§13/4)
*9	17.9: *foliation (s. xix)* (§13/4)
conspirarunt	17.13: *left margin*, latenter *(Th)* insurrexerunt (§14/1)
	17.14–15: *right margin full of notes in different hand, then scrawled through.*
et victum et fugatum	17.17: *above* Trahaern(um) (§14/2)
insertion mark	18.5: *after* [co]horte, *but insertion lost* (§14/3)
in ditionem	18.9: *above* ductores fiunt (§14/4)
prelium	18.14: *left margin*, bellum (§14/7)
caedes fit magna	18.15: *above* decertatum est (§14/7)
regis	18.16: *insert after* Griffini (§14/8)
centurias	19.3: *left margin*, cantredos (§14/9)
ignobilis	19.8: *insert after* proditorum (§14/10)
telo vibrato	19.9: *above* stricto gladio (§14/10)
c	19.10: *above* Gwyneus; c *added before* us (§14/11)
abduxit	19.11: *right margin*, aufert (§14/11)
*10	19.12: *foliation (s. xix)* (§14/11)
congressus	19.15: *left margin*, pugna *(Th)* (§14/12)
fortunae mutabilitate	20.1: *insert before* vincere (§14/13)
bellator	20.6: *insert after* dei (§14/14)

et bellator insignis (§14/16)	20.12: *above* numquam intermoritura
praecipua	20.13: *above* bella (§14/16)
par pari retulit	20.17: *left margin*, oppressoribus . . . resistere (§14/18)
quamvis iam aetate ingravescens	20.17: *above* oppressoribus poenas dignas (§14/18)
rege	21.2: *above* regibus (§15/1)
illum hortati sunt	21.3: *above* persuadere *glossing* persuadere conatur (§15/1)
et militibus	21.5: *above* instructis (§15/1)
*11	21.9: *foliation (s. xix)* (§15/3)
concuti	21.11: *above* contabescere (§15/3)
facultatum suorum	21.15: *above* reliquam (§15/4)
facultatem	21.16: *above* in Monam, *then deleted in same ink* (§15/4)
i	21.18: *added in* stipendia *(Th)* (§15/5)
ipsumque invitum secum abduxerat	22.2: *above* invito secum auferunt (§15/5)
remanserit	22.15: *left margin*, remansit *(Th)* (§16/3)
dispersus	22.16: *between deletions above deleted* dispersus (§16/3)
plaga	23.1: *left margin*, clades (§16/4)
fuit	23.1: *above* clades (§16/4)
asper	23.2: *above* ingressus (§16/4)
Inter haec	23.3: *above* cum iam (§17/1)
optimates	23.4: *above* viros (§17/1)
regiam	23.5: *left margin* classem (§17/1)
*12	23.8: *foliation (s. xix)* (§17/1)
inquit Griffinus	23.17: *above* et cuius (§17/4)
	23.10–18: *right margin full of notes in different hand, then scrawled through. The upper group reads* Ricar Myles's book.
modicae	23.18: *above* nuper regionis (§17/5)
impugnatus	24.1: *above* oppressus (§17/5)
sanctuario asylo	24.2: *left margin* hoc ... loco (§17/5)
ditionem	24.7: *left margin* dominationem (§17/8)
Venta	24.8: *above* Gwenta *(Th)* (§17/9)
Ventanis	24.9: *under* satellitibus *(Th)* (§17/9)
oppressorum suorum	24.12: *left margin* eorum qui Rhesi patriam clade affecerunt (§17/10)
certe	24.15: *above* meae tibi (§ 17/11)

animo	25.5: *before* laetus (§18/2)
ob suppetias	25.5: *above* laetus simul, *then deleted* (§18/2)
*13	25.7: *foliation (s. xix)* (§18/3)
unius diei	25.8: *above* iam itinere (§18/3)
sicque factum est	25.14: *above* dixerat praestabat (§18/6)
gladiis ferreis	25.17: *above* iacula ferreis (§18/7)
bellatorem	26.1: *insert after* Griffinus (§18/8)
adversarios disiiciens	26.2: *above* inimicos prosternens (§18/8)
chorustante	26.2 (*sic for* coruscante): *left margin* cuncto (§18/8)
filio praeter quod parentes memorandum	26.5: *left margin* famam post ... exaudient *(Th)* (§18/9)
strenue dimicant	26.10: *left margin* delerent (§18/11)
m̄ *or* inn	26.10: *uncertain* (§18/11)
rivuli	26.10–11: *left margin* flumina (§18/11)
Inter haec	26.11: *above* Tandem (§18/12)
mortuus prosternit	26.12–13: *above* pronus deiectus (§18/12)
in modum carnis	26.14: *above* ut carnem (§18/13)
Griffini militibus	27.2: *above* verterent (§18/13)
cum suis	27.3: *above* victor more *(Th)* (§18/14)
sequentem	27.5: *left margin* posterum *(Th)* (§18/14)
ex prelio *deleted*	27.5: *right margin added at end of line* (§18/14)
ex prelio	27.6: *insert after* aliquis (§18/14)
prelio confecto	27.7: *above* bello (§18/15)
ex parte	27.8: *above* Griffini (§18.15)
metuens	27.8: *left margin* (§18.15)
Griffini et suorum	27.9: *above* illius (§18/15)
ulli eorum	27.9: *above* nec in eius (§18/15)
*14	27.9: *foliation (s. xix)* (§18/15)
pugilem	27.14: *left margin* heroem *(Th)* (§18/17)
in plebem et domos	27.17: *right margin* (§18/18)
? in plebem caede assecit necit crudit domos *deleted*	27.18: *insert before* uxoribus (§18/18)
Post *deleted* Hinc	28.2: *above* Postremo (§18/19)
interceptis	28.4: *above* fusis (§18/20)
in propria	28.6: *left margin* paterna (§18/20)
bonis	28.9: *above* deliciis (§19/1)
ex baronibus unus	28.10: *left margin* Baro (§19/1)
*1070–1101	28.11: *left margin* Hugone comite Cestriae; *pencil note, s. xix* (§19/1)
hunc in modum	28.12: *above* prodidit (§19/1)

*1094–8	28.13–14: *left margin* Hugonem Salopiae; *pencil note, s. xix* (§19/2)
de Castro Baldwini	28.14: *left margin* Montegomerico (§19/2)
salve conductum	29.3: *above* eundi redeundique (§19/4)
cum suis	29.6: *above* mandarunt (§19/5)
manicis	29.7: *above* catenis (§19/5)
extraneos	29.9: *left margin* (§19/6)
*15	29.10: *foliation (s. xix)* (§19/7)
familiares	29.13: *after* domestici *(Th)* (§20/1)
colore venusto	29.16: *above* formosa (§20/1)
artubus	29.18: *left margin* membris (§20/1)
eloquentem	30.2: *above* excellentem (§20/1)
in domesticos	30.3: *above* munificum (§20/1)
strenuissimum	30.4: *insert after* fortissimum (§20/1)
statim eo capto	30.5: *insert after* Interim (§21/1)
damnis	30.12: *above* malis *(Th)* (§21/1)
ascendit	30.14: *above* ascendebat (§21/3)
ipse illos exaudivit	30.15: *above* tempore subsidium (§21/3)
praetorio	31.1: *above* palatio (§22/1)
manicis	31.2: *left margin* uinculis *(Th)* (§22/1)
arreptum	31.2: *above* abreptum (§22/1)
occulte	31.5: *left margin* tacite (§22/1)
robustiorem factum	31.6: *above* valitudineque (§22/2)
*16	31.9: *foliation (s. xix)* (§22/4)
statim	31.12: *above* ibi (§22/5)
Inde	31.18: *above* Iter (§22/6)
cum vidissent	32.3: *added after* moti (§22/7)
inferentem	32.11: *after* operantem *(Th)* (§22/9)
sensissent	32.11: *above* senserat (§22/9)
sagaces	32.13: *above* venatici (§22/9)
aestuarium	32.18: *left margin* flumine (§22/11)
rat	32.18: *above end of* solvebat (§22/11)
velis remisque	33.3: *left margin, insert before* adnavigavit (§23/1)
et periculis	33.7: *insert after* miseriis (§23/3)
volens	33.8: *right margin after* appulit (§23/4)
*17	33.9: *foliation (s. xix)* (§23/4–5)
acre	33.12: *insert after* saevum (§23/6)
caederet	33.17: *above* prosterneret (§23/7)
vitulorum marinorum	34.1: *above* phocarum *(Th)* (§23/9)
spondent	34.11: *after* tradunt *(Th)* (§23/10)
obsedit	34.14: *above* expugnavit (§23/11)

machinis	34.17: *left margin* instrumentis (§23/12)
densissimis quasi nymbis	34.17: *after* bellicis *(Th)* (§23/12)
et centum viginti quatuor	35.3–4: *left margin* aliique sexaginta quatuor (§23/12)
passim	35.8: *insert after* universum (§23/13)
*18	35.9: *foliation (s. xix)* (§23/14)
fruitur	35.12: *right margin after* usa est (§23/14)
Hocque ammota	35.13: *above* Nec praetereundum videtur (§23/15)
acerrime	36.4: *insert after* proelia (§23/15)
incepto itinere	36.5: *above* coeptum iter (§23/15)
musicorum princeps	36.9: *left margin* penkerd (§ 23/16)
Agharetam	37.3: *left margin* Angharat(am) (§24/1)
procerae	37.5: *left margin* ingenuae (§24/1)
magnis	37.5: *right margin* (§24/1)
sperie splendenti	37.6: *left margin* splendentibus *(Th)* (§24/1)
artubus robustis palidis, pedes rectos, digitos longos, ungues tenues, molles	37.6–7: *above* singulos etiam corporis (§24/1)
eloquentem, quoad cibum et potum liberalem, prudentem cautam et [...] consiliis	37.7: *above line* (§24/1–2)
*19	37.11: *foliation (s. xix)* (§24/2)
disposuit	38.6–7: *left margin* Aggressus est (§25/2)
Anglus neque laboris vel emolumentum quicquam secum praeter unica vacca retulit	39.1–2: nec perfidi ...vacca donatus *deleted and gloss added between lines 1 and 2* (§25/6)
multaque alia bona	39.4: *insert after* plurimos (§25/7)
ultus [...]	39.4: *above* concidit (§25/8)
devenire fecit	39.5: *above* devenit (§25/8)
interim	39.5: *after* quum *(Th)* (§25/8)
ditionem	39.7: *above* eius subditis (§25/8)
vel minimum	39.7: *insert before* nocerent (§25/8)
*20	39.9: *foliation (s. xix)* (§25/9)
compositis	39.12: *above* succedentibus (§26/1)
vlcisceretur	39.18 *(catchword): above* vlcisseretur (§26/1)
et cum eo conspiravit Hugo alter Salopiae Comes	40.1–2: Ad hanc rem ... Salopiae *deleted and gloss added between lines 1 and 2* (§26/2)
unanimi consensum	40.3: *above* simul (§26/2)
cum exercitu [*deleted*] copiis quas maximas possent	40.7: *insert after* suo (§26/3)
Cumque hoc innotuisset	40.8: *above* fuerat (§26/4)

et ad se pervenirent pecunia quantus vellent recepturi — 41.5: *insert after* relinquerent (§26/6)

proditionem — 41.10: *right margin* defectionem (§26/8)

precipit — 42.1: *above* praecipitus *(Th)* (§26/10)

*21 — 41.11: *foliation (s. xix)* (§26/8–9)

ut habet scriptura [*deleted*] divina scriptura — 42.4: *above* eorum perniciem *(Th)* (§26/10)

comites — 42.5: *above* comitibus (§26/11)

cunctatione seposita — 42.5: *over* et mora non fuit *(Th)* (§26/11)

cum triumpho — 42.5: *above* eorumque exercitui (§26/11)

ad vesperam usque — 42.6: *insert before* pervagari (§26/11)

*ti sunt — 42.6: *above end of* pervagari (§26/11)

trucidare — 42.6: *above* concidere (§26/11)

dedit — 42.10: *above* obtulit (§27/1)

confugerunt — 42.13: *above* se contulerunt (§27/1)

spectabat — 43.6: *above* spectantem (§28/1)

a barbaris — 43.8: *above* liberaret (§28/1)

deum — 43.9: *above* dominum (§28/2)

*22 — 43.11: *foliation (s. xix)* (§28/3)

dominus — 43.12: *right margin* eius princeps (§28/3)

effeminati — 43.17: *above* timidiores mulierculis (§28/4)

insidentes — 43.18: *above* sedentes (§28/4)

et cum tribus navibus in Regem feruntur — 44.1–2: *added between lines 1 and 2* (§28/4)

immobilis — 44.5: *left margin* ipse magnanimus *(Th)* (§28/7); *but should perhaps be read as* nobilis.

prora — 44.5: *left margin* puppi (§28/7)

procubuit — 44.7: *above* cadit *(Th)* (§28/7)

palpitantem — 44.7: *above* luctatur (§28/7)

casû — 44.8: *above* fortuito (§28/8)

*Virgilius (*hand sign pointing at* Virgilius) — 44.12: *left margin* Ferillus *(Th)* (§28/9)

divisos orbe Brytannos — 44.12: *beneath* Britannos a toto orbe *(Th)* (§28/9)

et penitus omniaque quae habebat — 44.14: *above* praedas (§29/1)

et animalia cuiusvis et spolia enumerata sunt et divisa. dimidium versus Cestriam secum abduxit — 44.15: *above* loca cantredorum . . . deduxerant (§29/1)

Vbi moram trahebant — 45.3: *above* cum aderant (§29/2)

pollicitationem Hugonis expectantes — 45.4: *above* illis prolixe promiserat (§29/2)

divinae scripturae — 45.7: *above* divinum (§29/3)

vndique

edaces consumptrices

pretium

*23

rerum potiebatur

suo more ut illi moris erat

ex

quosdam annos

desiderium petitionem

*consequutus

dispersit superbos [...]tis sui
    deposuit potentes de sede
        et exaltavit humiles

exaltat

ebant

entem

*24

ob persequutionem praedictam

cum libertatione asseruit

suppeditas

instructus

preliis assuetus

post *(deleted)* parva temporis
    interrapedione *(sic; for*
        interruptione?) interposita

militum delectum fecit

vulgo

*25

Trahermani

uit

vicinia

et in adiacentibus

opum et facultatum

in omni territorio

palatia

plura

colens

ut praeoccuparent

45.8: *above* ex singulis partibus (§29/4)

45.9: *above* inutiles *(Th)* (§29/4)

45.9–18: *right margin full of scrawled notes
and pen trials in a different hand (cf. p. 23)*

45.11: *insert after* proditionis *referring to*
mercedem *in previous line* (§29/4)

45.11: *foliation (s. xix)* (§29/4–5)

45.13: *above* imperabat *(Th)* (§29/6)

46.1: *above* consuetudine (§30/1)

46.1: *above* de (§30/1)

46.7: *above* annos complures (§30/2)

46.12: *above* interventu salutem (§31/1)

46.14: *insert after* est (§31/1); *italic hand s.
xvi/xvii*

47.1: *above* gratias agens (§31/1)

47.3: *above* honores evehit (§31/3)

47.5: *above end of* confugiunt *(Th)* (§31/5)

47.5: *after* confugiunt *(Th)* (§31/5)

47.15: *foliation (s. xix)* (§31/7)

47.14: *beneath* propter ... necessitates (§31/8)

47.15: *above* liberavit (§31/8)

48.1: *top margin above* ac pedites *(Th)* (§32/2)

48.4: *insert after* copiis (§32/3)

48.6: *left margin* sepius expertus (§32/4)

48.12: *above* transacto temporis perbrevi
(§32/7)

49.2: *above* recollegit (§32.8)

49.4: *right margin* colonis *(Th)* (§32.8)

49.12: *foliation (s. xix)* (§32/11)

49.13: *above* Trahaerni viri *(Th)* (§32/12)

49.16: *above end of* regnabat (§33/1)

49.16: *above* familiaritate (§33/1)

50.4: *after* terris (§33/1)

50.5: *above* bonarum omnium (§33/2)

50.7: *insert after* ecclesias (§33/2)

50.13: *left margin* (§33/3)

50.14: *left margin* amplius *(Th)* (§33/4)

50.18: *after* conservans (§33/5)

51.2: *after* immobilia (§33/5)

si	51.3: *left margin* (§33/5)
extraneorum	51.6: *above* alienorum (§33/6)
*26	51.11: *foliation (s. xix)* (§34/1)
post mortem suam	51.16: *insert after* quae (§34/2)
eius manet	52.2: *insert after* iustitia (§34/3)
pecuniae signatae	52.3: *insert after* solidos (§34/4)
fuit	52.4: *above* fuerat (§34/4)
autem	52.11: *after* dedit *(Th)* (§34/7)
religiosis	52.11: *above* clericis (§34/7)
pauperibus	52.12: *left margin* egenis *(Th)* (§34/7)
futuri	53.5: *above* eventuri (§35/2)
sicut	53.5: *above* ad similitudinem (§35/2)
olim	53.6: *insert after* Egypto (§35/2)
it	53.7: *above end of* benedixisset (§35/2)
*27	53.10: *foliation (s. xix)* (§35/3)
ducere	54.1: *above* vitam possent *(Th)* (§35/4)
tumulo	54.7: *next to* tumba (§35/7)
intra ecclesiam	4.8: *insert after* partem (§35/7)
in [...] in deum	54.9: *insert after* anima (§35/8)

Notes

The following notes are intended to supplement the compendious notes in *HGK*. Factual information is not supplied here unless the text edited here provides further or different information which alters or corrects details in *HGK*. The notes predominantly deal with textual matters and focus in particular on sections of the text where this text differs from the Welsh text in *HGK* (references are also supplied to the English translation in *MPW*). For recent discussions of Gruffudd ap Cynan, see the essays in Maund, *A Collaborative Biography*, and Pryce, 'Gruffudd ap Cynan', *ODNB*.

Title: the title has been lost from the top of the first page, but most of the derivative copies (and especially the immediate descendants, *B* and *D*) have the title *Vita Griffini filii Conani*, and it is reasonable to suppose this was the title in *A*. For the use of *vita* for a secular life, we may compare Einhard, *Vita Karoli Magni* (note that while Asser's 'Life' of Alfred has all the hallmarks of a biography, it is called *De rebus gestis . . .*, despite the attempts of editors to create the impression that it was entitled *Vita Alfredi* or the like). The Welsh translation is called a *historia*; for a detailed discussion of the range of the use of *historia*, see Brynley Roberts, '*Ystorya*' (cf. also Sims-Williams, 'Some functions of origin stories'). The term *buchedd* was also available but seems only to have been used in ecclesiastical and hagiographical contexts. It would appear that, while in Latin *vita* would be an appropriate title for a secular or religious biography, in Welsh a distinction was made between a *historia* (secular) and a *buchedd* (religious). We may, however, note the combination of the two in *Hystoria o Uuched Beuno* (*VSBG*, 16–22).

Griffini: the name is also sometimes spelt *Gruffinus*. It seems to be the standard Latin parallel to Gruffudd in this text and elsewhere (Morgan and Morgan, *Welsh Surnames*, 104); cf. *Grifinus f. Meredut* (*AC, s.a.* 1124, 1128), *Resus filius Griffini*, etc. (T. Jones, '"Cronica de Wallia"', *passim*), *Griffinus filius Wenhunwyn*

(Roderick, 'Dispute', *passim*). The early Welsh name seems to be a compound of *griff* 'griffin' (borrowed from Latin *gryphus*) and *iud* 'lord' (cf. Old Cornish *Gryfyið, Grifiuð*; see *GPC*, s.v. *griff*); for a detailed listing of *Gruffudd* names, see *EWGT*, 191, Lloyd-Jones, *Geirfa*, 590–4; see also Sims-Williams, *Celtic Inscriptions*, 113, n. 615, who offers as a parallel for a compound of *iud* with a fabled beast the inscriptional form from Cornwall, *LEUIUT* 'lion-lord'. The two elements of the compound seem less firmly bound than some, in that the second element can in some instances be replaced by *ri* 'king', for example, *Griphiud:Griphri* (*AC*, s.a. 815; *EWGT*, 113–14). Play on the connection between *Gruffudd* and *griff* is made by several poets; for example, in *Marwnad Ruffudd fab Llywelyn* by Dafydd Benfras: *Am Ruffudd gwaewrudd gwae finnau | Am riff ner lluch hyder Llachau* (*CBT* VI, 29. 24) 'Woe is me for red-speared Gruffudd, for the griffin, brilliant lord, the courage of Llachau'. A Latinized version of *Gruffudd* also occurs in some sources, notably in the account of Gruffudd ap Cynan's activities in *Vita Sancti Gundleii* (*VSBG*, 182–6): *Grifudus, Grifudo* (§12), *Grifudi* (§13), and in Orderic Vitalis: *Grit(h)fridus* (III, 138. 14).

In most cases, the Latin version of a Welsh name is more or less the same name with a Latin ending, for example, *Lewelinus, R(h)esus*, etc. In some cases, the Latin version preserves an earlier form of the name, for example, *Oudoceus : Euddogwy* (Book of Llandaf, *passim*), but it is relatively rare for the Latin form to be so different. *Maredudd* is found in some Latin sources as *Mareduc, Mareduko*, etc. (T. Jones, '"Cronica de Wallia"', *s.a.* 1198, 1201, etc.; Morgan and Morgan, *Welsh Surnames*, 160), where the final syllable has been modified. A particularly striking instance, where it is necessary to think in terms of replacement rather than modification, is the use of the Anglo-Norman name *Gervasius* for *Iorwerth* (T. Jones, '"Cronica de Wallia"', *s.a.* 1201, 1207, 1210; see Morgan and Morgan, *Welsh Surnames*, 140). The common element in these modified names is the presence of a final dental fricative which may have felt uncomfortable with Latin endings added to it; this general point is not made by Morgan and Morgan, though in each case they comment on the suitability of the modified name to carry Latin case endings (cf. also Welsh *Myrddin* beside Latin *Merlinus* where again the dental fricative may have been problematic (especially perhaps in an Anglo-Norman context)). In the particular case of *Griffinus*, Morgan and Morgan suggest that it may have been felt 'as a sort of translation', as the mythical griffin would have been a familiar image (*Welsh Surnames*, 104).

§1

§1 Only *dicto Hybernice Swrth* have survived of this first paragraph. On Sord Coluim Chille (anglicized as Swords) and the presence of Welshmen in the surrounding area in the twelfth century, see Flanagan, '*Historia Gruffud vab*

Kenan'; Duffy, 'The 1169 invasion', 104–5. The implication of §34/4 is that Swords belonged to Christchurch.

a domo suorum parentum: the Welsh text appears to refer to his mother and foster-mother at this point, *lle yd oed y vam a'e vamvaeth* 'where lived his his mother and his foster-mother' (*HGK*, 1. 6 = *MPW*, 53. 7), but this section of our text has been lost and may have been different. The focus on his maternal kin has encouraged the idea that his father, Cynan, may have died young; see Duffy, 'Ostmen, Irish and Welsh', 391.

§2

§2/1 *Cynannus erat rex Venedocie*: Cynan never had been king of Gwynedd. The *Brutiau* regularly refer to Gruffudd as the grandson of Iago (*ByT* (Pen. 20) 21b17 = tr. 16. 24; *ByT* (RB) 28.15; ByS 78.26 (*nei James*; note the confusion over the sense of *nepos*, for which see §35/4n. below)). For a discussion of the implications of the presentation of Gruffudd's genealogy, see Charles-Edwards, *Early Irish and Welsh Kinship*, 220–4; Maund, '"Gruffudd, grandson of Iago"'; Duffy, 'Ostmen, Irish and Welsh', 385–7. While it was important to emphasize the status of Iago, it is worth observing that 'grandson of Iago' would have been a more acceptable (and normal) mode of reference in Ireland than in Wales.

§2/2 *Prosapia quidem ...*: in the Welsh version Evans prints *megys y tysta ac a bonhed y reeni* (*HGK*, 1. 10–11), and in the notes (*HGK*, 38, n. 1. 10–11, and also p. ccxxiii, n. 16) expresses doubts about *ac* as to whether it is to be understood as *ach* 'lineage' or *ac* 'and'; if the latter, then something will have dropped out, leaving *a* as a verbal ending. He consolidates the latter view in *MPW* where he prints *megys y tysta ac [y traeth]a bonhed y reeni* 'as the pedigree of his parents testifies and relates' (*MPW*, 23. 13 (trans. 53. 13–14)). However, the rhetorical pattern of the Latin is working in doublets, *quam nobilis ac regia ... cum paterna tum materna*, and it is likely that the Welsh was echoing this. If so, the Welsh text should probably read *megys y tysta ac[h] a bonhed y reeni* 'as the lineage and pedigree of his parents testifies'. This may originally have been intended to correspond to the Welsh phrase, *ach ac edrydd*.

§3

§3 On these genealogies, see Sims-Williams, 'Historical need', Thornton, 'Genealogy of Gruffudd ap Cynan', 82–7; see also *EWGT*, 35–7, 134–6 (notes). The orthography of the names in the genealogy may not be reliable in that names would have been easy targets for modernization in the process of copying (see the Introduction pp. 34–5) or for replacement by more familiar forms of the names in other sources.

Broadly the genealogy matches that in *HGK*, but in comparison with the later fair copies of the Latin text and with *HGK* there are two gaps: the first seems explicable by eye-skip in that, in comparison with the Welsh text, a scribe seems to have jumped from *Catwallawn m. Catuan* to *Catwallawn Llauhir*, thereby omitting six generations; in the latter he has skipped from *fil. Gurwsti* to *fil. Bruti Ysgwydwyn* (the top of p. 3 is lost but the *Brutus* listed at the bottom of p. 2 is guaranteed as *Ysgwydwyn* (rather than *ducis Romani*) by the catchword *Ysg* deleted at the bottom of p. 2). Neither omission corresponds to a recognizable genealogical segment which could have been deliberately omitted; it is likely therefore that they are simply copying errors. For discussion of these omissions and their gradual restoration in the later copies, see the Introduction, p. 14.

§3/1   Cynan is not labelled as king in the Latin; contrast *y Gynan vrenhin* (*HGK*, 1. 12 = *MPW*, 53. 8). The Latin has *Elissae* rather than *Elissed* of the Welsh text, showing loss of the final -/ð/. Cf. *Esyllt* with *Etill* in Peniarth 17 but *Es(s)yllt* elsewhere in the Welsh versions. In view of the similarity between the *VGC* form and that in the other Welsh versions, the *Etill* form in Peniarth 17 may have been brought into the text from other genealogies, for example, *Etthil* (*EWGT*, 9 (Harleian Genealogies, 1)), *Ethellt* (*EWGT*, 47 (Jesus College, MS 20, 22)), *Dethild* (Exeter MS. 3514) (see Sims-Williams, 'Historical need', 22); if so, this would be an example of where Peniarth 17 has innovated in its reading (cf. also §§14/11, 21/1). Neither here nor in §3/2 is Rhodri given his usual epithet *Magnus* or *Mawr*; it has been added in the Welsh translation (*HGK*, 1. 22 = *MPW*, 54. 3). Note also that in the Latin and the Welsh versions, Rhodri, father of Cynan Dindaethwy, has been omitted; see Thornton, 'Genealogy of Gruffudd ap Cynan', 85.

§3/2   The Latin genitive ending is added from *Urbani* onwards. The scribe had difficulty distinguishing *Eu-* and *En-* in the run of names *Eudeyrn, Eudygant, Eudos*, etc. They have been regularized here to *Eu-*.

§4

§4/1–2 The punctuation of the manuscript requires adjusting: *aliarum complurium insularum* is followed by a punctuation mark and the next sentence seems to begin with *Rex* . . . However, that leaves a very clumsy genitival phrase coming after the relative clause, *qui e Scotia genus ducebat*, which seems to close the sentence. Moreover, the *ut* in the second sentence requires a balancing clause, i.e. 'he was regarded as king of X as much as king of Y'. Therefore, it is likely that the first sentence should end at *ducebat*, and that *aliarum complurium insularum* begins the next. In support of this, cf. the standard title *rex insularum*;

for discussion, see McLeod, '*Rí Insi Gall*'. This in fact then also matches the punctuation of the Welsh text: *Bonhed Gruffudd o barth y vam: Gruffudd vrenhin, m. Ragnell, verch Avloed, vrenhin dinas Dulyn a phymhet ran ywerdon ac enys Vanav, a hanoed gynt o deyrnas Prydein. A brenhin oed ar lawer o enyssed ereill, Denmarc, a Galwei, a Renneu, a Mon, a Gvyned ...* 'Gruffudd's pedigree on his mother's side: king Gruffudd, son of Ragnallt, daughter of Olaf, king of the city of Dublin, and a fifth part of Ireland and the Isle of Man, who came of yore from the kingdom of Britain. And he was king over many other islands, Denmark and Galloway and the Rinns, and Anglesey, and Gwynedd' (*HGK*, 2. 16–20 = *MPW*, 54. 30–55. 2). Note that *VGC* has *Arennae* which is taken in the translation to refer to Arran, although it corresponds to *Renneu* 'the Rinns (of Galloway)' in the Welsh.

Etchingham, 'North Wales, Ireland and the Isles', 158, has emended, translated and discussed the Welsh version of this passage. He would want to remove the comma between *enyssed ereill* and *Denmarc* so that they are the islands of Denmark, thus removing the claim that he was king of Denmark. However, the Latin text seems best translated to mean that he was king of several other islands just as he was king of Denmark, etc. One aspect is crucial, namely the precise geographical range of the term *Dania*. At various points the Welsh translator uses both *Denmarc* and *Llychlyn* to render *Dania*. In our text *Dania* is the standard term. It is quite possible that *Dania* is being used in some cases to refer to the whole sphere of activity of the Vikings and not just to Scandinavia; for example, at §23.1 *in insulas Daniae*, where Gruffudd goes to seek help from Godred, almost certainly refers to the Western Isles (Etchingham, 'North Wales, Ireland and the Isles', 159). *Lychlin* is used once in our text (§28/1) to refer to king Magnus as king of *Lychlin*. The Welsh translator seems to use *Llychlyn* to refer to mainland Scandinavia (for example, *HGK*, 3. 3, 4. 8, 25. 19). *Nordwei* is used at *HGK*, 4. 7 to translate the Latin *Northwegiae* (§5/9), but in this instance the term is being used etymologically to account for presence of the *Normanni* in France (the forms are collected in Appendix 2).

A second issue which is resolved by the Latin text is the antecedent of *a hanoed gynt o deyrnas Prydein*. It is assumed in Evans's translation (*MPW*, 54. 33–4) that it is the king of Dublin, Auloed (Amlaíb, Olaf), but Etchingham, following Arthur Jones's rendering (*HGC*, 105), translates without comment as if the antecedent were the Isle of Man: 'which was formerly part of the realm of Britain'. The Welsh is admittedly ambiguous, but the Latin *qui* makes it clear that Auloed must be the antecedent.

Note also that Latin *Scotia* has been translated by Welsh *Prydein*. This may be an error on the part of the Welsh translator or in the early transmission of the Welsh text where *Prydein* and *Prydyn* have been confused; see *GPC*, s.v. *Prydyn*; Pryce, 'British or Welsh?', 780, n. 24. Another possibility is that *Scotia* is being used in its sense of the 'land of the Scotti', and could therefore refer to

Ireland. Yet another possibility is that *Scotia* is being used rather like Irish *Alba*, which could be used to refer to Britain as a whole and not just Scotland (Dumville, 'Ireland and Britain'); this, however, is less likely on grounds of date, as by the twelfth century *Alba* seems to have acquired the narrower sense of 'Scotland'.

§5

§5/1–4 The story of the killing of Alanus by Twr: this story presents all kinds of difficulties of interpretation. *VGC* clarifies some but not all of these issues. On this section, see Van Hamel, 'Norse history', who argued that the description of Alanus/Alyn matches closely that of St Olaf. In §5/1 the Welsh text is unclear as to whether Alanus is the brother of the king, Harald's father, or one of Harald's brothers: *a bit honneit bot Harald Harfagyr a'e deu vroder yn veibeon y vrenhin Llychlyn. Ac Alyn y vrawt oed vrenhin kyssygredicaf ac enwocaf ymphlith holl Denmarc* 'Be it known that Harald Haarfager and his two brothers were sons of the king of Llychlyn. And Alyn his brother was the most hallowed and renowned in all Denmark' (*HGK*, 3. 1–3 = *MPW*, 55. 10–13). The matter has been much debated; see, for example, Thornton, 'Genealogy of Gruffudd ap Cynan', 90–3, and Jesch, 'Norse historical traditions', 144–6, both of whom hold to the view that he is one of Harald's brothers, but go on to argue about the identity of the Harald in question, whether *Harfagyr* or *Harðráði*. While in the Welsh the referent of the possessive pronoun of *y vrawt* is unclear, the Latin text almost certainly indicates that he is the brother of the king; *cuius* can only refer to the nearest masculine singular noun, namely *regis*. The only doubt is that *cuius fratrem* is restored from manuscript *B*, but the gap in our manuscript is sufficient for these two words and little more. Despite the uncertainty, it is anyway difficult to see how a simple reading of the text could make Alanus/Alyn another of Harald's brothers as all three, Harald, the one in Porth Láirge, and Rodulphus, are clearly accounted for; the only way to do so would be either to make Alanus/Alyn the brother established in Porth Láirge, which, given his fame in Denmark, seems perverse, or to go against the text and claim that there was a fourth brother.

It is clear that Twr kills Alanus. It was suggested by Van Hamel, 'Norse history', that *Alanus* (Welsh *Alyn*) represents a corrupt form of *Óláfr*. Now that we have the Latin form of the name available, it can be suggested that the original form in this text may have been *Alauus* (with the common confusion of *u* and *n*); a further refinement might be added, that a nasal was omitted after *A*-, or perhaps a suspension mark over the vowel, thus producing a form close to the Irish *Amlaíb* (cf. Welsh *Avloed*) or to Old English *Anlaf*, depending on the source of the name form.

Van Hamel, 'Norse history', 344, also suggested that *Thurkiawl*, the name which Twr subsequently acquires, is linked to his name in Norse tradition, *Þórir hundr* 'Thori the dog', since *kiawl* can be interpreted as 'doglike' in Welsh. Note that this section is lost in the Latin text, though the space would allow it to have been present, but what we do not have is any indication of the spelling of the name in the Latin text. It seems not to have been noticed that the account of Alanus' death whereby Twr is crippled, with his hands gripping the torc and his knees pulled up against his stomach, is itself an aetiological ex-planation of a canine epithet as the shape he adopts is precisely dog-like. However, *kiawl* would not be the expected Middle Welsh derivative of *ki* 'dog'; we would expect *kynawl* (see *GPC*, *s.v. cynol* where one example is attested). The canine link is extremely plausible but, if it is to be maintained, it looks as if the line of explanation would have to be reversed and the link with *Þórir hundr* may turn out to be secondary. On this account, we would start with a Welsh rendering of an Old Norse *Thurkell*, perhaps through an Irish source so that the Welsh spelling, *Thwrkiawl*, is an attempt to render /θurkˈəL/. If so, did this give rise to a narrative which was secondarily linked to that of *Þórir hundr* when the *-kiawl* element was connected to dogs? Another element which may be involved is a work of art: Giraldus Cambrensis (*Itinerarium Kambriae*, I.2) describes a torc which was said to have belonged to St Cynog (note the canine associations of the name) and was made of four sections and divided in the middle by a dog's head standing erect with its teeth bared. Could a torc of this type be associated with the development of the legend?

§5/7 The dating clause provided by the presence of descendants of Harald's brother in Porth Láirge *er henne hyt hediv* 'since then till today' (*HGK*, 3. 27 = *MPW*, 56. 8) has unfortunately been lost in our manuscript. However, the gap is consistent with it being present in the original version.

§5/8 *insulas Daniae*: these are probably to be understood as the Hebrides; see Etchingham, 'North Wales, Ireland and the Isles'.

inter mare Tyren et Daniam: The Welsh text has *rung mor Tyren a Denmarc* 'between the Tyrrhenian Sea and Denmark' (*HGK*, 4. 3 = *MPW*, 56. 12) and Evans makes uncomplimentary noises about the geographical competence of the author (*HGK*, 52, n. 4. 3). Our manuscript also contains the confusion with *inter mare Tyren et Daniam*, but a plausible emendation suggests itself. The text could be emended with little difficulty to *inter mare Tyren et Ioniam*, thus producing a satisfactory analogy between the position of the Hebrides as a chain of islands between Ireland and Scandinavia and the position of the Cyclades between the Tyrrhenian Sea (running down the west side of Italy) and Ionia with Scotland corresponding to the position of Greece. An early copyist, before the Welsh translation was made, misled by the frequency of *Dania* in this section of the text may have misread the original *Io* as *Da*. Note, however, that

Cyclas can be used as a synonym for 'island'; see, in particular, Orderic Vitalis' usage in a passage on the travels of King Magnus: *aliasque quoque Cycladas in magno mari velut extra orbem positas perlustravit* (*Ecclesiastical History*, X, 222. 12–13); for the parallel passage in *VGC* with strikingly similar wording, see §28/9. Another possibility is that the original version of the text simply had *Cyclades* or something similar in the sense of 'island' which was subsequently glossed with a classicizing phrase referring to the Tyrrhenian Sea.

§5/9   *quibus genus a Dania originem deducens*: in the manuscript this phrase begins with a capital letter and seems to start a new sentence, but it is better taken with the preceding sentence with the antecedent of *quibus* being the *viri Northwegiae*.

§5/10   *vel similitudinem ducum*: two different models are offered for the way in which Normandy was divided into twelve, according to the number of barons or like the leaders who divided up Brittany between them. The Welsh text has mis-understood that alternative explanations are being offered and runs them together: *herwyd y barwnyeit a'r tywyssogyon a doethant yn gyntaf...* 'according to the barons and leaders who came first' (*HGK*, 4. 9–10 = *MPW*, 56. 19–20); note Evans's doubts about this passage in the Welsh text (*HGK*, 53, n. 4. 10–11).

Wallice: used only once in *VGC* and there is no corresponding phrase in the Welsh text (*HGK*, 4. 10–11). *Cambrice* occurs only once in our extant text (§12/6), but it is also found once in text imported from manuscript *B* to fill a gap (§4.2); cf. also *Hibernice* 'in Irish' (§1/1). The term *Wallia* for the country only occurs once (§22/4: *in australibus partibus Walliae*) and does not occur in the corresponding part of the Welsh text (*HGK*, 18. 22 (= *MPW*, 71. 15): *en Deheubarth*). On the other hand, *Cambria* and *Cambri* 'the Welsh' occur three and nine times respectively (for details, see Appendix 2). For possible implications, see the discussion in the Introduction, p. 45.

§6

§6/2 *Slani:* changed to *Alam* by Thelwall. This indicates that he did not have to hand the Peniarth 17 version of *HGK* which has the reading *Slani* (*HGK*, 4. 25 = *MPW*, 57. 4); all the other manuscript versions have *Alam* (*HGK*, 4. 25, n. 4), the source of Thelwall's correction. On Sláine, see Duffy, 'Ostmen, Irish and Welsh', 392–3.

Ryeni: this is probably to be understood as *Bryeni*; cf. *Vrien* (*HGK*, 4. 25). It is possible that the capital *B*- was misread as *R*-, and *Rryeni* then corrected to *Ryeni*. It is worth pointing out that there was a ruling dynasty named Uí Ríain, but they were of the Uí Dróna in Leinster.

Innen: *HGK*, 4. 26 has *Muen* (< Irish *Mumhan*) and *Innen* is probably a misreading of the five minims at the beginning of the word.

duas partes: Evans (*HGK*, 54 (n. 4. 26)) refers to the division of Munster into two. By 1137 or later, Munster was divided into Túathmuman (Uí Bhriain) and Desmuman (Meic Charthaigh), rather than the early east/west split deriving from the political grouping of the Eoganachta.

§6/3 *Gurmlach*: on Gormlaith, see now Ní Mhaonaigh, 'Tales of three Gormlaiths', esp. 18–24.

Sutrilii: it corresponds to Sutric in the Welsh text (for example, *HGK*, 4. 27). There may have been a misreading of a high *c* at some point in the transmission.

§6/4 *cui ferunt tres filios*: most of this passage has been lost from the top of the page and we are reliant on later copies. However, as they stand, they confirm the text of the Welsh, *Ac y hvnnw y bu tri meib* (*HGK*, 4. 28 = *MPW*, 57. 8), which Simon Evans suggested should be emended to *y honno* referring to Gormlaith (followed by Ní Mhaonaigh, 'Tales of three Gormlaiths', 19–20, n. 121). In the Latin the immediate and obvious antecedent of *cui* is *Murchathum regem Laginiae patrem* (though only *Murchathum* has survived in the manuscript). We cannot admittedly know whether the text has been annotated and altered by Thelwall; but, since the tradition that Murchadh was the father of Donnchadh, Sitric and Máel Sechnaill is preserved in the triads (*Trioedd Ynys Prydein*, 256, 258), it may be sensible to retain the reading of the manuscripts in *HGK*. There is a confused tradition here: both the Latin and the Welsh texts seem to be saying that Murchadh was the father of Donnchadh, Sitric and Máel, but that Gormlaith was mother only to Sitric. But Murchadh is also said to be Gormlaith's father. There is then the further confusing coda about Máel Mórda being Gormlaith's son by Murchadh. For discussion, see Ní Mhaonaigh, 'Tales of three Gormlaiths', 18–21.

§6/5 On the Ua Mathgamna, see *HGK* pp. clxxvii–clxxix; Duffy, 'Ostmen, Irish and Welsh', 391–2.

quatuordecim: this is deleted and changed to *quadraginta* by Thelwall which corresponds to the Welsh *pytheunos a mis* 'in a fortnight and month' (*HGK*, 5. 6 = *MPW*, 57. 16). Evans (*HGK*, 55–6, n. 5. 6) draws attention to the parallel phrases in Irish, such as *na teora cóicthiges* and *cóicthiges ar mís*. The Welsh phrase may well be correct and it is possible that the reading *quatuordecim* in our text is an error. Perhaps the text originally had a phrase broadly equivalent to the Irish phrases and either *et mensem* was lost after *quatuordecim* or *ter* (*vel sim.*) was lost in front of it. Another possibility is that the original had something like *quater decem*.

binas partes: elsewhere this text talks of *duas partes* (for example, §6.2) and it is difficult to know whether this change in phrasing should be taken seriously. If it is, then the implication is that it refers not to two of the five parts of Ireland as *duas partes* would mean, but rather to '*the* two parts of Ireland', i.e. the northern and southern halves. On Rinaldus mac Mathgamna, see Duffy, 'Ostmen, Irish and Welsh', 391–2.

§6/6 *monstrum marinum*: cf. Irish *muirgelt*. Cf. *Llemhidyd anryved oed* 'he was a wondrous leaper' (*HGK*, 5. 7 = *MPW*, 57. 17); *llemhidydd* can also be used of sea-creatures.

§6/7: *Isliniach*: the Welsh text has *Islimach* (*HGK*, 5. 9 = *MPW*, 57. 20).

§6/9 *Ethminach Gawyn*: on Áed mac Mathgamna, king of Ulaid (killed in 1127), see Duffy, 'Ostmen, Irish and Welsh', 391.

§7

§7 The Welsh version of this section is far less wordy than the Latin. The first part has been lost at the top of p. 9, and so the reading is not secure.

§7/1 *ea*: is this nom. sg. fem. or abl. sg. fem. of the pronoun, or is it the ending of a word from the preceding line?

ille psalterii versus: The Welsh text personifies this sentence with the subject as *tad sant* 'the saintly father' (*HGK*, 5. 16 = *MPW*, 57. 29). The quotation is from Psalms 81.6.

§8

§8 The text of the prophecy is very close but not identical to the Latin version of the prophecy given in *HGK*, 5. 27–9 (= *MPW*, 58. 10–12); *HGK* has *quia multos corrumpet*, while *VGC* has *multosque corrumpet*, which corresponds more closely to the Welsh version and does not draw any etymological conclusions about him being a source of corruption. *VGC* has not preserved the Welsh version, but only the Latin translation of it. The original must have had the Welsh as well; for discussion of the translation, see below. For discussion of the prophecy, see *HGK*, 57–8, and the references given there, to which Williams's discussion in *AP*, pp. xli–xlv should be added. The implications of Williams's arguments were not pursued by Evans. Williams drew attention to the close verbal parallels between the prophecy in *HGK* and part of a prophecy preserved in *BT*, 70. 16–71. 6 which he thought could be regarded as *Armes Prydein fychan* corresponding to *Armes Prydein fawr* (*AP*, p. xli). The section in question could well be taken to refer to Gruffudd ap Cynan and/or Rhys ap Tewdwr: *Rydybyd llyminavc auyd gvr chwannavc ywerescyn mon a rewenyav gvyned. oe heithaf oe pherued oe dechreu oe diwed. A chymryt gwystlon. Ystic y vyneb nyt estvg y neb na chymry na saesson* 'There will come a *llyminawg* who will be a predatory man to conquer Môn and lay waste to Gwynedd from her furthest border to her centre, and from her beginning to her end, and take her hostages. Angry his face who submits to nobody, neither Welsh or English' (text from *BT* 70. 25–71. 1; Williams's trans. (*AP* p. xlii)). The use of *llyminavc* in the *HGK* prophecy is suggestive in the light of the above passage which refers to Gwynedd and Môn, and might have been intended to call that passage to mind. It is striking too that *lletfer*, used to describe the *llyminavc* in *HGK*, finds an echo in *Armes Prydein* in the *pennaeth lletfer* 'oppressive rule' (lit. 'half-fierce rule') (*AP*, 38). Given the detail in the *Book of Taliesin* passage quoted above, it is likely that the *HGK* prophecy is an allusion to it rather than vice versa. The attribution of the prophecy in *VGC* and *HGK* to Merlin is presumably an assumption made by the author, but probably implies that the prophecy was in existence before he created his narrative. Certain factors, however, may have determined his choice of this particular prophecy. The Latin version is certainly a translation. *Llyminauc* is a derivative based on *llam, llemain* 'leaping' (see Russell, *Celtic Word-Formation*, 117–18), and so originally had the sense of 'leaper', but then developed into 'warrior', etc. Latin *saltus* 'leap' is a poor translation. But was the choice of *llyminauc* also intended to echo the achievements of his uterine brother Ranaldus? Compare §6/6 *cui similem ... saltandi peritia Hybernia non habuit* (cf. *Llemhidyd anryved oed* (*HGK*, 5. 7)). Likewise, *ferinus* 'savage, wild' seems to have been determined as much by an intention to echo the second element of *lletfer* as to produce an accurate translation. But again was the original sense of *llet-* intended to draw attention to the half of Gruffudd's ancestry which was not Welsh? A final observation on the prophecy: if the parallels with and allusions to the *Book of Taliesin* prophecy can be upheld, it hardly seems to be a prophecy which could have been used in Gwynedd to predict the rise of Gruffudd, perhaps another indication that *VGC* was composed outside Gwynedd.

§8/3 *antiquorum more*: this seems to have turned into the *hen gyvarwydyt* 'old account' of the Welsh text (*HGK*, 6. 5 = *MPW*, 58. 18). *VGC* has no mention of an ancient authority.

§9

§9/1   The first two lines of this section have been heavily overwritten, leaving it difficult to read both the original text and some of the corrections.

quam crudelis iam tyrannus: the Latin text focuses on the cruelty of the tyrant in possession, while the Welsh text is generic, *a pha ryw dreisw(y)r* . . . 'and what kind of oppressor(s)' (*HGK*, 6. 11 = *MPW*, 58. 27–8). The manuscripts of the Welsh version also hesitate between singular and plural (sg. ChEFFfGH, pl. ABCDDd).

§9/2 *multoties*: while the Latin text refers to him thinking things over time and time again, using the multiplicative, the Welsh text turns this into a period of time, *llawer o dydyeu* 'every day' (*HGK*, 6. 13 = *MPW*, 58. 25).
Murchathi: see Duffy, 'Ostmen, Irish and Welsh', 394–5, for the possibility that the author had in mind Muichertach Ua Bríain.

querelas ... gravissimas: the Latin text is damaged here, but if *gravissimas* is what the original had, referring to the complaints, then in the Welsh text it has been turned into a superlative adverb, *en benhaf* 'chiefly' (*HGK*, 6. 15 = *MPW*, 58. 32), referring to Murchadh, perhaps understood or read as *gravissime*. The word order of the Latin, by delaying the adjective, *gravissimas*, until the end of the clause, might equally support either interpretation.

paternam hereditatem: the Welsh translate this with *dadaul deyrnas* 'paternal kingdom' (*HGK*, 6. 16 = *MPW*, 58. 33–59. 1); *tadaul* seems to be a loan-translation of *paternus* and is rarely used outside a broadly Latinate context or contexts with a Latinate flavour.

§9/3 *Consensum*: at this point the Welsh version adds *A thruanu urthav a orugant* 'They took pity on him' (*HGK*, 6. 18 = *MPW* 59. 2–3), an emotion merely implied in the Latin, but perhaps for the Welsh version it was important to emphasize the sympathy of the Irish kings.

§10

§10/2 *in Cambria*: the Welsh version (*HGK*, 6. 23 = *MPW*, 59. 9) omits this phrase which marks a shift in the broad geographical context from Ireland to Wales; again perhaps an indication of a narrower interest in Gwynedd.

rex Powisiae: in the Welsh version Cynwrig is downgraded to the diminutive *brenhinyn* 'a petty king' (*HGK*, 7. 2 = 59. 12).

§10/4 *adventus causas querunt*: in the Latin they ask him why he has come, but in the Welsh they welcome him: *a dywedut urthaw, 'O damunet ry doethos'*, 'and told him "Your coming is welcome"' (*HGK*, 7. 7–8 = *MPW*, 59. 19–20).

§10/5 *(siquidem . . . dominari)*: the subject of *spectabat* is not immediately clear and the verb should probably be taken in the sense of 'pertain, relate to'. That is the sense of the Welsh *canys ef oed eu hargluyd priodaur* 'because he was their rightful lord' (*HGK*, 7. 10 = *MPW*, 59. 21–2). The use of different parts of *ille* does not help to clarify matters: *ad illum* refers to Gruffudd, *in illos* probably to the people of Gwynedd and Angelsey. Note that the Latin does not have any technical term corresponding to *argluyd priodaur* in the Welsh, such as *proprietarius*; for discussion of these terms, see Smith, 'Treftadaeth Deheubarth', 34–5 (and n. 65).

§10/6 *secreto*: omitted in the Welsh, where it is simply *y kyngor* 'the council' (*HGK*, 7. 13 = *MPW*, 59. 25), perhaps with an implication of secrecy.

vel ... vel: the imprecision as to his exact movements is characteristic of the Latin text. According to the Latin text, he goes either to Robert of Rhuddlan or to Hugh of Chester. The Welsh version (*HGK*, 7. 15–16 = *MPW*, 59. 28–9) has created precision by removing the 'either ... or', and by making Hugh the uncle of Robert (*nei y Hu yarl Caer* (*HGK*, 7. 15–16)). This relationship is not supported elsewhere: according to Orderic Vitalis he was *consobrinus* 'cousin' to Hugh of Chester but nephew to Hugh de Grentesmaisnil (*Ecclesiastical History*, VIII, 138. 14). The variation between the Latin and Welsh may be the result of a textual error in the transmission of the Welsh text. A direct translation of the Latin text would have been *hyt ar Robert Rudlan ... neu y Hu yarll Caer*, and it is possible that *neu* was misread or misunderstood as *nei* 'nephew'. In the Welsh version the person who accepts his appeal for support is simply *ynteu*, but that has to refer to Robert, as Hugh has been downgraded to a mere relative. The equivalent phrase in the Latin text (§10/7) has unfortunately been lost; the fair copies of the Latin have *Robertus*, but they are simply following the Welsh text in this (in the text *Robertus* has been bracketed to indicate the uncertainty). But, if the original Welsh version maintained the alternative sources of help, Robert or Hugh, *ynteu* would then have assumed a more significant role as the differentiating pronoun. According to Mac Cana, 'Conjunctive pronouns', 418–19, a conjunctive pronoun can be used to refer to the last mentioned person when several have been mentioned (in his second example, p. 419, from Branwen (*Pedeir Keinc y Mabinogi*, 31. 10) the *ynteu* must surely refer to Matholwch and not to Manawydan). If so, the help and support for Gruffudd, which in the Welsh version came from Robert, may well have come from Hugh and not from Robert. Indeed, §13/1 *ut cum Roberto castris custode et aliis Francis pugnaret* (cf. *HGK*, 9. 23 = *MPW*, 62. 3–4) would support the idea that it was Hugh who was supporting Gruffudd. According to *HGK*, 8. 6 (= *MPW*, 60. 17–18) Robert is supporting Gruffudd in the campaign against Cynwrig, but the relevant section in *VGC* (§12/2; see below) is damaged and it is not clear whether Robert is involved or not, though *Tegeinglia* is legible and would imply that Robert is present (see §12/2n.). A secondary consequence of all of this is that there is no evidence that Robert was the nephew of Hugh of Chester.

§11

For an image of this section, see Plate 1.

§11/1 *(suum cognatum existentem)*: it is likely that for reasons of space this phrase was not in the original.

§11/2 *optimam ex* < > *Griffini*: there is a space in the text between *ex* and *Griffini. et tunicam* has been added above *optimam ex* with an insertion mark between the two words. Over the space *yskin, id est pelle* has been added. Presumably, the scribe had difficulty reading what followed *ex*.

§11/3 *a thesauris*: for *a(b)* denoting official duties, see *DMLBS*, s.v. 3 *a*, *ab*, 8(b). For classical examples, see *OLD*, s.v. *ab*, 24 (c).

§12

For a brief notice of the events described in this section, see *ByT* (Pen. 20), 21b16–18 (= tr. 16. 24–5), *ByT* (RB), 28. 15–16, *ByS*, 78. 26–27, and, for discussion, *HGK*, p. cxxii.

§12/2: this sentence is badly mangled in the manuscript (see Plate 1). It runs from the bottom of p. 13 to the top of p. 14. Most of it has been deleted and heavily emended by Thelwall and not all of the underlying text is legible. In addition large portions of it are missing at the top of p. 15. The major emendation to bring it into line with the Welsh text suggests that the underlying text was trying to saying something different, but what that was is now probably irrecoverable. The significant variation between our text and the Welsh text means that it is impossible to substitute elements from the subsequent Latin fair copies; hence the gaps in the edited text at this point.

The general sense is clear: Gruffudd is gathering allies in his attempt to wrest Gwynedd from Cynwrig and Trahaearn and those allies seem to include the sons of Merwydd (listed in §10/3), Robert of Rhuddlan and troops from Anglesey. The Welsh text (*HGK*, 8. 3–4 = *MPW*, 60. 13–14) says that Gruffudd sent the sons of Merwydd who were in sanctuary in Clynnog through fear of the threats of the men of Powys. But our text, insofar as it is legible, suggests that he sent the sons of Merwydd to a sanctuary in Clynnog; that is, there is no relative pronoun to subordinate the clause about Clynnog. The presence of Robert of Rhuddlan is implied by the surviving phrase [*ex*] *Tegenglia elegerat* since Robert controlled Tegeingl (but cf. the note above to §10/6). There is no evidence surviving that forces from Anglesey were involved but there are sufficient gaps in the text for them to have been there.

§12/4 *omen*: this corresponds to *coelfain* 'boon' in the Welsh text (*HGK*, 8. 15 = *MPW*, 60. 28) and seems to carry the sense of a reward for the delivery of good news.

The parallel drawn between Anian, *iuvenis quidam Arvonensis*, and the *iuvenis quidam Amalechita* is made explicit by the verbal parallel. However, the parallel runs only as far as the delivery of news. In 1 Samuel 31 and 2 Samuel 1, the young Amalechite who brings the news of Saul's death is executed by David because he boasted that he had killed Saul (at Saul's own request) to prevent him falling into the hands of the Philistines. The Welsh text has him being given an arm-band (*HGK*, 8. 20 = *MPW*, 61. 1), and not the concubine, Dylad, as he requested. In our text Anian is rewarded but, as the text is lost at the crucial point, it is not clear with what. The text is fragmentary but seems to end with *et* followed by a large space; it is possible that this section may have been illegible in the exemplar.

in Philistino bello: the Welsh text has *hyt en Philistiim* 'to the land of the Philistines' (*HGK*, 8. 19 (varr. *Philistin*) = *MPW*, 60. 32). According to 2 Samuel 1, David was in Ziklag.

§12/5 *missi*: it has been deleted in the manuscript, but the deletion may be by the original scribe and not by Thelwall. It was originally in an odd position splitting *victoria ... ovantes*, the preceding words are lost but I suspect the original had *reversi milites in expeditionem superiorem missi victoria ovantes*, and that *missi* had been omitted and then inserted one word later.

lustrare: the meaning is unclear; it can mean 'purge, cleanse', 'wander, roam over' or 'illuminate'. The second sense is unlikely, given that the preceding clause has *circuiret* which means much the same. There is nothing corresponding in the Welsh text (*HGK*, 8. 28–9 = *MPW*, 61. 10–11).

Angliae conterminos: Evans (*HGK*, 64, n. 8. 26) suggests that this refers to Tegeingl, and the areas attacked by the Normans from Chester, Shrewsbury and Hereford. But it is far from clear that Gruffudd ranged that far east. Tegeingl was controlled by Robert who seems to have been on Gruffudd's side against Trahaearn.

§12/6 *in loco vallis Kyning, Cambrice dictus Gwaeterw*: the Welsh text has *yg glynn kyving, y lle a elwir yg Kymraec Gvaet Erw* 'in a narrow glen, the place called in Welsh Gwaed Erw' (*HGK*, 9. 4–5 = *MPW*, 61. 16–17), where *kyving* is treated as an adjective 'narrow'. Lloyd, *History of Wales*, 380–1 (and n. 76) suggested that 'Glyn Cyfing' refered to the valley now called Dyffryn Glyncul where a mill of Keuyng was noted in the *Record of Caernarvon*, 275; see also J. B. Smith, 'Age of the Princes', 7–8. While it would be possible to emend to *kyuing* in our text (assuming confusion of *n* and *u*), there are a number of difficulties: first, our manuscript clearly has an initial capital *K-* implying that it is being regarded as a name, not an adjective; secondly, this Latin text does not as a rule contain stray Welsh adjectives (all Welsh words are carefully identified and explained; cf. in this sentence *Gwaeterv, vel ager sanguinis*, §14/11 *in insulam Adron (quae et focarum insula dicitur)*). We would expect to find *in loco vallis angustae*, or *in valle angusta* or something similar to §25/5 *in angustiis viarum insidias collocans* which refers to Gruffudd placing ambushes to attack William Rufus (translated in the Welsh text as *en lleoed keuing* (*HGK*, 22. 20 = *MPW*, 75. 6–7)). Furthermore, the phrasing of *in loco vallis Kyning* suggests that the author is thinking of a place name of the form 'in the valley of –', perhaps beginning with *Cwm-*. Assuming that we do not have the Old English word 'king' here, a possible candidate is *Cwmgwnin* (in the parish of Llanelltyd). The following forms are attested: 1209 *Cumgwenyn* (Llywelyn's Charter, 55); 1293 *Coumgwynnin* (*Merioneth Lay Subsidy Roll*, 74); 1352 *Cumgwenyn* (*Record of Caernarvon*, 200. 14); 1574 *Congwynyn alias Cwingwnym* (*Peniarth Estate Papers*, III, 814 (item NA12) = *Schedule*, item 473); 1612 *Cwm gwuning* (*Peniarth Estate Papers*, III.820 (item NA31) = *Schedule*, item 463); *c*.1700 *Kwm Gwning, Afon Wnning o Gwm Kwnning* (*Parochalia*, I, 2). The same name element may appear in *Afon Wnni*. If the identification is correct, there is some support in the other forms for the spelling with final *-ng*. However, the original element seems to have begun with /g/- (it is unlikely that Lhuyd's form *Gwm Kwnning* can be taken seriously in the face of the overwhelming evidence for an initial *G-*). It could be argued that, in the process of being taken into a Latinate context, it was thought that *G(w)yning* was lenited and so the form *Kyning* was produced as a back-formation; it might also have been felt that, when shifting from Welsh *cwm* (masc.) to Latin *vallis* (fem.), it was important to show that nouns were not lenited after feminine nouns in Latin.

Cwmgwnnin (modern Cwm yr Wnin) is a small valley running south (from OS SH 709227 to 716192) to join the upper end of the Mawddach estuary just to the west of Llanelltyd and Cymer Abbey, on the border between Merioneth and Ardudwy. The flat area near to the point where it joins the Mawddach would be an appropriate location for a battle with Trahaearn defending Merioneth from forces coming from the north.

The battle of Gwaederw is not mentioned in the *Brutiau*, but it does figure in Meilyr Brydydd's *Marwnad* for Gruffudd ap Cynan; see *CBT*, I, 3, l. 128, and Williams, 'Meilyr Brydydd and Gruffudd ap Cynan', 181 (l. 128), 185 (translation); J. B. Smith, 'Age of Princes', 8.

§12/7 *(conservatus) ex bello*: the text is damaged here. The text of the fair copy must have been expanded as it is too long to fit into the space.

§12/8 *quasi gigas ad currendam viam*: cf. Psalms 18.5–7: *ut gigas ad currendam viam.*

ab iniquis et paganis dominis: in the Welsh text there is no equivalent to *iniquis et paganis*: *o'r argluydi a dothoed idi o le arall* 'from the masters who came to it from elsewhere' (*HGK*, 9. 14 = *MPW*, 61. 31–2). However, the omission of the adjective in the Welsh breaks down the rhetorical parallel with the *regum infidelium* in the following analogy with Maccabaeus.

§13

§13/1 *ad habitandum commigrarent*: again this is less forceful than *dothoedent y wledychu* 'had come to rule' (*HGK*, 9. 25 = *MPW*, 62. 6–7) where *gwledychu* has connotations of rule missing from *habitare*.

§13/2 The precise details are unclear as the right-hand corner of the page is missing. But the fair copies suggest that there was nothing parallel to the *bailli* 'bailey' of the Welsh text (*HGK*, 9. 26 = *MPW*, 62. 9).

e castris: the text before *castris* has been lost. The Welsh text is quite different (*HGK*, 9. 25–7 = *MPW*, 62. 7–10).

§13/4 *reges*: this has been changed in the Welsh text to *vrenhin Ywerdon* (sing.) 'king of Ireland' (*HGK*, 10. 2 = *MPW*, 62. 13–14) and the *cognati Griffini* have been removed.

§14

For a brief mention of the battle of Bron yr Erw, see *ByT* (Pen. 20), 22a1–5 (= tr. 16. 31–2), *ByT* (RB), 28. 22–3, *ByS*, 80. 1–2; see also *HGK*, p. cxxii.

§14/1 *nocte quadam intempesta*: the Latin is more specific about it being in the dead of night, while the Welsh *hyt nos* 'by night' (*HGK*, 10. 6 = *MPW*, 62. 20) simply suggests that it happened during the night.

Hybernis: this applies to the horsemen in the Latin text. The Welsh text *yn e wlat o'r Gwydyl* ... (*HGK*, 10. 7) is translated as 'in the country of the Irish' (*MPW*, 62. 20), but it is unclear in the Welsh whether *o'r Gwydyl* should go with *yn e wlat* or with the following number. In the Latin *Hybernis* has to refer to the fifty-two horsemen. Jones interprets the Welsh similarly, though he is mistaken about the number, 'two hundred and twenty of the knights of Gruffudd' (*HGC*, 119).

§14/2 *consanguinei*: cf. *Kenwric y gar* 'Cynwrig his kinsman' (*HGK*, 10. 13 = *MPW*, 62. 27) which Evans notes is ambiguous (*HGK*, 66, n. 10. 13). The Latin text does at least make it clear that Cynwrig is a relative.

§14/5 *accepto ... Kellinawc vawr*: according to the Latin text Tewdwr and Gollwyn commit treachery against Gruffudd even though that had received Clynnog Fawr from him. The Welsh text states that they received a gift from him *in* Clynnog Fawr: *eu kyuarws yg Kellynauc Vaur* (*HGK*, 10. 21–2 = *MPW*, 63. 3–4). It is conceivable that something has fallen out of the Latin text, but two errors would have to have been made: the loss both of a word corresponding to *kyuarws* and of the preposition *in*. However, while there is some material inserted at this point in the text, there is nothing added by the main hand.

§14/8 *complures iacebant, captique in prelio nonnulli*: by means of a chiastic word-order pattern the Latin contrasts the relatively large number killed with the small number captured. The Welsh text dispenses with any such distinction: *llawer a digvydassant ... a llawer a dalyassant* 'many fell ... and many were captured ...' (*HGK*, 10. 27–8 = *MPW*, 63. 11–12).

§14/9 *Keritus, nutricius, Varudri princeps et dominus Cruc Brendan*: there is no conjunction between the two names (as there is in the Welsh text (*HGK*, 10. 28 = *MPW*, 63. 13)) and so it is not clear that in the Latin text Keritus and Varudri (probably a corruption of mac Ruaidrí (see *HGK*, 67, n. 11. 1)) are intended to refer to two separate people; it is possible that Gruffudd's foster-father was called Kerit(us) mac Ruaidrí *vel sim.* and was lord and master of Cruc Brendan. On Cruc Brendan, cf. also *The Song of Dermot and the Earl*, 122–3 (l. 1653). On the other hand, it has been suggested that Keritus (Welsh Cerit) was a corruption of [*ma*]*c Eric*; see Duffy, 'Ostmen, Irish and Welsh', 394.

§14/10 *rex Frigiae*: Agamemnon was never king of Phrygia. The same error, *brenhin Frigia*, has been maintained in the Welsh text in Peniarth 17 (*HGK*, 11. 7 = *MPW*, 63. 21), though it was corrected to *brenhin y Groegwyr* in the archetype of the other manuscripts; for the stemma of the manuscripts of the Welsh version, see the Introduction, Figure 1. It may prove interesting if the source of this error can be traced.

§14/11 *ut ad naves deducat*: the Welsh text adds *o'e anvod* (varr. *o'e anvon*) (*HGK*, 11. 11 (and n. 3) = *MPW*, 63. 27). The Latin is correctly rendered by *o'e anvon*, and so the Peniarth 17 version of the Welsh text, in reading *o'e anvod*, contains a copying error.

in Insulam Adron (quae et focarum insula dicitur): cf. in the Welsh text *hyt en enys Adron, sef lle oed hvnnv enys y moelronyeit* 'to the island of Adron, namely the island of the seals' (*HGK*, 11. 12–13 = *MPW*, 63. 29–30). This can be taken together with §23/9 *in quandam insulam (quae Dinieuyt vocatur)* corresponding to *en ron enys, nyt amgen enys dinewyt e mor* 'in the island of Ron, namely the island of the seals' (*HGK*, 20. 9–10 = *MPW*, 72. 29–30), which must refer to the same place. Both probably refer to the Skerries, islands also known as St Daniel's Isle or Ynysoedd y Moelrhoniaid. There is no evidence apart from *HGK* (and now also *VGC*) for Ynys Dyniewaid (see Melville Richards, *Atlas Môn*, 160; *Enwau Tir a Gwlad*, 21), and it is therefore likely that it is a paraphrase of 'seal island' or the like.

The name *Adron* is problematic: the *quae ... dicitur* clause is intended to explain *ron*, the Welsh rendering of Old English *hrán* 'seal', implying that it was regarded a separate word at the stage of transmission when the explanation was added; it is preserved in Welsh in the compound *moelrhon* (see Lloyd-Jones, '*Rôn*'; I. Williams, 'Llywelyn Foelrhon'; Meyer, 'Zur keltische Wortkunde', 946 (§125); there seems to be no Old Norse comparandum (except possibly for the name of a sea-goddess, *Rán*). Given that a version of OE *hrán* is used here, it is odd that it is apparently compounded with *ad-*. However, while *Adron* is written as one word with an initial capital, in the context it could be taken as *ad Ron*. It is slightly awkward with the preceding *in insulam*, though not impossible. Perhaps the original of our Latin text had *ad Ron insulam .i. focarum insula* and this was translated into Welsh as *en ron enys*, etc. in the second instance. In the first occurrence it is possible that *ad Ron* was taken as a single name and thus the whole phrase was rewritten as *in insulam Adron quae et focarum insula dicitur*. It follows, therefore, that the misunderstanding of *ad Ron* as *Adron* had already happened before the Welsh text was produced. At §23/9, to judge from the Welsh text, *en ron enys*, the original Latin text may have had something like *ad Ron insulam* but this was changed to a vaguer *in quandam insulam* perhaps through uncertainty as to whether this was the same island as in §14/11. A further implication is that the Welsh version was made from a Latin text which was at least one copy removed from the original. Alternatively, the original Latin could have had the vaguer phrase, *in quandam insulam*, and the Welsh text made things more precise. This would fit well with the suggestion that the Latin life treats Gwynedd as if it were at a distance and can be rather vague about details; see the Introduction, pp. 41–2. If the broad argument in this note is correct, then *Adron* would disappear as a real place name along with any link to Ptolemy's *Androu/Adrou/Edrou* (see Sims-Williams, 'Old Irish *feda*', 472–3).

§14/13 *cum primis*: this phrase is understood here as adverbial 'usually, for the most part'. The Welsh version seems to assume that it means 'from the beginning' and translates it by *er y dechreu* 'from the beginning' (*HGK*, 11. 17–18 = *MPW*, 63. 37). Alternatively, it is possible that the Welsh translator understood the Latin phrase as 'among leaders' and so transferred it to the preceding clause where it was translated *y'r tywyssogyon* 'for the leaders' (*HGK*, 11. 17 = *MPW*, 63. 36); this phrase, however, only occurs in the Peniarth 17 version and so may well be a later addition.

§14/14 *infidelis*: in the translation this is taken with *Demetrii regis* (as it is at *HGK*, 11. 20) since *populus* is already qualified by an adjective, but its position in the sentence could allow it to be taken with *populus Israeliticus*, possibly a deliberate positioning of the word to emphasize the parallel between Iudas Maccabaeus and Gruffudd in having to deal with an unreliable populace.

ut gygas vel leo: the comparison with Iudas Maccabaeus is verbally explicit; cf. 1 Macc. 3.3–4: *sicut gigans ... similis factus est leoni*. The same Maccabaean reference is used at §18/8.

§14/17 *in civitate*: cf. the Welsh text, *yg Caer Llwytcoet* 'in Lincoln' (*HGK*, 11. 28 = *MPW*, 64. 15).

§15

§15/2 *Quorum vocibus acquiescens*: there is nothing in the Welsh text corresponding to this (cf. *HGK*, 12. 8 = *MPW*, 64. 22).

sulcantibus: the manuscript has *sultantibus* or *saltantibus*. This has been changed by Thelwall to *sulcantibus* matching the Welsh *gan rwygaw dyvynvoroed* 'cleaving the deep seas' (*HGK*, 12. 9 = *MPW*, 64. 26). It is likely that the original had *sulcantibus* as syntactically *saltantibus* would require a preposition with *mare* and possibly a different case of the noun. It is not impossible that *saltantibus* was originally a misreading of *sulcantibus* written in an insular hand; see Introduction, p. 43.

§15/4 *quem eorum opere aequificaret*: there is nothing corresponding to this in the Welsh text (cf. *HGK*, 12. 16 = *MPW*, 64. 35). There is a parallel relative clause *a gavas onadunt* 'as many of them as he found', but it does not correspond in sense.

§15/5 *indignati cives domesticique eius*: the unhappy companions are identified in the Welsh text as Danes, *Daynysseit* (*HGK*, 12. 19 = *MPW*, 65. 5). Likewise in §15/6 the treachery is *civium suorum* but is identified as betrayal by the Danes in the Welsh text (*HGK*, 12. 24 = *MPW*, 65. 13). It is at least as likely that the disenchanted companions and members of his household were Irish as Danish, given that they take him off to Ireland. It is possible that the Welsh translator with his more Gwynedd-centred interests may have been reluctant to portray the people of Anglesey and Gwynedd as treacherous.

depopulati: the manuscript has *de v* (confirmed by the catchword). It is likely that the scribe could only partially read the word and it was overwritten with *depopulati* by Thelwall.

navibus spoliis onustis: in the Welsh text the *spolia* are specified in greater detail as *deneon a goludoed* 'men and riches' (*HGK*, 12. 22–3 = *MPW*, 65. 10–11); cf. Evans' note (*HGK*, 71, n. 12. 22–3).

§16

§16/3 There is nothing in the Latin text corresponding to Welsh *beunyd* 'daily' (*HGK*, 13. 5 = *MPW*, 65. 24).

relinquunt: the corresponding Welsh version, *y hadaussant* (*HGK*, 13. 6 = *MPW*, 65. 25), is unclear; see Evans's note (*HGK*, 72, n. 13. 6). It perhaps offers another example of where the Latin text is clearer than the Welsh.

adeo ut: the consecutive clause is marked in the Welsh text by *ac odyna* (*HGK*, 13. 6–7) which in view of the Latin might be better translated 'and as a result . . .' than the weaker 'and then . . .' (*MPW*, 65. 26).

haberetur: the manuscript reads *habebaretur* which looks like the scribe intended to write an imperfect indicative *habebatur* but then realized that a subjunctive verb was required in the consecutive clause, and so added the subjunctive ending without deleting as much of the verbal stem as he should have done.

quasi: the Latin text implies that many of the people of Gwynedd remained but suffered *as if* they had been exiled. The Welsh version (*HGK*, 13. 7–8 = *MPW*, 65. 29) simply assumes that they went elsewhere (and few returned).

§17

§17 The structure of this chapter seems to have the air of a charter narrative, for example, the list of people from St David's, the verbal agreements then used to justify later acts of aggression.

§17/1 *trivisset curiam* < >: the text is difficult to read under the deletions and there is a gap after *curiam*; in the Welsh version this phrase is rendered by *yn trwydet* 'as guest' (*HGK*, 13. 14 = *MPW*, 66. 2).

a(pud) Diermit: the copyist seems not to have recognized the personal name as he copied it without a initial capital. The text reads *a diermit*, possibly to be read in the first instance as *ad Diermit*; however, *ad* may be a misreading of an abbreviation for *apud*. Alternatively, the *a* may be the ending of the preceding word which the main hand had difficulty reading.

civibus Hybernis ac Britannis: the Danes are added in the Welsh text (*HGK*, 13. 16 = *MPW*, 66. 5).

archepiscopali: how far this is related to the claims of St David to metropolitan status is discussed elsewhere; see the Introduction, pp. 46–7. It is suggested in *HGK*, 73, n. 13. 19, that the original Latin might have had *metropolis* here.

§17/2: the emphasis on St David's is striking; see the Introduction, pp. 45–7.

§17/6–13 For this section, see Plate 2.

§17/7–9 *tres Cambriae reges praecipui*: these are subsequently listed in §17/9 as Caradog of Gwent, the inhabitants of Morgannwg (king unnamed), and Trahaearn with the men of Arwystli. The changes made by Thelwall, which match the Welsh text, have the effect of amalgamating the inhabitants of Morgannwg with the forces of Caradog and adding Meilyr ap Rhiwallon with the men of Powys. The Welsh text also differs in referring not to 'three noble kings of Wales' but rather to *tri brenhin o'r gwladoed pennaf o Gemry* 'the three kings of the chief lands of Wales' (*HGK*, 14. 4–5 = *MPW*, 66. 24–5) which would have to be taken to include Powys. Note the absence of Meilyr ap Rhiwallon; on what little is known of him, see Maund, *Ireland, Wales and England*, 94.

§17/11 *Dimidium ... ditionis meae*: possibly a justification for the invasion of Ceredigion by Owein Gwynedd in 1136. For the possible significance of this for the composition date of *VGC*, see the Introduction, pp. 46–7.

§17/13 *D. Davidis*: in a twelfth-century text we might have expected *S(ancti) Davidis*. *Divi* is common from the fifteenth century onwards, and it may be a late replacement in the text. However, it could also be a product of scribal error; in the type of secretary hand found in Peniarth 434 and earlier manuscripts capital *S* and *D* are very similar and perhaps vulnerable to confusion.

§18

§18 For a discussion of the textual variation between the narrative of the battle of Mynydd Carn here and in the Welsh version, see the Introduction, pp. 27–9. For notices in the *Brutiau*, see *ByT* (Pen. 20), 23a15–26 (= tr. 17. 22–6), *ByT* (RB), 30. 14–17, *ByS* 80. 24–8; see also *HGK*, p. cxxii.

§18/1 *Kyndelw filius* < > *Monensis*: cf. *a Chendelu m. Conus o Von* (*HGK*, 14. 23 = *MPW*, 67. 14). There is a gap between *filius* and *Monensis* which may have contained the patronymic. The lack of agreement is puzzling (the reading of the manuscript has been retained in the edited text); we would expect *Kyndelw filio* [*Conusi*] *Monensis*. Perhaps *Kyndelw*, encouraged by the ambiguous *Monensis* after the gap, was not recognized as an ablative and treated instead as nominative.

§18/2: there is some finely nuanced characterization of Rhys in this sentence: his small number of followers (*perpaucis australibus*) in contrast to Gruffudd's large retinue; the striking use of the emphatic prefix *per-* on the adjectives *perpaucis* and *perbelle*; his self-satisfied but mistaken analysis of how things were going.

§18/3 *montes*: cf. §18/17 *montes autem in quibus ... montes Carn...* The plural *montes* is in contrast to the singular *menyd* of the Welsh (*HGK*, 15. 2, 16. 13, 14).

§18/4 *differamus bellum*: for a possible parallel to this unwillingness to fight which is rejected by a heroic king, cf. 1 Macc. 3.17–19.

§18/5 *inquit Griffinus*: the Welsh text adds *dan igyon* 'with a sigh' (*HGK*, 15. 6 = *MPW*, 67. 24), thus adding an indication of Gruffudd's feelings which is missing in the Latin.

quousque tibi placuerit: the Latin is far more dismissive than the Welsh *os mynny* 'if you wish' (*HGK*, 15. 6 = *MPW*, 67. 24–5).

§18/8 *non secus ac gigas vel leo*: this analogy has already been used of Iudas Maccabaeus at §14/14 (cf. 1 Macc. 3. 3–4).

§18/9 *in quo ne filius quidem patri pepercit*: in the Welsh this clause was removed and replaced by a blander phrase about sons celebrating the battle after the death of their parents *y chof* (varr. *clyf, klyw*) *y'r etiued wedi eu ryeni* 'to be remembered by the descendants after their forebears' (*HGK*, 15. 17–18 = *MPW*, 68. 4–5). Was this done to remove the implication of civil war and that families were split over their support for Gruffudd?

§18/12 *quasi herbas viventibus carpere dentibus ex armis*: cf. the Welsh *en pori a'e danhed y llyssyeu ir* 'chewing with his teeth the fresh herbs' (*HGK*, 15. 24–5 = *MPW*, 68. 15) where the adjective has been shifted to agree with *herbas*. The Latin version is far more striking with its unexpected patterns of agreement and word-order; it implies that Trahaearn in his death throes was gnawing at the grass and that the only things left alive were his teeth. On the other hand, it is not impossible that a copying error has crept into the Latin whereby the eye of the scribe skipped from the last two syllables of *viventes* to *dentibus* and added the wrong ending to *viventibus*. The Welsh seems to expand on the notion of death throes: *ac en palualu ar warthaf ei arveu* 'and groping on top of his arms' (*HGK*, 15. 25–6 = *MPW*, 68. 15–16). For a similar description of death throes, cf. the death of Hugh, earl of Shrewsbury, at §28/7. The phrase *ex armis* may be misreading of *exermis* 'disarmed, unarmed', but it may simply mean that he has lost his weapons or that he had been disarmed.

§18/13–18 For this section, see Plate 3.

§18/13 *ut carnem suillam in lardum*: Gwcharki preserved Trahaearn's body in salt in the same way as pork was turned into bacon. The Welsh text seems to have shifted the point of the analogy: *a wnaeth bacwn ohonaw ual o hwch* 'made bacon out of him as of a pig' (*HGK*, 15. 26–27 = *MPW*, 68. 17).

§18/15 *societate uni tam illustris*: the text has been heavily deleted, but *uni* is clear and, unless it is to be emended to *unius*, can only be explained as a medieval genitive singular of *unus*.

§18/20 *in paternam hereditatem*: in the Welsh this is rendered as *y'u briodolder a thref y dat e hun* 'to his own proper possession and patrimony' (*HGK*, 16. 24–5 = *MPW*, 69. 14–15); on *priodolder* in *HGK*, see Charles-Edwards, *Early Irish and Welsh Kinship*, 294–6.

§19

§19/1 *illi fidelitate obstrictus*: according to the Welsh text Meirion's treachery is because of 'the devil's arrow', *o saeth diauwl* (*HGK*, 16. 28 = *MPW*, 69. 19). This may be an allusion to Ephesians 6.16, *tela nequissimi ignea*. If so, it may be a case where the Welsh translator reveals a preference for the New Testament over the Old; cf. §26/10 *propter metu Iudaeorum*.

§19/3–4: for the kidnap plan, we might perhaps compare the attempted kidnap of Iudas Maccabaeus at 1 Macc. 7. 28–9.

§19/3 *adulatoriis*: not in the Welsh text (*HGK*, 17. 6 = *MPW*, 69. 26).

§19/4: the Latin text has the invitation made to Gruffudd alone, but the Welsh text adds *a'th wyr dieither* 'with thy foreigners' (*HGK*, 17. 8 = *MPW*, 69. 28); cf. §19/6 below where the Latin text implies that there were others accompanying Gruffudd but that they were his *famuli* not his 'foreigners' (again *wyr deithyr* in the Welsh text (*HGK*, 17. 13 = *MPW*, 69. 34–5)).

§19/5 *annis duodecim*: We would have expected an accusative plural *annos* here. Cf. §22/1 *post sedecim annorum spacium* (*vn vlyned ar bemthec* (*HGK*, 18. 10 = *MPW*, 70. 29–30)). For discussion of the discrepancy between the two different lengths of time given for Gruffudd's imprisonment, which are to be found in both the Latin and the Welsh texts, see *HGK*, pp. cxxviii, cl, ccxl, 80, n. 17. 8, Lewis, 'Gruffudd ap Cynan and the Normans', 68–9 (twelve years fits well between Mynydd Carn and the Welsh rebellion of 1093), Moore, 'Gruffudd ap Cynan and the mediaeval Welsh polity', 36–9 (was Gruffudd involved in 1293?). It is possible that the discrepancy arose from textual confusion either between *duodecim* and *sedecim* or between the Roman numerals *xii* and *xui*. The latter requires loss of a minim at some point. In neither case is it clear that the confusion would necessarily go in one direction or the other; while confusion between Roman numerals might require *xui* to be prior, that may itself be a misreading of, for example, *xiii* or *xiu*. Note that other sources seem confused over the length of Gruffudd's imprisonment; see the references to *HGK* above. A further observation might be made about the historical background: when Gruffudd escapes, he goes off to Godred Crovan of Man (§23/1 *Gothreum*). According to the *Cronica regum Mannie*, fol. 33v and various annalistic sources (Thornton, 'Genealogy of Gruffudd ap Cynan', 95, n. 68), Godred died in 1095 in Islay, fourteen years after Mynydd Carn (see Duffy, 'Irishmen and Islesmen', 106–8); if so, the sixteen-year period must be inaccurate, but that does not make the twelve period correct. Alternatively, if one wished to hold on to the sixteen-year period, the identity of *Gothreus* would have to be questioned. For further details on Godred Crovan, see the note on §23/1 below.

§19/6 *famulos*: see the note above on §19/4.

§19/7 '*Percutiam pastorem, et dispergentur oves gregis*': a quotation from Matthew 26.31. This passage is recycled from memory by the Welsh translator and added after §26/10 at *HGK*, 24. 23–4 (= *MPW*, 77. 5); see §26/10 for further discussion.

§20

§20 The physical description of Gruffudd follows the usual top to bottom sequence of medieval descriptions; for a similar description in a biography, cf. Einhard, *Vita Karoli Magni*, §22.

§20/1: many of the corrections were intended to maintain the *oratio obliqua* of the main description; thus, *perpolitus* and *excellens* were changed into accusatives and the main verb of that clause, *fuerat*, deleted. Since the accusatives continue in the final clause of the sentence, the clause about Gruffudd's linguistic skills looks like a parenthetic afterthought which stands outside the syntax.

coaetanei: this is a more general description than *kedemdeitheon gvahanredaul* 'special acquaintances' (*HGK*, 17. 18 = *MPW*, 70. 4).

externarum linguarum excellens: the Welsh text emphasizes the number of languages in which he was competent, *huaudel en amravaellyon yeithyoed* (*HGK*, 17. 23–4 = *MPW*, 70. 12).

in hostes magnanimum: the Welsh text is harsher, *a chreulaun wrth y elynyon* 'cruel towards his enemies' (*HGK*, 17. 25 = *MPW*, 70. 14).

§21

§21/2 *ad* ...: there is a gap in the text here which Thelwall filled with the words *eorum defensionem*. The Welsh text (*HGK*, 18. 6 = *MPW*, 70. 18) has nothing corrresponding to this, and it is possible that the copy used by the Welsh translator was also corrupt at this point. Given that the following clause has to do with inflicting cruelty and that this text has a liking for gerunds, it is perhaps more likely that the original had something like *ad depopulandum*.

pedites sagittariosque: the Peniarth 17 version of the Welsh text has *a phedyt saethydyon* 'archers on foot' (*HGK*, 18. 7 = *MPW*, 70. 24–5) against *a phedyt a saethydyon* 'infantry and archers' of the other manuscripts (*HGK*, 18, n. 1). In comparison with the Latin text, the other manuscripts preserve a better reading.

§21/3 *ipseque ... subsidium tulit*: the Welsh text has a different text, *ac enteu a'e guerendewis wy* 'and He listened to them' (*HGK*, 18. 9 = *MPW*, 70. 28). The first part of this sentence is biblical and it may have triggered in the Welsh translator the usual biblical continuation, *et (ex)audivit (Deus)*, or the like; cf. Exod. 2.23–4, *ascendit clamor eorum ad Deum ab operibus et audivit gemitum eorum*; Deut 26.7, *et clamavimus ad Dominum Deum patrum nostrorum qui exaudivit nos*; 1 Sam 7.9, *et clamavit Samuhel ad Dominum pro Israhel et exaudivit eum Dominus*. The same replacement has happened at §28/2.

§22

§22/1 *post sedecim annorum spacium*: see the discussion above at §19/5.

in palatio civitatis: the Welsh text (*HGK*, 18. 14 = *MPW*, 71. 3) has *ym plas e dinas* 'in the city square' (*HGK*, 18. 14 = *MPW*, 71. 3) implying that Gruffudd was out in the open and so it was easier to remove him. The Latin suggests that Cynwrig rescued him from inside a building.

in amplexibus: the Welsh text has Gruffudd being carried on Cynwrig's back, *ar e geuyn* (*ef*) (*HGK*, 18. 14–15 = *MPW*, 71. 4). The implication of both texts is that Gruffudd was not in a fit state to walk.

vespere: the Welsh text has *pyrnavn* (*HGK*, 18.16), translated in *MPW*, 71. 6 as 'afternoon', but the Latin shows that 'evening' would be more appropriate.

§22/4 *in australibus partibus Walliae*: the corresponding phrase in the Welsh text is *en Deheubarth* (*HGK*, 18. 22 = *MPW*, 71. 15). *Walliae* looks like a late addition here; cf. §5/10n. above, and the Introduction, p. 45.

§22/5 *nonus*: cf. *a'r nauvet* (*HGK*, 18.23 = *MPW*, 71. 16).The use of the ordinal to refer to one of the number is characteristic both of Celtic languages and of Latin written by native speakers of Celtic languages.

§22/7 *Collwini*: cf. Welsh *Gollwyn* (*HGK*, 19. 5 = *MPW*, 71. 26). There is hesitation in the source material as to whether the name begins with *C-* or *G-*; see *HGK*, 83, n. 19. 5.

ad se receperunt: the Welsh text has the sons of Gollwyn taking pity upon him, *y truanassant urthau* (*HGK*, 19. 7 = *MPW*, 71. 27).

§22/8 *cum sexaginta viris*: the Welsh text has a hundred and sixty men at this point, *wyth ugeinwyr* (*HGK*, 19. 8 = *MPW*, 71. 29). It is possible that the Welsh translator misunderstood *cum* or perhaps the abbreviated form with the *m* as a suspension mark, as in this manuscript, as an abbreviation for *centum*.

quasi erro quidam: this is not preserved in the Welsh text (*HGK*, 19. 8–9 = *MPW*, 71. 30). Perhaps a Gwynedd-based translator preferred not to portray Gruffudd as a runaway slave. Did the original author wish to imply a comparison with Spartacus? §22/9 *ipsi milites*: the Welsh text has locals involved in pursuing Gruffudd as well as the Normans, *eu hemlyn a wnaethant ac wynt a chivdaut e wlat* (*HGK*, 19. 12–13 = *MPW*, 71. 35–6), while in the Latin only the *Franci* are engaged in his pursuit.

cervum: the Welsh text has a tired stag, *carv blin* (*HGK*, 19. 14 = *MPW*, 71. 37).

§22/10 *remigum importunis laboribus*: the Welsh text (*HGK*, 19. 16 = *MPW*, 72. 3) omits to mention the heroic efforts involved in rowing to Ireland. On rowing between Wales and Ireland, see Hudson, 'Changing economy', 40.

§22/11: This stage of the narrative ends with Gruffudd returning to Wales, presumably to Aberdaron, from where he then sets off again in §23 to visit Godred. In the Welsh text another sentence relates his immediate return to Ireland: *ac odeno y kerdus eilweith dracheuen hyt yn Iwerdon* (*HGK*, 19. 18–19 = *MPW*, 72. 6–7).

§23

§23/1 *in insulas Daniae*: these are probably the Western Isles or perhaps more specifically Islay; see Etchingham, 'North Wales, Ireland and the Isles', 159.

ad Gothreum regem: he is identified by Evans (*HGK*, 84, n. 19. 21) as Godred Crovan, perhaps to be identified with the individual known in Irish sources as Gofraid Méránach or Gofraid mac mic Arailt; for more recent discussion, see Duffy, 'Irishmen and Islesmen', 106–8, where the identity of these named characters is accepted (but cf. Moore, 'Gruffudd ap Cynan and the mediaeval Welsh polity', 38, n. 276, who by implication thinks that Godfrey Méránach and Godred Crovan are different characters) ; if the *Cronica regum Mannie* are correct (compiled at Rushen Abbey no earlier than 1137 but perhaps as late as 1249 (see *Cronica Regum Mannie*; Blom, 'Chronicles of the Kings of Mann', 31–2)), Godred Crovan ruled Man from 1079, and died in Islay in 1095. If Gruffudd goes to Godred *in insulas Daniae*, it may well be that Godred still maintained his headquarters elsewhere than Man (Duffy, 'Irishmen and Islesmen', 107, n. 70). If *Gothreus* has been correctly identified, then Gruffudd's imprisonment at Chester cannot have lasted for sixteen years from the battle of Mynydd Carn in 1081; see the note at §19/5 above.

ad res suas: the text reads *aliaque res suas necessaria* which has to be emended either to *ad res suas* or to *rebus suis*; at §17/1 *ad* is used with *necessariis*, and so the same pattern is used here.
adnavigavit: rendered in the Welsh text as *y kerdus o hwyl a rwyf* 'he voyaged by sail and oar' (*HGK*, 19. 20 = *MPW*, 72. 9).

§23/2 *primis suis temporibus*: Gruffudd is confident of gaining help from Godred not because it is the first time he went and asked (as the Welsh translator supposed, *canys ena gentaf ry dothoed* 'for then had he first come to him' (*HGK*, 19. 23 = *MPW*, 72. 11–12)), but because he had made a similar successful request in his youth (*primis suis temporibus*). Presumably, Godred was one of those who supported Gruffudd in his early attempts to gain power in Gwynedd (cf. §9/2). The *suis* is crucial in making it clear that *temporibus* refers to a stage in Gruffudd's own life.

§23/4 *ex insulis*: throughout this section *insulae* (pl.) seems to refer to the *insulae Daniae*; cf. §23/8 below, where all of the ships, except for Gruffudd's, return to the *insulae Daniae* after the battle.

§23/6 *ad vesperam*: the Welsh text has *hyt byrnhavn*, again better translated as 'evening' (*MPW*, 72. 21 'afternoon'), especially in view of §23/8 *nox proelium diremit*. Cf. §22/1 above.

§23/7 *bipennibusque armatos*: in the Welsh text it is Gruffudd who is armed with the two-headed axe, *o'e uwyall deuvinyauc* (*HGK*, 20. 6 = *MPW*, 72. 24–5).

§23/8 *in insulas*: see §23/4 above.

§23/9 *in quandam insulam (quae Dinieuyt vocatur)*: see §14/11 for discussion.

§23/12 *iacula torserunt ... defensitarunt*: the Welsh translator evidently had a much better grasp of Norman military terminology than the Latin author: *en burv ergydyeu a saytheu ac a chwareleu ac a thafleu ac a magneleu en gawadeu* 'among blows and arrows from quarrels and slings and mangonels in showers' (*HGK*, 20. 19–20 = *MPW*, 73. 7–9; a better translation might be 'blows from arrows ...'). Note the use of *bailli* (*HGK*, 9. 26) where the term does not seem to be used in the Latin text (§13/2: certainty is impossible as the text is damaged at this point).

Wallorum: elsewhere in the text the Welsh are referred to as *Cambri*, and the usage here is striking, not least because the usual term based on *Wallia* is *Wallensis* (see Pryce, 'British or Welsh?', and the Introduction, p. 45), and there is no evidence for a term *Wallus* 'Welshman' (cf., however, *inter Walos et Anglos* in the *Quadripartitus* version of the Dunsaete Ordinance; see the Introduction, p. 45 n. 120, for details). That the original was understood as having a term referring to the Welsh at this point is indicated by the Welsh text, *o beunydyawl emlad e Kemry* 'by the daily fighting of the Welsh' (*HGK*, 20. 21–2 = *MPW*, 73. 9–10). Did an early version of the text have something like *certamine vallorum* 'contest over the ramparts'?

sexaginta quattuor: the Welsh text has *a phetwar gvyr a chue ugeint* 'a hundred and twenty four' (*HGK*, 20. 23 = *MPW*, 73. 11). The Welsh translator seems not to be very competent at rendering Latin numerals into Welsh; he makes the same error at §23/15 below, and cf. also §22/8 where *sexaginta* becomes *wyth ugeint*. In the present case it is possible that he misunderstood the -*ginta* of the Latin numeral as equivalent to *ugeint* and so ended up doubling the number.

§23/15 *sexaginta*: see the discussion above at §23/12.

§23/16 *cytharaedus, penkerd*: in the Welsh text his status is ambiguous as he is called *telynor pencerdd* (*HGK*, 21. 14 = *MPW*, 73. 34–5) which could mean 'harpist to the *pencerdd*', but it is clear from the Latin that it is intended to mean 'harpist, i.e. *pencerdd*'; see J. E. C. Williams, 'Meilyr Brydydd', 169.

§23/17 *perpolitum*: the Welsh text renders this with a noun, *drybelitet* (*HGK*, 21. 15 = *MPW*, 73. 36). Lambert, 'Two Middle Welsh epithets', 105–6, has suggested that *trybelid* was part calque and part loan-word deriving from Latin *perpolitus*, a suggestion amply confirmed by this text.

Homerum: in the Welsh text the author compares himself to Virgil rather than Homer, *ac a Maro vard* (*HGK*, 21. 19–20 = *MPW*, 74. 5). The Latin text seems curiously unwilling to refer to Virgil (see Introduction, p. 43); at §28/9 the Welsh text (*HGK*, 26. 21–2 = *MPW*, 78. 22–4) adds a reference to Virgil's *Eclogues* on the remoteness of Britain, which is not in the Latin text. In the present instance, it is possible that there has been a copying error between *Homerum* and *Maronem*, with confusion between capital *H*- and *M*- and between lower case -*r*- and -*n*-; the latter would be easier to envisage in an insular style of script.

§24

§24/1–2: the text has been heavily overwritten by both Thelwall and Thomas Wiliems; not only is the original text difficult to recover but it is also hard to distinguish the two sets of additions; see the apparatus for details.

§24/1 *oculis ac* < >: a gap, where the exemplar was illegible, was left after *ac* into which *splendentibus* was inserted.

§24/2 *habita ac gesta quam decoram*: in the Welsh text this is replaced by reference to her hospitality: *a da o uwyt a llyn* (*HGK*, 22. 2 = *MPW*, 74. 14).
§24/3 *liberi*: more specifically in the Welsh text *veibeon a merchet* (*HGK*, 22. 8 = *MPW*, 74. 18).

§25

§25/1 *ut ne canem mingentem ad parietem relinqueret*: for discussion of this phrase as an example of Thelwall's *modus operandi*, see the Introduction, pp. 25–6. The phrase is biblical but modified to produce a greater impact. In Samuel and Kings, not to leave anyone pissing against a wall is a common phrase for exterminating all the males and implies brutal slaughter; see, for example, 1 Kings 16.11, *percussit omnem domum Baasa et non dereliquit ex eo mingentem ad parietem et propinquos et amicos eius* (also 1 Samuel 25.22, 25.34, 1 Kings 14.10, 21.21, 2 Kings 9.8). To leave not even a male dog alive adds even greater force, implying presumably the prior extermination of all the male humans. The Welsh translator removed the biblical phrase and rewrote it as *hyt na bei en vyw kemeint a chi* 'so that there would not be alive as much as a dog' (*HGK*, 22. 14 = *MPW*, 74. 30–1). It is still brutal but does not retain the Old Testament implications of total massacre. The phrase was well known in medieval Britain and seems to have been in vogue in the twelfth century; for other examples, see Dumville, 'Celtic-Latin texts in northern England', 24–6; for a seventeenth-century instance, see L. M. Davies, 'The Tregaer manuscript', 269 (stanza 54). The most striking instance is the use of the phrase by Giraldus Cambrensis in *Descriptio Kambriae*, II. 7, where he uses it of Harold's incursion and depredation of Wales, and it is tempting to wonder whether he was familiar with its use in *VGC*.

§25/2 *ne vel umbra quidem*: this is a rhetorical doublet to not leaving even a dog pissing against a wall, namely cutting down all the trees so that not even a shadow is left. The Welsh text emphasizes the extended sense of *umbra* as 'protection', *hyt na bei wascaut nac amdiffyn* 'so that there would not be shelter or protection' (*HGK*, 22. 15–16 = *MPW*, 74. 32–3).

imbecilliores: this adjective is omitted in the Welsh text, but they are identified as Venedotians, *e'r Gwyndyt* (*HGK*, 22. 16 = *MPW*, 74. 33–75. 1). It may have been omitted because it was taken to be disparaging, though it may just be assuming that the weaker element in the population of Gwynedd would take shelter in the woods, or alternatively it may mean that the men of Gwynedd were in this campaign the weaker side without any pejorative implication.

§25/3 *castra intra castella muris cincta*: only in the Welsh text (*HGK*, 22. 17 = *MPW*, 75. 2) is this identified as Mur Castell (Tomen y Mur; see *HGK*, 101, n. 29. 6). Likewise at §32/3 *VGC* has *positis castris intra murata castella* and this identified again as Mur Castell in the Welsh version (*HGK*, 29. 6 = *MPW*, 80. 25–6). §25/5 *in angustiis viarum*: the Welsh text has *en lleoed keuing* (*HGK*, 22. 20 = *MPW*, 75. 6–7); cf. §12/6 for discussion of a similar phrase.

§25/6 *per intestina terrae*: this phrase looks like a calque on Welsh *perfedd* 'middle part, intestines' (see *GPC*, s.v.), and indeed the Welsh text has *trwy berued y wlat* 'through the middle of the land' (*HGK*, 22. 22 = *MPW*, 75. 9). However, rather than being a literal translation, given the direction of William's retreat from Gwynedd to Chester, it is possible that it is to be taken as a calque on the place name *Perfeddwlad*, the area of Gwynedd east of the Conwy (a possibility not envisaged in *HGK*). Even so, it is worth bearing in mind that the use of *intestinum* (and its adjective) in this sense is classical; cf. *Mare Intestinum* 'the Mediterranean Sea'.

nec perfidi ductores: *VGC* emphasizes the fact that with the departure of William Rufus even the treacherous guides gained no reward. This is omitted in the Welsh text (*HGK*, 22. 24 = *MPW*, 75. 11–13) perhaps to avoid drawing further attention to the fact that he had been aided by Welshmen.

nisi forte unica ... vacca donatus: this clause provides an ironical anticlimax to the ambitions of William Rufus and his treacherous guides: it holds out the possibility (and the subjunctive implies that it is only a possibility) that they got only one cow each and they did not even capture that.

§25/7 *currus*: the reading is not secure as the word has been heavily deleted. If it is correct, then the Welsh redactor has adjusted the text, and again as elsewhere (cf. *HGK*, 9. 26, 20. 19–20) introduced Norman terminology, *acueryeit* 'esquires' (*HGK*, 22. 25 = *MPW*, 75. 14; see also *HGK*, 90, n. 22. 25).

§25/9 *ut olim David se gessit contra Saulem*: cf. 1 Samuel 24.1–8: David and his men are hiding in a cave and Saul comes in unawares to relieve himself (*ut purgaret ventrem*). David's men want to kill him but David refuses to allow them as Saul is God's anointed one. The implication might be that Gruffudd had them at his mercy but held back as a matter of honour (because William was God's anointed?). As elsewhere (cf. §§12/4, 34/2, 35/1, 35/4), the biblical references should perhaps not be pressed too hard.

---

§26

For the events of §§26–30, see the brief account in the *Brutiau* for 1098: *ByT* (Pen. 20), 28a22–29b4 (= tr. 20. 33–21. 28); *ByT* (RB), 36. 21–38. 20; *ByS* 88. 30–92. 2; see also *HGK*, p. ccxxii.

§26/1 *malorum omnium architectus*: the Welsh text has *gureid er holl drwc* 'the root of all the evil' (*HGK*, 23. 11 = *MPW*, 75. 27). The first time Antiochus Epiphanes (for details, see *HGK*, 91, n. 23. 11) appears in 1 Maccabees, he is described as a *radix peccatrix* 'an evil scion' (1 Maccabees 1.11). This matches the Welsh version better than the Latin.Was the Welsh translator elaborating on the Maccabaean analogies already present in the text? Gruffudd's role as the Iudas Maccabaeus of north Wales has been well established from §12/2 onwards. Throughout this portion of the narrative Hugh is portrayed as Antiochus to Gruffudd's Maccabaeus. At §32/2 there are also hints that Henry might also be being aligned with Antiochus.

iam saltem in Cambros vlcisceretur: this clause does not appear in the Welsh text (*HGK*, 23. 14 = *MPW*, 75. 32).

§26/2–5 For this section, see Plate 4.

§26/3 *phalanges suas in terras Griffini ducunt*: although a fleet has been mentioned above (§26/1) and ships occur later in the narrative, no mention is made of a sea-borne landing here; cf. the Welsh text, *ac eu llu en eu llonges ar vor* 'with their host in their fleet by sea' (*HGK*, 23. 17 = *MPW*, 76. 1–2).

Yweino ap Etwin: Gruffudd's father-in-law; on his career and genealogy, see Maund, *Ireland, Wales and England*, 95–6.

Vchtrico fratre suo: on his career and genealogy, see Maund, *Ireland, Wales and England*, 48–51 (and fig. 29). The form of the name seems corrupt; it is invariably spelt with a final -*t* or -*d* in other sources. It is possible that the -*c*- is a misreading of an insular -*t*-. Alternatively, compare the use of *Mareduko* for *Maredudd* (see above, Notes, p. 126).

§26/4 *vel ore*: or perhaps *velere*. The reading is very uncertain as it has been heavily deleted; there is an insertion mark after the *l* which is usually placed between words, and so it may be two words. A word such as *more* or *voluntate* might have been expected. If the reading above is correct, then *os* may be being used in the sense of 'appearance'.

§26/5 *Kadwgan et Meredith*: the manuscript has *Kadwallawn* for *Kadwgan*, but that is almost certainly an error; cf. later in the narrative (§26/9) where Cadwgan ap Bleddyn appears. There seems to be no pair of brothers operating in eleventh- and twelfth-century Wales called Cadwallawn and Meredith. On Cadwgan and Maredudd, sons of Bleddyn ap Cynfyn, see Maund, *Ireland, Wales and England*, 103–5.

maturo capto consilio: from this point on, the text of *HGK* used for comparison changes; the fragmentary Peniarth 17 version has broken off and Evans's edition uses the Peniarth 267 version; the break comes at *HGK*, 23. 23.

§26/7 *totam insulam ... tradiderunt*: the corresponding Welsh text is *y tywalldassant oll yr ynys* 'they all poured into the island' (*HGK*, 24. 7 = *MPW*, 76. 22–3), where presumably the last phrase in the Welsh should be read as *y'r ynys*, as *tywallt* only seems to take that which is being poured as a direct object (*GPC*, 3685, s.v. *tywalltaf*), and there is nothing at all about handing the island over. There seems to be some confusion in that *oll*, which presumably corresponds to *totam*, has been transferred to the Irishmen.

§26/8 *consilii dubius fuit*: the Latin text has Gruffudd in a dilemma as to whether he should first tackle the French or the defection of the fleet. The Welsh text simply has him not knowing what to do about these problems (*HGK*, 24. 10–11 = *MPW*, 76. 26–7).

§26/9 *Cadwgan ap Bleddyn*: see §26/5 above. The Welsh text adds that he is the son-in-law of Gruffudd, *y daw* (*HGK*, 24. 12 = *MPW*, 76. 28).

§26/10 *multis modis miserabilis*: not in the Welsh text (*HGK*, 24. 16–17 = *MPW*, 76. 33–4).

ut in specubus subterraneis, locis palustribus, sylvis, lucis, agris incultis, cisternis, paludibus, ruderibus, ac rupibus locisque aliis absconderet: a listing of hiding places for fugitive peoples is familiar from the Old Testament; cf. Judges 6.2, 1 Samuel 13.6, and also Gildas, *quin potius de ipsis montibus, speluncis ac saltibus, dumis consertis continue ebellabant* (*De Excidio*, 20. ii); *alii montanis collibus minacibus praeruptis vallatis et densissimis saltibus marinisque rupibus ...* (*De Excidio*, 25. i).

Francorum aliarumque externarum gentium metu: the Welsh text has *rhag ofyn yr Iddewon, nit amgen, y Ffreink a chenedloedd ereill* 'for fear of the Jews, namely the French and other peoples' (*HGK*, 24. 21–2 = *MPW*, 77. 2–3). It is not immediately clear why at this point the Jews are introduced in this way as all the analogies employed in this text would make the men of Gwynedd analogous to the Jews. The allusion is probably New Testament; cf. *propter metum Iudaeorum* 'because of fear of the Jews' (John 7.13, 19.38, 20.19) where it is used in the context of followers of Christ being persecuted by the Jews. The Welsh translator would seem then to be introducing a New Testament layer of allusion to a narrative mainly framed in Old Testament terms; cf. perhaps also §19/1. After this sentence the Welsh text introduced another sentence, *Kanys megys y dyweit dwywawl ymadrawdd: 'digwyddaw a orug y bobl hep tywyssawg'* 'For as the Holy Word says: "the people fall without a leader"' (*HGK*, 24. 23–4 = *MPW*, 77. 4–5). This is similar to the concluding sentence of the section on Gruffudd's imprisonment and the consequent suffering of the people where

Matthew 26.31 is quoted (see §19/7 above (= *HGK*, 17. 15–17 = *MPW*, 70. 4–5)). The sentence here in the Welsh text may well have been carried over from the earlier passage. The biblical reference is unclear and is likely to be a quotation from memory; cf. Zachariah 13.7, Matthew 26.31 for similar sentiments.

§26/11 *pervagari*: the Welsh text adds *yn orawenus* 'gleefully' (*HGK*, 25. 2 = *MPW*, 77. 7).

§27

§§27–8 The episode of King Magnus and the death of Hugh was well known both in Welsh and Norse sources: see *ByT* (Pen. 20), 28a22–29b2 (= tr. 20. 33–21. 22); *ByT* (RB), 36. 21–38. 13; *ByS*, 88. 30–90. 27; Giraldus Cambrensis, *Itinerarium Kambriae*, II. 7 (p. 129); for a discussion of the Old Norse sources, see Jesch, 'Norse historical traditions'; see also *Cronica Regum Mannie*, fol. 34v, for a brief notice.

§27/1 *qua a Francis animadversa ... contulerunt*: the latter part of this sentence has been rewritten in the Welsh text, *a phan welet honno, anhyfrydu a orug y Ffreink a'r Daenysseit bratwyr a dwyllessynt Ruffudd* 'and when it was seen, the French and the Danes, the traitors who had deceived Gruffudd, became dejected' (*HGK*, 25. 7–8 = *MPW*, 77. 13–15). The Latin text has nothing about the dismay of the French and does not involve the Danes except to remark that they would have been overcome had the French not resorted to their usual deceptions.

§27/4: this sentence has been heavily rewritten. Our understanding is not helped by the inability to read *v...d. spe* (possibly *vivida spe*). The French trick the Welsh on Anglesey into making peace so that they can deal with the threat of the approaching fleet. The last clause is difficult; it seems to mean that the French did this so that future generations might forget the great disaster. The Welsh translator has rewritten this clause and turned it into another general comment about recollection of their suffering being handed down the generations, *a allei dyfot ar gof y'r etifedd wedy y ryeni* 'which could be remembered by descendants after their forebears' (*HGK*, 25. 16–17 = *MPW*, 77. 26–7); cf. §18/9 where a powerful phrase about the horror of civil war is replaced by a much more generalized phrase about the remembrance of suffering.

§28

The first two sentences are very difficult to read in places.

§28/1 *Llychlin*: only at this point is he called the king of Llychlin; later in the narrative his men are called *Dani* (§28/6–7 = *Llychlynwyr* (*HGK*, 26. 11–12, 17 = *MPW*, 78. 11–12, 19)). In the Welsh text he is later identified as *Magnws* (*HGK*, 26. 24 = *MPW*, 78. 26), but nowhere is he named in the Latin text, though there is a gap in the text (where the exemplar was illegible) corresponding to the point where he is named in the Welsh (§29/1).

singularis anima: this is uncertain; it has been heavily deleted in places but the manuscript seems to have *singulari ama*, and perhaps a suspension mark has been omitted above the standard abbreviation for *anima* (cf. §27/1 (p. 42, l. 11 of the manuscript) *animadversa* where *anima-* has likewise been abbreviated). It has to be the subject of the verb *dignata est*, hence the emendation to *singularis*. *praessuris*: the reading is uncertain, as it has been heavily deleted, and suggested with hesitation. What is visible is the abbreviation for *prae-/pre-* followed by *ss*, then two or three unclear letters and a final *s*. The Welsh text has *o'e trugaredd* 'in his mercy' (*HGK*, 25. 19–20 = *MPW*, 77. 29) which refers to God and not to the suffering of the Welsh.

§28/2: The singular *clamavit* and the pronoun *eam* indicate that the subject is *plebs* carried over from the subordinate clause in the preceding sentence.

et Deus eam salvam fecit: the Welsh text has *a Duw ag eu gwerendewis* (*HGK*, 26. 1–2 = *MPW*, 77. 32). For this pattern of rewriting, see §21/3 above and the discussion there.

§28/3 *per intrepretes*: the Welsh text translates this by *yeithydd* 'interpreter' (sg.) (*HGK*, 26. 2 = *MPW*, 77. 33–4), but there is no need to assume that there is a language issue here; *intrepres* can mean 'someone who explains, expounds', and in this context could simply mean 'guide'.

§28/6 *ut ficus de arboribus*: the use of the 4th declension plural *ficus* and the negative connotations of the 'bad' fig suggests that this may well be a biblical echo; cf., in particular, Jeremiah 29.17 *ecce mittam in eis gladium et famem et pestem et ponam eos quasi ficus malas quae comedi non possunt eo quod pessimae sint* (cf. also Nahum 3.12 *omnes munitiones sicuti ficus ... cadent*).

§28/7 *rex e puppi sagittam* < >: there is a gap in the manuscript text here which Thelwall filled with *torquens*. At this point the Welsh text has added *yn ddigyffro* 'unruffled' (*HGK*, 26. 12 = *MPW*, 78. 12). It is possible that the section which was illegible to the main scribe of our manuscript either contained something corresponding to *yn ddigyffro* or this section was also illegible to the Welsh translator and he made up something appropriate. The Welsh version of this sentence differs in several respects: *ynteu a ddigwyddws o'e ochrum y'r ddaear yn vwriedig ddieneit y ar y farch arfawg* 'and he fell a humped back to the ground mortally wounded from his armed horse' (*HGK*, 26. 14–15 = *MPW*, 78. 14–16). The phrase *o'e ochrum* presumably means 'hunched-up'. There is nothing in the Latin about him falling from his horse, though presumably he did so. The phrase *licet armatus* is emphasizing that, though fully armoured, he was still hit in the eye by the arrow.

cum ferro luctatur: either he is struggling to pull the arrow out, which is contradicted by the *exanimatus*, or he is in his death throes. The Welsh text has *dan ymffustyaw ar y arfeu* 'beating upon his arms' (*HGK*, 26. 15 = *MPW*, 78. 16), which would imply the latter. The treatment of the death of Trahaearn (§18/12) is comparable, notably in the way it is rewritten in the Welsh version; see §18/12 and notes.

§28/9 *quae totius orbis ultimae habentur*: at this point the Welsh translator has added a translated quotation from Virgil, *megys y dyfot Fferyll bot y Brytanyeit yn ddieithredig yn gubyl o'r holl vyt* 'as Virgil said, "the Britons were entirely separated from the whole world"' (*HGK*, 26. 20–3 = *MPW*, 78. 22–4), corresponding to Virgil, *Eclogues*, I. 63, *et penitus toto divisos orbe Britannos*. Cf. the comment of Orderic Vitalis on the voyage of King Magnus around Britain (*Ecclesiastical History*, X, 222. 12–13; see also §5/8). On the Welsh translator's use of Virgil, see §23/17.

§29

§29/1 *aliique Franci < > laetitia perfusi*: the gap in the text was filled by Thelwall with *ob discessum magni regis Norwegensium*. The Welsh text has *yn llawen o ymchwelyat magnws vrenhin* 'joyous at the return of king Magnus' (*HGK*, 26. 23–4 = *MPW*, 78. 24). In the Latin text mention of Magnus may have been lost in the illegible section of the exemplar.

praedas: at this point the Welsh text (*HGK*, 26. 24–27. 1 = *MPW*, 78. 27) has them leading off the people of Gwynedd as well as their possessions.

cantredorum Monae: the Welsh text has them transporting their plunder to the cantref of Rhos, *hyt yg kantref Ros* (*HGK*, 27. 1 = *MPW*, 78. 28), while in the Latin text he withdraws to a safer place on Anglesey.

sunt partiti: the Welsh text added that they sensibly counted them first, *ag yna y rhifwyt* (*HGK*, 27. 2 = *MPW*, 78. 30).

frumenta bovesque: translated in the Welsh text as *ysgrybyl… a'e anrheith* 'cattle and plunder' (*HGK*, 27. 2–3 = *MPW*, 78. 30). But *ysgrybyl* is intended to translate *frumenta* and *anrheith boves*. At *HGK*, 28. 7 (corresponding to *VGC*, §31/2) *anrheithieid* 'possessions' (*MPW*, 79. 28) is used to render *praedis*. Evans (*HGK*, 96, n. 27. 3) suggests that *anrheith* can be used to refer to animals. *GPC*, s.v. *anrhaith*, quotes the latter passage from *HGC*, 150 (translated as 'possessions' (*HGC*, 151)) but, probably following *HGK*, 96, puts it under the heading 2(b) 'farm animals, herds'. The present passage would support that interpretation.

§29/2 *prolixe*: not in the Welsh version (*HGK*, 27. 6–7 = *MPW*, 78. 35).

amplissimum perfidiae praemium: not in the Welsh version (*HGK*, 27. 8 = *MPW*, 79. 2).

§29/3 *ut fidelis infidelibus, ut illud divinum confirmare*: the author probably had in mind St Paul's Letter to the Corinthians where the phrase occurs several times; cf. 2 Corinthians 6.15, *quae autem conventio Christi ad Belial aut quae pars fideli cum infidele?* Another passage perhaps further implies the linguistic differences between the French and the Danes: 1 Corinthians 14.22, *itaque linguae in signum sunt non fidelibus sed infidelibus, prophetia autem non infidelibus sed fidelibus*. The overall implication seems to be that the exchange will end badly.

§29/4 *obeses*: the Welsh text has *gormessawl* 'troublesome' (*HGK*, 27. 11 = *MPW*, 79. 5), but Evans (*HGK*, 97, n. 27. 11) suggests that *gormessawl* might mean 'repulsive', which would be closer to *obeses*.

§29/5 *mancipiorum squalentem catervam*; this vivid phrase was not translated in the Welsh text.

alios morte: not in the Welsh version (*HGK*, 27. 15 = *MPW*, 79. 9–10)

§29/6 *in exilio perpetuo*: on the notion of exile in *VGC* and *HGK*, see Lewis, 'Gruffudd ap Cynan and exile'.

§30

§30/3 *in illo cantredo*: the location of this cantref is not stated here or in the Welsh text (*HGK*, 27. 21). In our text Thelwall added *de Rossia*, i.e. Rhos, presumably on the basis of what the Welsh text says at *HGK*, 27. 1 (= *MPW*,

78. 28) corresponding to §29/1 above, where Hugh takes his plunder off to Rhos. However, at this point the Latin text (§29/1) does not refer to Rhos but to *cantrefi* in Anglesey (see the discussion at §29/1). In fact, Anglesey would fit well with the other evidence cited by Evans (*HGK*, 97, n. 27. 21).

§31

§31/1: Gruffudd's visit to Henry is probably to be dated to *c*.1100 or a little after; see *HGK*, 97–8. If the bishop of Bangor who intervenes on his behalf is Hervé (*Erfyn* in *HGK*, 28. 4–5 = *MPW*, 79. 25), then his visit must have been before 1109 when Hervé was translated to Ely (*HGK*, 98, n. 28. 4–5). However, the Latin text does not mention the name of the bishop of Bangor (that has been added in the Welsh translation (*HGK*, 28. 4–5 = *MPW*, 79. 25)). Even so, the bishop in question is likely to be Hervé as after his departure in 1109 the see was not filled until 1120 when David the Scot (who was present at Gruffudd's deathbed (§35/1 below)) became bishop; see Richter, *Giraldus Cambrensis*, 30–1.

vitam: presumably this means that Henry granted him the resources or where-withal for living. The Welsh text at this point has *rubuchet* 'good-will' (*HGK*, 28. 3 = *MPW*, 79. 24).

§31/2: on the granting of lands to Gruffudd by Henry I, see R. R. Davies, 'Henry I and Wales', 138–40.

§31/3 *qui deponit potentes de firmis suis sedibus ... eundem ad honores evehit*: parts of this have been heavily deleted and altered and are thus difficult to read. The alterations in the Welsh text seem to be stylistic rather than substantive (see *HGK*, 28. 9–12 = *MPW*, 79. 31–80. 1). The author may have had the words of the Magnificat (Luke 1.52–3) in mind and then elaborated upon it: *deposuit potentes de sede et exaltavit humiles, esurientes implevit bonis et divites dimisit inanes.*

§31/8: The Welsh version makes more explicit the return of the people from exile which is implicit in the Latin text with the analogy of the Israelites returning from captivity in Bablyon, *a dwyn a wnaeth y holl giwdawt o amrafael alltudedd, y rhei a aethoeddynt y alltudedd o'r ymlitfa a ddywetpwyt uchot* 'and he brought all his people from exile in various parts, those who had gone into exile from the pursuit mentioned above' (*HGK*, 28. 21–3 = *MPW*, 80. 12–14).

§32

§32/1 *Comes*: Henry's attack on north Wales is dated according to the *Brutiau* to 1114, by which time the earl of Chester is Hugh's son, Richard. Hugh had died in 1101; see *HGK*, p. cxxiii, 90, n. 29. 1; Harris, *History of the County of Cheshire*, II, 1. See *ByT* (Pen. 20), 58a19–62a6 (= tr. 37. 5–38. 38); *ByT* (RB), 78. 1–82. 6; *ByS*, 120. 13–122. 31.

§32/2: *maximos sumptus*: the words have been heavily deleted and the reading is uncertain, particulary the ending of *maximos*.

erogando: the manuscript reads *erogand* without an ending; it is possible that it was unclear in the exemplar. Elsewhere in this text the ablative of the gerund is regularly used in the function of a present participle, for example, §§5/6 *mactando fugandoque*, 12/8 *irruendo*, 23/13 *pugnando*, 29/6 *mulctando*, 35/2 *bendicendo*, and that has been restored here. The Welsh version of this sentence differs in several respects; Henry pays money to horsemen and foot-soldiers, *y farchogyon a phedit* (*HGK*, 29. 4 = *MPW*, 80. 22), which do not figure in the Latin text except by implication. He also brings the king of Scotland et al. with him, *a dwyn ganthaw vrenhin Yskotlont ...* (*HGK*, 29. 4–5 = *MPW*, 80. 22–4). This is a misunderstanding of the Latin *erogando et in regem Scotiae*; *erogare* + *in* (with acc.) is a technical term meaning 'to pay someone out of the public purse'. For this ransacking of the treasuries to fund an expedition, perhaps cf. Antiochus at 1 Macc. 3.28; is there an implicit aligning of Henry with Antiochus? At §26/1 Antiochus is used as an explicit model for Hugh of Chester.

§32/3 *positis castris intra murata castella*: see the discussion above at §25/3.

§32/4 *nivosi montis*: this may be an etymological acknowledgement of its English name 'Snowdon'.

§32/7 *transacto temporis perbrevi spacio*: this episode seems to the one related in the *Brutiau* for 1121; see *ByT* (Pen. 20), 79b1–80a13 (= tr. 47. 36–48. 10); *ByT* (RB), 104. 24–106. 2; *ByS*, 138. 26–140. 7; see also *HGK*, p. ccxxiii.

in ore gladii: a well established Old Testament phrase: Exod. 17.13, Num. 21.24, Deut. 13.15, 20.13, 17, Joshua 6.21, 10.30, 32, 35, 37, 40, Judges 1.8, 25, 4.15, 18.27, 20.37, 1 Samuel 15.8, 22.19, 2 Samuel 15.14, Judith 7.17, 15.6, 1 Macc. 5.51, Jeremiah 21.7, and also Luke 21.24. It has been translated literally in the Welsh as *yg geneu y kleddyf* (*HGK*, 29. 16). It is unlikely that the phrase would have been used in the Welsh had it not been translated from the Latin; *GPC* records no other examples of the phrase in Welsh.

§32/8 *Verum*: the Welsh text adds at this point *A phann glywyt hynny* (*HGK*, 29. 16 = *MPW*, 81. 4) which has no correspondence in the Latin text, though it looks as if it might translate something like *quo audito* or *quibus auditis*.

§32/10 *Comites*: the Welsh text makes this refer specifically to the earls of Chester (*HGK*, 29. 24 = *MPW*, 81. 14), presumably father and son, Hugh and Richard, but the Latin text simply has *comites*, thus including the earls of Shrewsbury, Hereford and Rhuddlan who have also been involved in attacking Gruffudd; see §16/2.

§32/11: this sentence was omitted in some of the fair copies made of this text and provides a useful diagnostic feature for fixing the relationship of the descendants of Peniarth 434; see the Introduction, pp. 11–12.

§33

§33/1 *exantlatos*: a relatively rare word; cf. *DMLBS* s.v. *exantlare*. It generally seems to mean 'draw out, drain out'. The verb may have been unfamiliar to the Welsh translator who replaced it with a simple time phrase, *A gwedy hynny* 'And after that' (*HGK*, 30. 3 = *MPW*, 81. 20).

arbores plantare, pomaria, hortos ...: The general gist of this passage may be that the Welsh were not the primitive pastoral barbarians as portrayed by some Anglo-Norman writers from the 1120s onwards; cf. the note on *Romanorum more* below. Note also the comment about Gwynedd by Giraldus Cambrensis to the contrary: *non pomeriis utuntur, non hortis. Utrorumque tamen fructibus, eis aliunde porrectis, libenter vasci solent. Agris igitur plurimum utuntur pascuis, parum cultis, floridis parce, consitis parcissime* (*Descriptio Kambriae*, I. 17).

§33/2 *stagnis*: not in the Welsh version (*HGK*, 30. 12 = *MPW*, 81. 31–2).

edificia: in the Welsh text they are 'walled buildings', *adeiladeu murddin* (*HGK*, 30. 13 = *MPW*, 81. 32), presumably meaning buildings with walls around the outside to protect them.

fructus: the Welsh text has *frwytheu y ddaear* 'fruits of the earth' (*HGK*, 30. 13–14 = *MPW*, 81. 33).

Romanorum more in usum colligere: this probably carries an implication of sophisticated agriculture. More specifically, it could mean 'to gather in and store for later use', so that they can live off the produce and be self-sufficient, a reference to Roman farming methods as described in, for example, Cato's *De Agricultura*, Varro's *De re rustica*, Columella, Virgil's *Georgics*. However, the phrase *in usum* can mean 'for profit', and it may imply the development of a more sophisticated economic infrastructure where surplus produce could be sold at market. Alternatively, it might refer to the Roman custom of taxing produce, which would arise naturally from the latter explanation. The notes in *HGK* are silent on this. The Welsh text simply has *ymborth* 'live on' (*HGK*, 30. 13 = *MPW*, 81. 32).

§33/3 *quae* ...: another example of a clear relative clause in the Latin being confused in the Welsh translation. The *quae* can only refer to the *palatia*, but in the Welsh it is turned into a separate clause referring to courts and feasts and then it goes off on another tangent about the honour and status of courts: *ag adeiladoedd y lyssoedd a gwleddeu yn wastad yn anrhydeddus* 'and he held his courts and feasts always honourably' (*HGK*, 30. 16 = *MPW*, 81. 35–82. 1).

§33/4 *quid vero eflueret?*: the rhetorical question is omitted from the Welsh text (*HGK*, 30. 14 = *MPW*, 81. 34).

§33/5: a difficult sentence. The text is uncertain as the main verb seems to be missing, probably lost in the gap after *splendere*, but it may have been *videbatur* or *visa est*. There seems to be an analogy being drawn between the churches and dedications of Gwynedd on the one hand and stars in the firmament on the other. Are the churches like stars in the firmament of Gwynedd, or are the dedications like stars in the firmament of the churches?

ecclesiis: the Welsh text has *egleysseu kalcheit* 'with lime-washed churches' (*HGK*, 30. 17–18 = *MPW*, 82. 2), perhaps intended to emphasize the notion of gleaming churches. Cf. *HGK*, 104, n. 30. 17–18, where Evans draws attention to the line of Llywelyn Fardd in *Canu Cadfan* (*CBT*, II, 1), *eglwys wenn wyngalch wynhaed*; it has been emended in *CBT*, II, 1, l. 34, to read *eglwys wenn wyngalch ualch wynhaed* 'a white, bright-chalk church, finely whitened' in order to achieve the correct number of syllables (cf. also other suggestions, *CBT*, II, p. 27, n. 34). It is tempting to wonder whether the Welsh translator was familiar with the poem of Llywelyn Fardd.

dedicationibus: under the deletion the manuscript seems to read *didioeibus*, and the restored reading assumes a lost suspension mark and some misread letters.

praepositos coll[ ]*velit*: the text is uncertain, but the first word is almost certainly the noun *praepositi* 'overseer' and has been restored as such. The latter looks more like a verb.

quasi < >: in the Welsh text the simile is *mal mur agkyffroedig* 'like an immovable wall' (*HGK*, 30. 23 = *MPW*, 82. 9) and it is likely that the Latin text had something similar but it was illegible to the main scribe.

§34

§34/1 *in secretiorem quendam locum secedere*: for the language we may compare Luke 5.16, *ipse autem secedebat in deserto et orabat.*

§34/2 *Ezechias*: this is a curious analogy; the example of Jacob the patriarch used at §35/2 would better fit the context. This sentence and §35/2 act almost as doublets. For the account of Hezechiah, see 2 Chronicles 29–32; for his wealth and his building works, see 2 Chronicles 32.27–9, Isaiah 39.2. For the account of his extended life, see Isaiah 38.1 where, after much weeping and lamentation, his life was extended by fifteen years. The reference to Hezechiah fits reasonably well with the following section about the distribution of Gruffudd's wealth, and with the account in the previous section (§33/2) of Gruffudd establishing the agricultural infrastructure of Gwynedd. Furthermore, it can also be seen as a continuation of the general analogy between Gruffudd's exploits and the house of David. However, as with many of the biblical analogies in this text they cannot be pushed too far. Hezechiah is also used as the paradigm of the good king who is succeeded by a bad son, Manasseh; it is reasonable to assume that the author would not have wished that implication to be followed through.

§34/3: for other examples of a king on his deathbed distributing his wealth, cf. Einhard, *Vita Karoli Magni*, §33; Suger, *Vie de Louis VI*, 274–6.

§34/5: this sentence has the feel of an afterthought. The text seems to be running from the bigger legacies to the smaller. If so, then the legacy to Bangor, which is the biggest, is in the wrong place.

§34/6: there is a difference in order of the churches who were to receive ten pieces of silver: the Welsh text has Llanarmon and Dinerth at the end. In geographical terms, both lists begin in Anglesey (Caergybi and Penmon), the Latin text then moves to Is Conwy (Llanarmon and Dinerth), and then to Uwch Conwy (Clynnog and Enlli), and finally to Powys (Meifod). The Welsh text moves in an arc from Anglesey to Uwch Conwy to Powys and then finally north to Is Conwy (*HGK*, 31. 20–32. 2 = *MPW*, 82. 33–83. 1). There may be some significance to this or it may have just been a copying error in the translation; that is, the translator mistakenly omitted Llanarmon and Dinerth and then added them at the end. On the other hand, if Clynnog can be associated with the Welsh version, its promotion in the list may be significant (see the Introduction, pp. 43–4).

§34/7: This sentence is difficult to read because the Welsh text has undergone some major rewriting in order to turn the sentence into a first person commendation to the Holy Spirit, *y daoedd hynny a gymynnaf i y amddiffyn yr Yspryt Glan* 'these goods do I commend to the protection of the Holy Spirit' (*HGK*, 32. 5–6 = *MPW*, 83. 4–5).

Haec: this was deleted and *Bona illa* added at the end of the line by Thelwall to clarify the referent, i.e. the legacies.

episcopis, archidiaconis: in the Welsh text, these are singular, *y esgob ag archddiagon* (*HGK*, 32. 3–4 = *MPW*, 83. 2), perhaps intended to refer to David, bishop of Bangor, and the archdeacon Simeon mentioned below in §35/1.

§35

On Gruffudd's death, see *ByT* (Pen. 20), 88a7–b12 (= tr. 52. 9–19); *ByT* (RB), 116. 3–12; *ByS*, 146. 8–9.

§35/1 *Simeon archidiaconus*: in the Welsh text he is further described as *gwr addfet o oet a doethinap* 'a man mature in years and wisdom' (*HGK*, 32. 10 = *MPW*, 83. 9–10); see following note.

prior Monasterii Cestriae homo et doctrina et sapientia insignis: the reference is presumably to the Abbey of St Werburgh (*HGK*, 107, n. 32. 10–11), the same institution as was mentioned above at §34/4 as receiving a legacy of 20 *solidi*. The presence of a representative of St Werburgh's may not be surprising; in 1093 Earl Hugh made a number of grants to St Werburgh's of land and rights in Anglesey and Rhos: two manors in Anglesey, one in Rhos, the tithe of the fisheries of Rhuddlan and Anglesey, and the right to have engaged in Anglesey a ship carrying ten nets (Dugdale, *Monasticon Anglicanum*, II, 386; Lloyd, *History of Wales*, 392). The eulogistic phrase about the prior is omitted in the Welsh text (*HGK*, 32. 11 = *MPW*, 83. 10), though something similar is said of Simeon of Clynnog. It is possible that the description has been transposed in one direction or the other. It is not known who the prior of the monastery of Chester was in 1137. Given the sizeable legacy and that there was an abbot at this time, namely William, who was elected in 1121 and died in 1140, it is perhaps curious that the prior was sent to the deathbed of Gruffudd; on William, see *Annales Cestrienses*, I, xxvi, 18, 20; *The Chartulary or Register of the Abbey of St. Werburgh*, I, xxvi; Kettle, 'The Abbey of Chester', 144; Knowles et al., *Heads of Religious Houses*, 39. Gruffudd's legacy is not mentioned in Kettle, 'The Abbey of Chester'.

iuxta praeceptum Iacobi Apostoli: see James 5.14 *et orent super eum unguentes cum oleo in nomine Domini*. Again the biblical reference is not entirely appropriate; James is referring to anointment by oil as a means of healing, while the context here has to do with Gruffudd's death.

§35/2: this is in some respects a more detailed doublet of the passage at §34/2. *quae illis olim eventura essent, ad similitudinem Iacobi patriarchae*: for the reference to Jacob the patriarch and his prophecies to his sons, see Genesis 49. The words here seem to be an echo of the biblical words at Genesis 49.1: *quae ventura sunt vobis diebus novissimis.*

postremis suis temporibus: the Welsh text has *yn y ddiwedd ddyddyeu* 'in his day' (*HGK*, 32. 18 = *MPW*, 83. 29); Evans (*HGK*, 107, n. 32. 18) suspects that something is wrong and wonders whether *ddiwedd* is a misunderstanding of *diewed*, an early plural of *dydd*. However, *postremis suis temporibus* shows that the Welsh is not in error (though it may be a cumbersome translation). It is likely that the Latin phrase is an attempt (but possibly mistaken) to render the Latin of Genesis 49.1 *diebus novissimis* (see note above) which in its context seems to mean 'in days to come'.

§35/3 *cum porticibus Abermeney*: this seems to mean the harbour of Abermenai (cf. *HGK*, 32. 20 *porthloedd*) and presumably the dues from it. But Latin *porticus* usually means 'colonnade, portico', and it is possible that the author has mistaken the word.

§35/4–9. For this section, see Plate 5.

§35/4 *filiorum nonnulli*: since Gruffudd's sons have already been mentioned (§35/2), these are probably the sons of his daughters alive in 1137 (for whom, see Maund, *Ireland, Wales and England*, 91 (fig. 51)). The Welsh translator attempted, but failed, to clarify matters by rendering *filiorum nonnulli* with *neieint* 'nephews' (*HGK*, 32. 21 = *MPW*, 83. 33). There are two possible ways of accounting for this: first, Welsh *nai* seems originally to have meant 'grandson' (Charles-Edwards, 'Some Celtic kinship terms'), and it is perhaps possible that *neieint* here preserves the original meaning, but it would be an implausibly unique survival. Alternatively, and more likely, the error is Latinate. If the translator thought that *filiorum nonnulli* were 'grandsons', that in Latin would be *nepotes* which can, however, also mean 'nephews', and he mistranslated it as *neieint* rather than *ŵyr*.

§35/5 *Iosue filium Nun*: see Joshua 23–4 and, for his death, Joshua 24.29, where there is no reference to mourning. On the other hand, we might compare the wording of the lamentation after the death of Iudas Maccabaeus (1 Macc. 9.20): *et fleverunt eum omnis populus Israhel planctu magno et lugebant dies multos.*

Appendix 1

The orthography of the Welsh names in Vita Griffini filii Conani

The material is gathered in phonemic groups, front and mid-vowels, diphthongs, labio-dental fricatives, dentals and dental fricatives and gutturals. For discussion, see the Introduction, pp. 34–5. For the mode of presentation and an explanation of the focus on certain areas of the sound system, see, for example, Charles-Edwards and Russell, 'The Hendregadredd manuscript', 420–5. Note that, where it is unclear which segment of the word is under consideration, it is underlined. Distinction between final and internal consonants is sometimes difficult to maintain, especially when a Welsh name has been Latinized by the addition of a Latin ending. Names have only been taken from the base text of Peniarth 434 itself; no use has been made of the supplementary text from Cotton Vitellius C.ix.

/ə/	/i/	/ɨ/	/u/
y	*i*	*i*	*w*
Cynani 2/1, 3/1, 7/1	is coet 17/9	Evyonid 23/10	Alkwm 2/1
Prydein 2/1	Hir 22/1	Nevin 23/9	Olbiwch 11/1
Dyvynarthi 2/2	Enlli 34/6		Gwrganum 11/3
Lydaw 5/10		*y*	erw 12/6, 14/12
Kynwricus 10/1		Meirionyth 21/1	Llwchgarmaw[n]
Lywarch 11/2			14/11
Kelynnawk 12/1		Dyffryn 23/10	
Dylad 12/4		Bleddyn 26/9	*v*
Kyning 12/6		Eivionyd 31/2	Theodvr 17/2
Kyndelo 18/1			Morgannvc 17/9
i			*o*
Rivedeti 2/1			Kyndelo 18/1
Kelliniawc 14/5			

/ʉ/	/ʉw/	-/w/-
v	*v*	*u*
Rvc 19/2	vch 17/8	Dinieuyt 23/9

/au/	/eʉ/	/aɨ/
au	*eu*	*ay*
Anarauti 2/1	Meurik 1/2	Dyndaythwy 2/1
Kelynnauk 12/1	Gwrgeneu 16/2	Ayre 22/2

aw
Cadwallawn 2/1 (cf. 26/5)
Einiawn 2/1
Godebawc 2/1
Meirchiawn 2/1
Lydaw 5/10
Meiriawn 10/3
vawr 14/5
Llwchgarmaw[n] 14/11

But cf. also Rhiwallon 10/2,
   Cadwallon 24/3

ae
Gwaeterw 12/6

/eɨ/	/uɨ/	/aɨa/
ey	*ui*	*ea*
Abermeney 10/1, 12/1, 14/11	Guidawc 2/1	Trahearn 10/2
Porth Cleys 17/1		

ei

wy
Dyndaythwy 2/1

ae
Trahaern(i) 12/7, 14/2,
   18/2, 18/18

Einiawn 2/1
Meiriawn 10/3
Seisill 11/2
Meirianus 19/1
Meivot 34/4

Tangwystl 11/1
Gollwynus 14/5
Llwyd 14/17
Llwyt 14/17
Llwyn 14/17
Ardudwy 15/4
  et passim
Clwyt 23/10

aea
Trahaearn 17/9

wi
Collwini 2/7

/v/-
v
vawr 14/5

-/v/-
v
Rivedeti 2/1
Avallach 2/1
Arvon 21/2, 23/10
Edenyved 22/7
Nevin 23/9
Evyonid 23/10
Eivionyd 31/2
Meivot 34/4

w
Tegwan 2/1

-/v/
f
Sandef 23/2

/f/
ff
Cloff 2/1
Dyffryn 23/10

-/d/-
t
Rivede̲ti 2/1
Keritus 14/8

d
Ederni 2/1
Rhodri 2/1
Cadwaleder(i) 2/1, 24/3
Godebawc 2/1
Caradoci 10/2
Ardudwy 15/4, 31/2
Theodvr 17/2
E̲denyved 22/7
Aberdaron 22/10
Cadwgan 26/9

-/d/
t
Gwryat 2/1
Gwaet(erw) 13/6
Llwyt 14/7
Coet 14/7
Dinieuyt 23/9
Clwyt 23/10
Angharat 24/1
Meivot 34/7

d
Edenyve̲d 22/7
lwyd 14/6

-/ð/-
d
Cunedae 2/1
Rive̲deti 2/1
Rudlan 10/5
Kyndelo 18/1
Hodni 22/4

-/ð/
d
Evyonid 23/10
Penkerd 23/26
Merwyd 10/3, 14/4, 22/7
Arllechwed 31/2

t
Rutlan 16/2

dd
Bleddyn 12/4, 26/9
Cuneddae 2/1

th
Meredith 26/5
Meirionyth 21/1

dd
Merwydd 12/1,
   14/1

-/g/-
c
Caercybi 34/7

g
Gwrganum 11/3
Gwrgeneu 14/3, 16/2

-/g/
c
Kelliniawc 14/5
Llienawc 23/15
Gelynnawc 34/7

k
Meurik 2/1
Kelynnauk 12/1

/gw/-
gv
Gventa 17/8

gw
Gwaeterw 12/6

Appendix 2

Names of countries and nationalities in Vita Griffini filii Conani

Names for countries and nationalities are listed in regional order. References are to the chapter and sentence of the text. Italicized references refer to the supplementary sections of text from Cotton Vitellius C.ix.

Wales

Cambria	10/1, 10/2, 23/17
Cambri	8/3, 15/7, 17/2 (australes), 25/4, 26/1, 27/3, 27/4, 32/2 (australes), 35/5
Cambrice (adv.)	*4/2*, 12/6
Wallia	22/4
Walli	23/2
Wallice (adv.)	5/10

Areas within Wales

Ardudwy	15/4, 22/6, 23/10, 31/2
Arllechwed	31/2
Arvon	21/2, 23/10
Arvonia	*10/3*, 12/5, 14/6, 15/4, 15/5
Arvonensis	12/4
Arwystli	17/9
Arwistlensis	18/18
Dyffryn Clwyt	23/10
Edeirnion	19/4
Edernensis	22/1
Eivionyd	31/2
Evionydd	14/4

Evyonid	23/10
Lleyn	14/1, 23/9, 23/10, 31/2
Lleyna	12/5
Llino	10/3
Llyen	15/4, 15/5, 16/2
Llyn	12/2
Meirionyth	21/2
Merioneth	12/6, 15/4
Mona	4/2, *10/3*, *12/2*, 12/5, 14/5, 14/6, 14/9, 15/5, 15/6, 21/2, 22/2, 23/4, 23/11, 23/15 (*tris*), 28/1, 31/6
Monensis	14/11, 18/1
Powisia	14/2, *14/3*, 16/2, 18/19, 26/4, 32/11
Powisenses	12/1
Ros	23/10, 31/5
Tegenglia	12/2
Venedotia	4/2, 10/2, 12/5, 12/8 (*bis*), *14/2*, 16/1, 16/4, 18/20, 22/8, 23/14 (*bis*), 25/1, 26/4, 31/7, 31/8, 33/2, 33/5

Ireland

Hybernia	1/1, 5/5, 5/6, *5/8*, 5/8, 6/1, 6/6, *9/2*, 13/4, 14/11, 15/1, 17/1, 22/3, 22/10, 23/17, 26/5, 26/9, 28/9, 29/5, 30/1, 33/1, 34/4
Hibernus	18/13
Hyberni	1/1, 14/1, 14/6, 14/9, 15/2, 17/1, 18/1, 18/7, 35/5
Hybernice (adv.)	1/1

Provinces of Ireland

Innen	6/2 (leg. Muen)
Laginia	6/1
Ultonia	6/5

Other countries

Scotia	4/1 (*HGK, Prydein*)
Scoti	32/2
Golowidia	4/2
Arenna	4/2

Anglia	1/1, 5/12, 12/5, 13/1, 16/4, 25/1, 31/1, 32/1, 32/6, 33/1
Anglus	25/6, 25/7, 25/9
Saxones	23/15
Normanni	16/4, 17/9
Franci	13/1, 19/2, 21/1, 22/6, 22/9, 23/4, 23/7, 23/12, 23/15, 25/1, 25/8, 25/9, 26/7, 26/8 (*bis*), 26/10, 27/5, 28/4, 28/6, 28/8, 29/1
Britannia	28/9 (Britain)
Britanni	17/1
Britannius	8/1 (British)
Britannia	5/10 (Brittany)
Lydaw	5/10
Dania	4/2, 5/1, 5/3, 5/8 (leg. Ionia? see note), 15/6
Dani	5/3, 15/2, 18/1, 18/7, 27/1, 28/6, 28/8, 29/2, 29/4, 35/5
Danmarci	14/6
Llychlin	28/1
Northwegia	5/9
insulae Daniae	*5/8*, 23/1, 23/17, 33/1
Gallia	5/9 (*bis*)
Galli	5/9, 13/3
Normannia	5/9, 5/12
mare Tyrrhenum	5/8

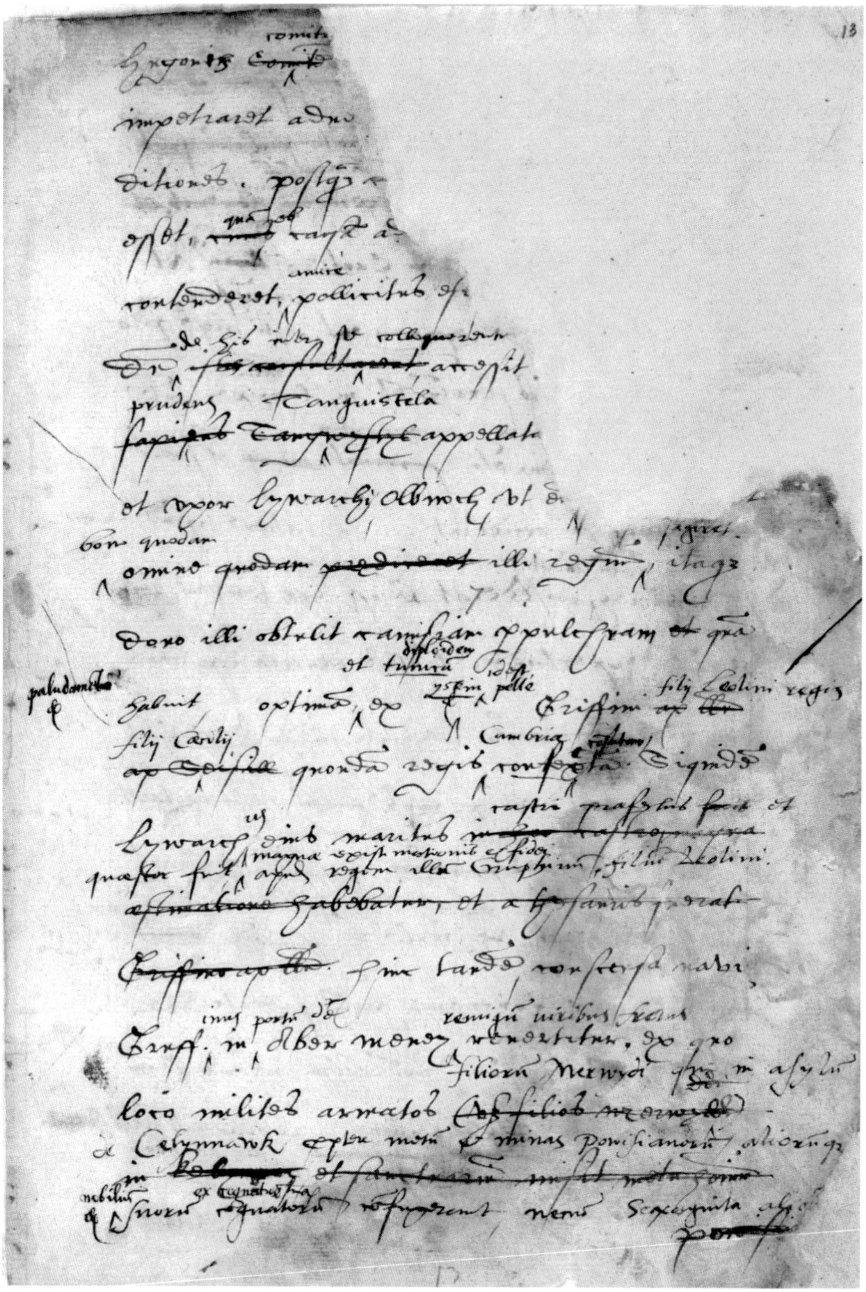

Plate 1 Peniarth MS 434, p. 13.
Reproduced by permission of the *National Library of Wales*, Aberystwyth.

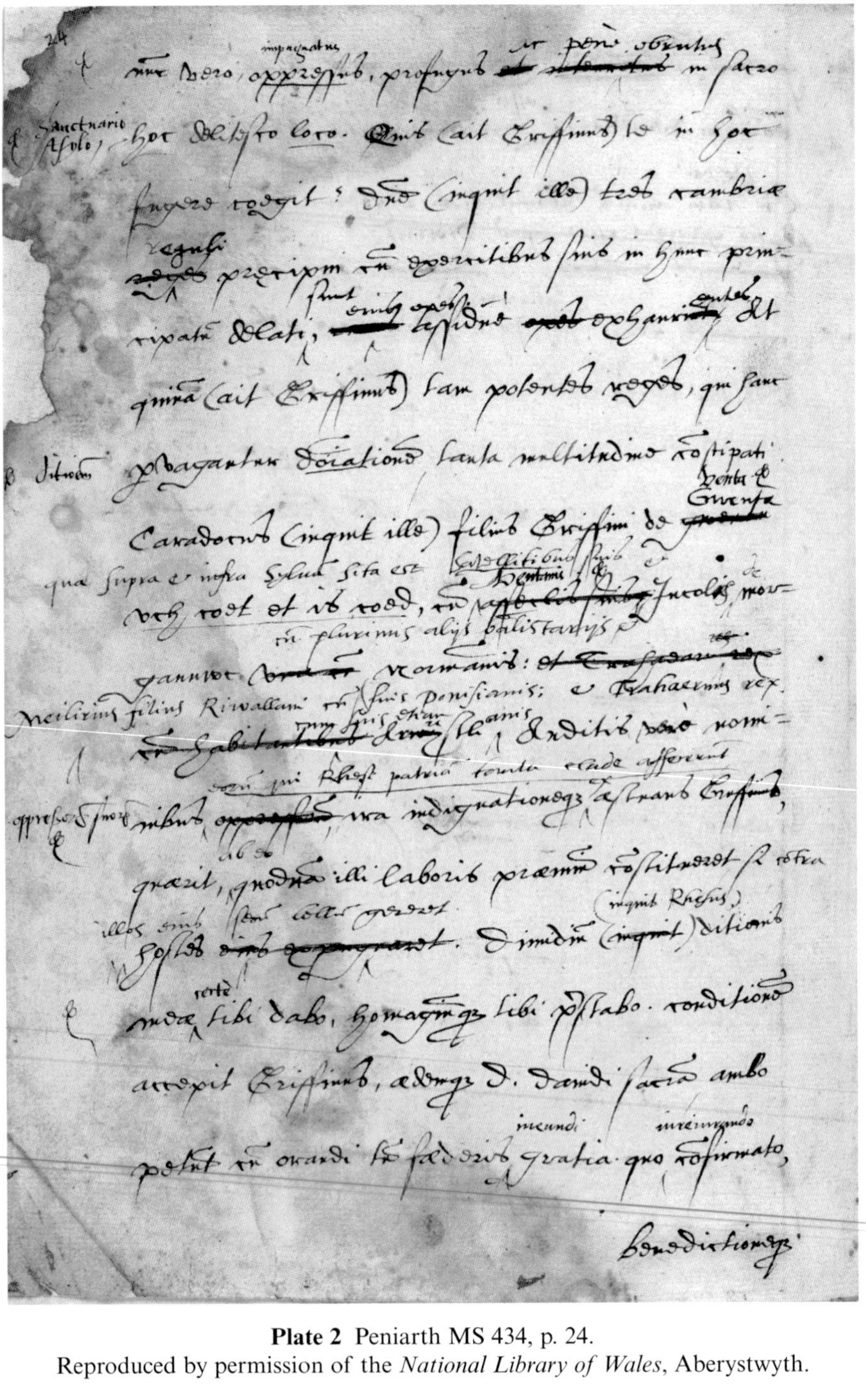

Plate 2 Peniarth MS 434, p. 24.
Reproduced by permission of the *National Library of Wales*, Aberystwyth.

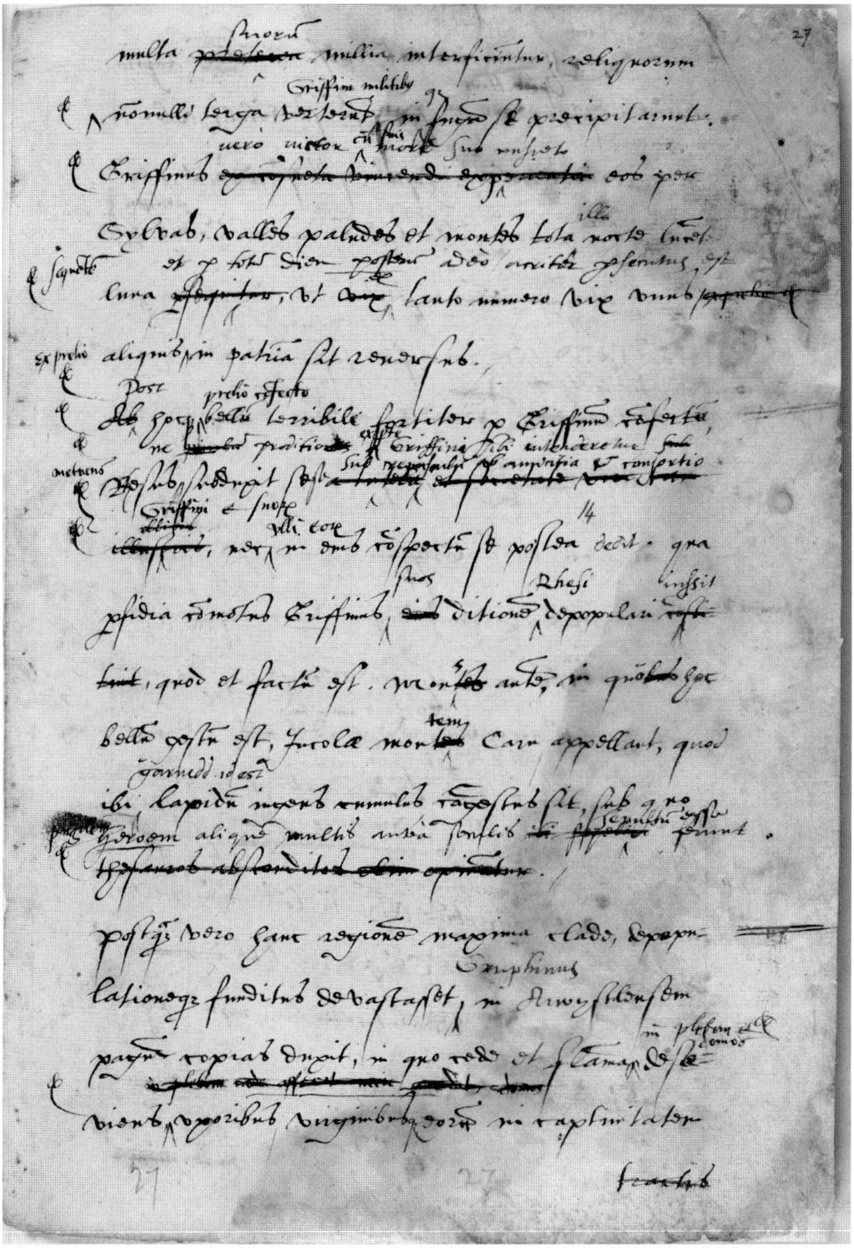

Plate 3 Peniarth MS 434, p. 27.
Reproduced by permission of the *National Library of Wales*, Aberystwyth.

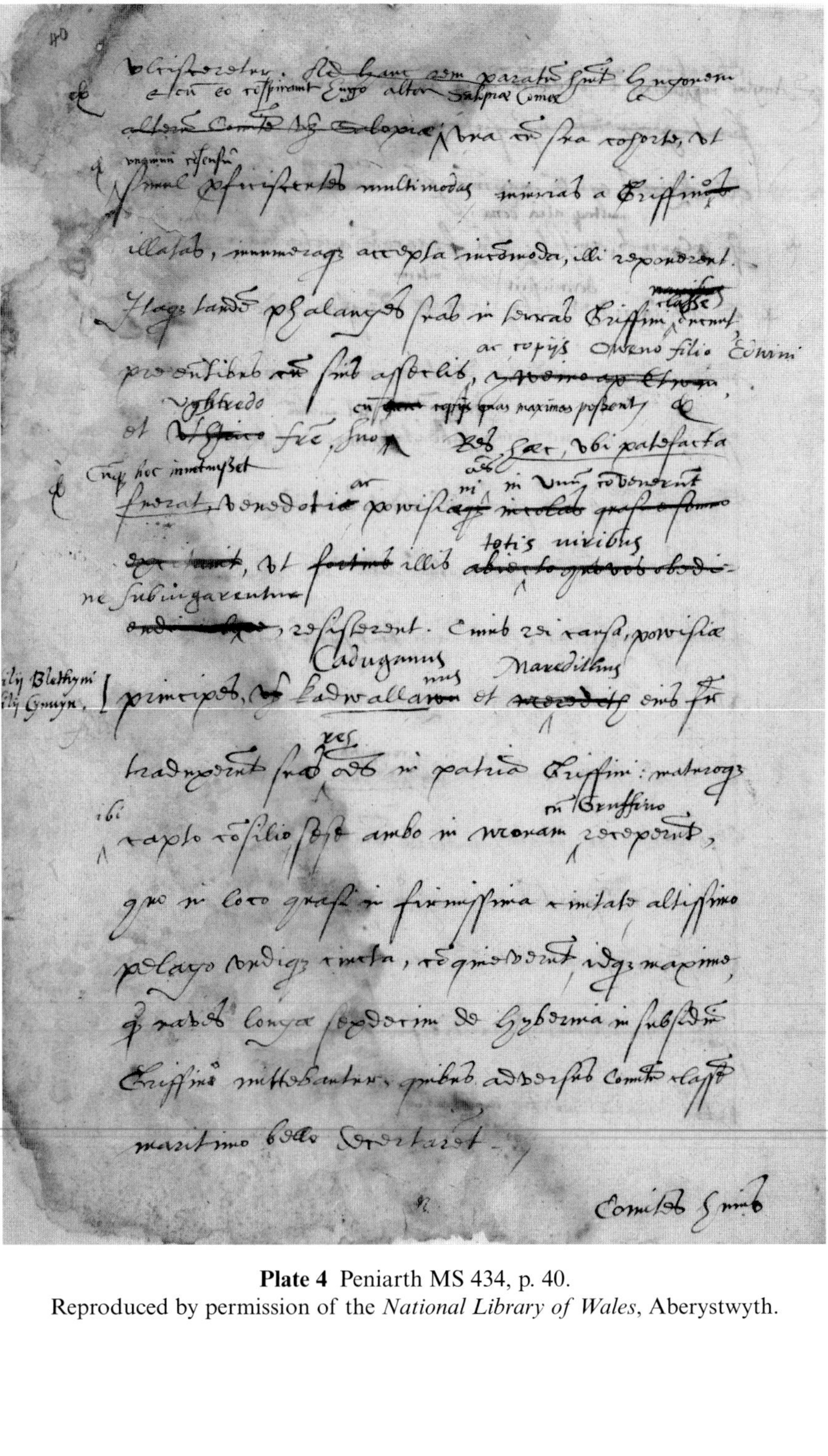

Plate 4 Peniarth MS 434, p. 40.
Reproduced by permission of the *National Library of Wales*, Aberystwyth.

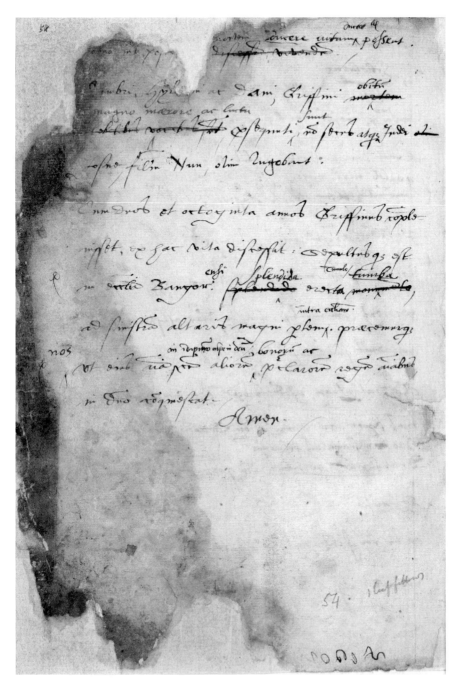

Plate 5 Peniarth MS 434, p. 54.
Reproduced by permission of the *National Library of Wales*, Aberystwyth.

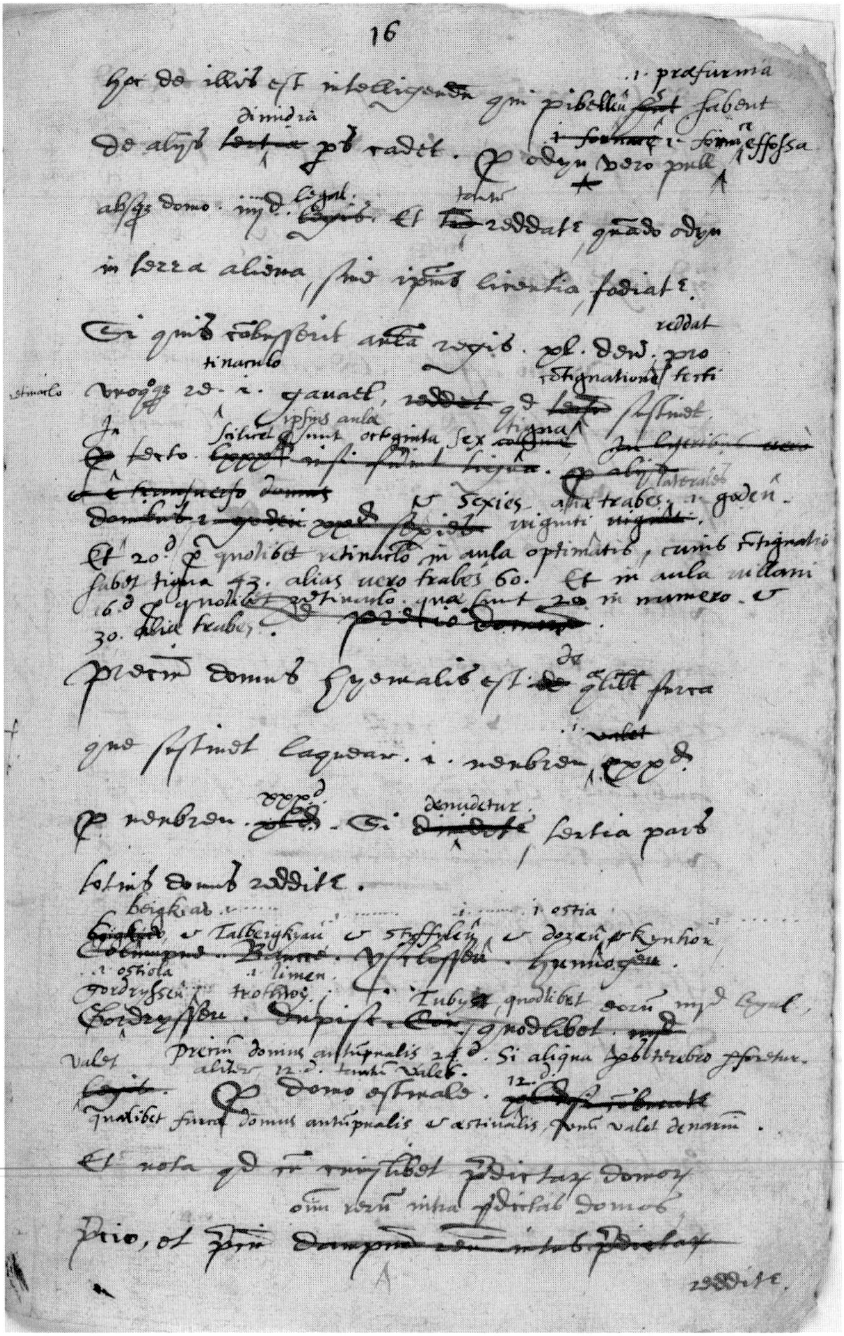

Plate 6 Peniarth MS 256, fol. 16r.
Reproduced by permission of the *National Library of Wales*, Aberystwyth.

...no miretur hominum rerum uicissitudines, &c. interdum ...et, interdum fugere sit necesse; proditio siquidem regnat ab initio.
...t enim in manibus Demetrij Regis infidelis populus Israeliticus
Iudam Maccabeum Regem ac Principem suum tradiderunt; uerum Bellator
hic Deus, ut Gigas uel Leo, scripsit ultus est in utrosque.;
Iulius Caesar qui continuis bellis orbem terrarum sibi subiugarat,
a senatoribus Romanis in ipso Capitolio Romano proditione, ac
pugionibus confoditur, Arthurus etiam, Regni totius Britanniae
Rex praenobilis, et fama (unquam intermoritura dignus) duodecim
bella contra Saxones ac Pictos gessit; In quorum primo fusus
fugatusque erat, ex proditione, in ciuitate Alwyd roet, quae et Alwyn
Alwyt Dd, hodie Eurolnia; At in reliquis, de Saxonibus Pictisque
subditorum suorum oppressoribus poenas dignas sumpsit, cui ne semel
quidem resistere potuerunt

At Sufflinus in Hyberniam appulsus, de proditoribus oppressoribus
que acerbissime conquestus est, coram Regibus, Principibusque ibidem
qui tanta indignitate commoti persuadere conantur, ut statim in patriam nauibus iam reparatis, rebusque necessarijs retutertur
quouis uoribus acquisitis, sed triginta nauibus Hyberniorum Da-
numque militibus plenis, mare aequiduo fulcantibus, in patriam fe-
uehitur, portumque Aberment; occupat; ubi Trahatruid domine
reperit, qui audito classis Regiae aduentu, cepit tristitia affini,
suspiria alta ducere, timore et tremore contabescunt, ac suos
oes qui illi in Leyn et Ardudio fauebant, pecunias suas ac facultates secum deducentes subito transmigrare fecit ad se, in Cantredum de Mcirionyth, / Cum que aduerso, Sufflinus eiusque exercitus item reliquam Leyn et Ardonie, in Mona transportat,
ut ibi incolumes in eius tutela arquie sceret. At indignati ami-
ciarij Dam, suique satellites praetorij, quod comissa Stipendia illa
non sint persoluta, maxima Mona item depopulati sunt, ac in pau-
redni nauibus spolijs onustis festinant, ipsisque inuito secum auferunt.
Nec fuit haec domestica suorum ad Sufflinus opprimendum proditio uenis sor, q illa prius Cambrorum: huic mala immer-
in Deuendotia exorta sunt.,
Ad haec miseriis accessit quod paulo post, Hugo Comes
Cestriae, alijque belli Duces, ut Robertus de Rulan, Swaring
de Salopia, Swalterus Herfordiae Comet, exercitu
amplissimo

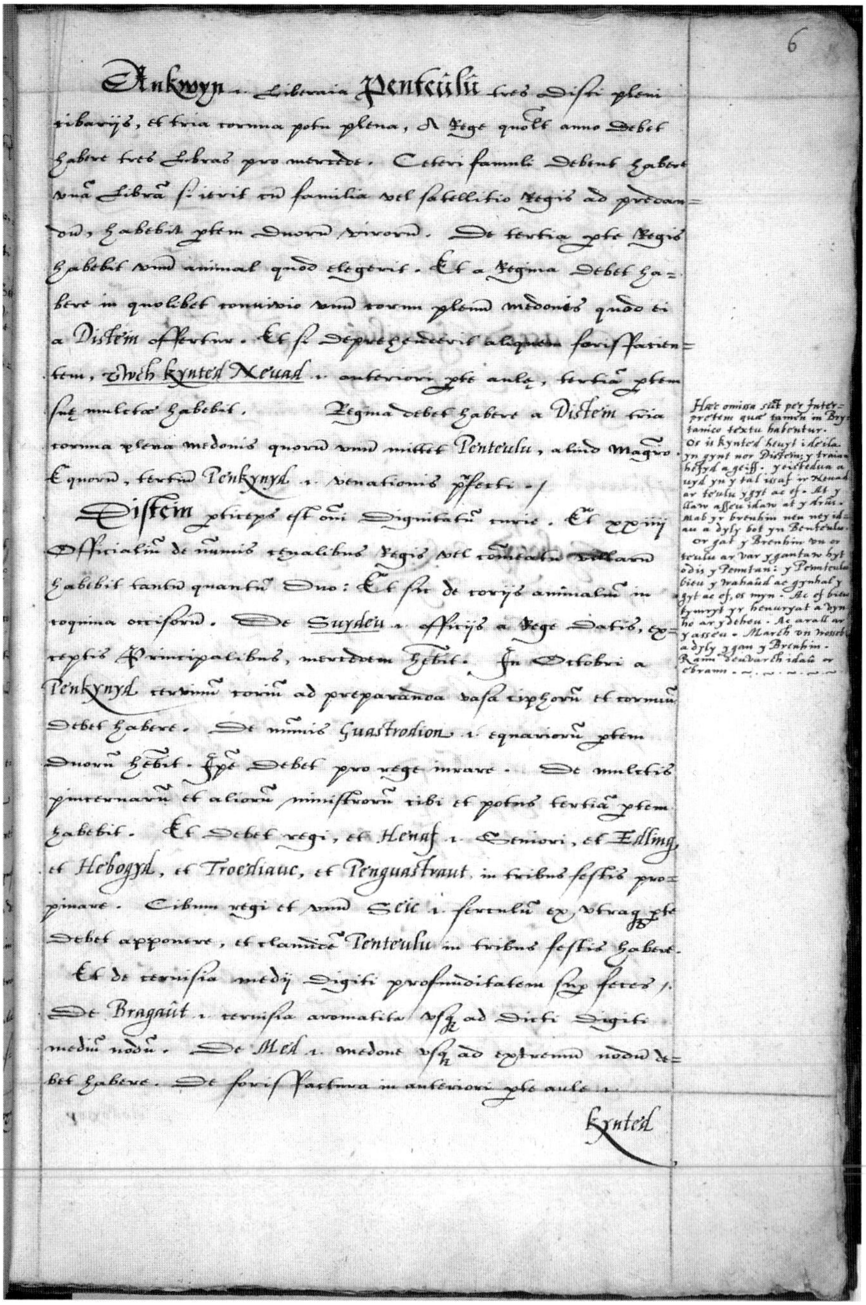

Plate 8 Oxford, Merton College MS 323, fol. 6r.
Reproduced by permission of The Warden and Fellows
of Merton College, Oxford.

Appendix 3

The fair copy of Peniarth 434 in BL, Cotton MS, Vitellius C.ix, fols. 133r–143v

The text presented below is in the hand of Maurice Kyffin who acted as a Welsh amanuensis for Dr John Dee (see Introduction, p. 10). The text is printed as in the manuscript; bold and italic sections correspond to sections written in a heavier lettering and a more italic style respectively. Most of the personal names and place names have been underlined, probably by a later annotator; the underlining is not indicated in the notes. The notes indicate annotations, corrections or glosses, and other points of interest. The paragraph division corresponds to that of the main edition above. The manuscript was singed in the Cottonian fire of 23 October 1731. The damage only affected the text of the top outer corner of the pages, and the loss of text was slight, at most a couple of words per page: on the verso the text can usually be restored from the catchword at the bottom of the preceding page, and on the recto the text has been restored from Peniarth 276, which was copied from this manuscript before 1731. For detailed discussion of the manuscript and its relationship to Peniarth 434 and to the other later Latin versions, see the Introduction, pp. 10–15. For an image of fol. 136v, see Plate 7.

[fol. 133r]   ¹Vita Griffini filij² Conani,
                              Regis Venedotiae Vel Northwalliae

§1

Cum in Anglia regnaret Edwardus (dictus Confessor) et apud Hybernes³
Therdelachus Rex; nascitur in Hybernia, apud civitatem Dublinensem Gruffinus
Rex Venedotiae, nutriturque in loco Comoti Colomkell, dicto Hybernice Swrth
Colomkelle⁴ per tria miliaria distante a domo suorum parentum.

§2

Eius pater Cynanus erat rex Venedotiae, mater vero Racvella, filia Auloedi regis
Dublini civitatis, ac quintae partis Hyberniae; prosapia quidem quam nobili ac
regia oriundis⁵ erat Gruffinus, cum paterna, tum materna, quemadmodum
genealogiae recto ordine a parentibus deductae monstrant, quarum series
sequitur.

§3

Siquidem Griffinus filius fuit Cynan filij Jacobi, filij Idwali, filij Elissae, filli
Meurick, filij Anarawti, fil. Roderi magni, fil. ⁶ Essyldis, quae fuit filia Cynani
de Castro Dyndaythwy, fil. Idwali Dyre (i. Capriae), fil. Cadwaladeri Benedicti,
fil. Cadwallani⁷ Longimani, fil. Eniani Yrth, fil. Cuneddae regis, fil. Ederni, fil.
Paterni vestis ceruleae, fil. Tageti, fil. Jacobi, fil. Guidauci, fil. Keni, fil. Caini,
fil. Gorgaini, fil. Doli, fil. Gurdoli, fil. Dwyn, fil. Gordwyn, fil. Anwerit, fil.
Onnet, fil. Diawng, fil. Brychweni, fil. Yweni, fil. Avallach, fil. Avlech, fil. Beli
Magni. At rursum Rhodericus Magnus fuit filius Mervyn Vrych, .i.
versicoloris, filij Gwryat, fil. Elideri, fil. Sandef, fil. Alkwm, fil. Tagiti, fil.
Gwen, fil. Dwc, fil. Llywarch senioris, fil. Elidir llydanwyn (.i. lati candidi), filij
Meirchiani Macri, fil. Gorwst lledlwm (.i. subnudi), filij Keneu, fil. Coeli
Godebawc, fil. Tegvani claudi, fil. Deheweint, fil. Urbani, fil. Gradi, fil.
Rivedeli, fil. Rydeyrni, fil. Endeyrni, fil. Endiganti, fil. Endos, fil. Endolei, fil.
Avallach, fil. Aflech, fil. Beli magni. fil. Manogani, fil. Eneit, fil. Kyrwyt, fil.
Crydoni, fil. Dyvynarthi, fil. Prydein, fil. Aet magni, fil. Antonij, fil. Seirioel,
fil. Gurwsti, fil. Riwalloni, fil. Regatae, filiae Lyri, fil. Rudi, filli Bladudi, fil.
Llywelit, fil. Bruti humeri candidi, fil. Eboraci, fil. Membricii, fil. Madauci, fil.

---

¹ Vita Griffini Regis Venedoti[ae a Thelwello] Iurisperito in Latinum conversa *added in top margin in*
   a later hand. Text in [ ] lost in burnt corner of page but added from NLW, Llanstephan MS, 150, a
   copy of this manuscript.
² *Added in small hand above with insertion mark after Griffini.*
³ *Sic.*
⁴ *Final* e *uncertain.*
⁵ *Sic.*
⁶ fil. Idwali *added in right margin in a later hand with no location mark.*
⁷ *In comparison with the Welsh text and later Latin versions the following is missing*: fil. Catmani, fil.
   Iacobi, fil. Beli, fil. Runi, fil. Maglocuni, fil. Caswallani.

Locrini, fil. Bruti ducis Romani, fil. Sylvii, fil. Ascanij, fil. Aeneae ysgwydwyn, .i. humeri candidi, fil. Anchisis, fil. Capis, fil. Assaraci, fil. Trois, fil. Erictonij, fil. Dardani, fil. [fol. 133v] Jovis, fil.[8] Saturni, fil. Coelij fil. Creti, fil. Cyprij, fil. Javan,[9] fil. Japhet,[10] fil. Noe, fil. Lamech, fil. Mathusalem, fil. Enoch, fil. Javet, fil. Mahaleel, fil. Cainan, fil. Enos, fil. Seth, fil. Adae, fil. **Dei.**

§4

Nobilitas Griffini ex stirpe materna deducitur sic: Griffinus Rex filius Racvellae, filiae Auloedi Regis Dubliniae, et quintae partis Hyberniae ac Insulae Mevaniae vel Mannae, qui Olim e Scotia genus ducebat, et Rex nuncupabatur aliarum complurium insularum et regionum ut Daniae, Galovidiae, Arran in occidentali Hyberniae mari, Monae, et Venedotiae, vbi castellum (dictum Castellum Auloed) fossa et muro quam munitissimum construxit, cuius rudera apparent, et vocabatur Castellum Auloedi, quamvis Cambrice appelletur Bon y Dom.

Auloed iste fuit filius Sutrici regis, fil. Auloed regis Cirian, fil. Sutrici, fil. Auloed regis fil. Harfageri Regis qui filius fuerat Regis Daniae.[11]

§5

Animadversione hoc dignum est fuisse Haraldum, Haraldum Harfagyr, et suos binos fratres filios regis Norvegiae, cuius fratrem Alanum Regem et religionis sanctitate, et virtutis gloria inter Danos praestantem, Twr quidam Princeps inter preliandum interfecit. At dum spolia illi detraheret, ac precipue collo torquem aureum ponderis gravissimi (quo ornamenti genere reges nobilesque tum utebantur) extorqueret, adhaesit manibus torques genuaque defixa ventri iungebantur. Atque hoc fuit primum, quo eum miraculo ornaverat Deus. Deinceps vero Dani eum Divorum numero adscripserunt, et honoribus sunt persecuti non modicis, adeo ut templa ad eius nominis gloriam erigerent, ac per Daniam cultus ei perficerent, maxime vero nautae illum continuo invocabant, sacrificia donaque alia illi offerentes, si quando inter navigandum in pericula inciderent. Caeterum qui illum occidit princeps, post hoc facinus Thurkiawl est appellatus, qui tantae innocentiae regem peremisset. Neque hoc praetereundum videtur, tres istos fratres mari longe lateque perlustrasse cum classe regio more instructissima, ac tandem in Hyberniam pervenisse. Verum non multo antea Haraldus Harfagyr exercitum ducens copiosum eam erat ingressus, totamque Hyberniam pertransierat summa crudelitate incolas mactando fugandoque, sic maximam eius partem sibi subiugarat. Ipse vero civitatem Dublinensem

---

[8] Iovis, fil. *lost in burnt corner of page but restored from catchword at the bottom of the preceding page.*

[9] an *lost in burnt corner of page.*

[10] phet *lost in burnt corner of page.*

[11] *Stroke at end of paragraph repeated in left margin with addition in later hand.*

aliasque civitates, castella atque munitiones edificabat, ubi iam in huius regni possessione confirmatus acquieverat, fratremque alterum in una illarum quas condiderat urbium praefectum constituit, quae illorum usitato sermone vocatur Porthlarg, cuius posteritas in hodiernum diem eius urbis dominio potitur. At ipse Haraldus totam Hyberniam insulasque[12] cunctas Daniae regebat, que ex illo latere Scotiae adiacent, ut insula [fol. 134r] Cycladis inter mare Tyren et Daniam. Tertius fratrum (viz. Rodulphus)[13] in Gallias naves direxit, ubi fortiter se gessit, variisque proeliis[14] Gallos perdomuit, Galliae portionem non modicam sibi subiecit, quam hoc tempore Normaniam vocitamus: quod viri Northwegiae ex Septentrionalibus regionibus originem deducentes ibi sedes fixerant. Hanc regionem in duodecim provincias sunt partiti, ad numerum Baronum, vel similitudinem ducum, qui in aliam Galliae partem Britanniam citeriorem, Wallice Lydaw dictam, olim advenerant. Hic civitates multas condiderunt ut Rodwn .i. Rothomagum ad Rodulfi regis primi conditoris perpetuam memoriam, ut Roma a Romulo nomen acceperat, et a Remo Rhemi: necnon alias urbes, castella, locaque presidiis firmata constituit. Ab hoc Rodulpho genus deducunt reges[15] Normanniae qui Angliae regnum armis sibi acquisiverunt. Scilicet Willhelmus, Normannus rex, et eius filij duo, qui ei in regno successerunt: Wilhelmus Longa Spata, vel Rufus, Henricus, neposque eius Stephanus, qui coetanei regis Gruffini fuerunt. Huiusmodi ergo fuerat stirpis Gruffini series, quae paternam maternamque nobilitatem spectat.

§6

Atque ut paulo longius progrediamur, Aviae maternae genus non ignobile fuerat. Siquidem Racvella, mater Gruffini, filia erat prenobilis feminae, Vaelcorcre, filiae Dunlugi, qui filius erat Tethel regis Laginiae (quintae viz. partis Hyberniae). Preterea Alam mater Auloed Regis filia erat Vryeni regis Innen, que Hyberniae duas partes continebat. Gurmlach[16] etiam mater Sutrici regis erat: Haec Marchathum regem Laginiae patrem habuit: cui ferunt tres filios nobilitate insignes fuisse, viz. Duncathum regem Innen, Sutricum Regem Dublinensem, atque Moelchelen Regem Midiuiae suscepisse necnon tradunt Murcathum Regem Laginiae ex hac Regina Maelmordam filium.[17] Erant Griffino fratres duo uterini Ultoniae reges ambo, viz. Ranaldi fil. Mathganyn, qui tanta fortitudinis gloria precelluerit, ut intra dies quadraginta Hyberniae binas partes sibi subiugarit. Admirandum quoddam quasi monstrum marinum erat, cui similem vel virium robore vel saltandi peritia, Hybernia non habuit. Equum aluit multis

---

[12] inulasque *MS.*
[13] z Rodul *lost in burnt corner of page.*
[14] *Lost in burnt corner of page.*
[15] *Underlined and* Duces *added in right margin in a later hand*I
[16] Gurmlach *and* Haec *at the beginning of the next sentence joined by a line.*
[17] susepisse *added above in a later hand.*

naturae dotibus ornatum, ac velocitatis gloria celebrem cui Isliniach nomen inditum erat: neque ei saltandi agilitate inferior erat Rinaldus. Comparandus hic quidem equus erat Cinnari equo Achillis, vel Bucephalo equo Alexandri [fol. 134v] Imperatoris.[18] Alter Griffini frater, Ethminach Gawyn Rex etiam[19] Ultoniae fuerat.

§7

Quam huc usque delibauimus generis nobilitatem, ea quoniam Gruffinum humano quodam modo, et secundum rerum terrenarum rationem attingit, operae praetium me facturum spero, si eius quasi caelestem prosapiam et divinum genus exordiar: de quo ut communi etiam cum alijs hominibus ille psalterij versus testatur, vos dij estis, et filij excelsi omnes, ita ut vere illud affirmetur, fuisse Griffinum Kynani, Kynanum Adae, Adam vero Dei filium.

§8

Quam celebris ergo habenda cum sit Griffini nobilitas, cum terrena, tum caelestis. Sumamus illud Merlini Britannorum Bardorum facile principis oraculum, qui de Griffino sic prophetasse dicitur. *Saltus ferinus presagitur venturus, De mari insidiaturus, Cuius nomen corruptor quia Multos Corrumpet.*

Charissimi mihi Cambri, quos fraterna dilectione complector, Griffinum cernitis cum terrena generis nobilitate, cum Merlini vaticinio commendatissimum: festinandum itaque videtur (hijs tamen faeliciter iactis fundamentis), ad eius praeclare res gestas, operaque magnifica, quae [20] antiquorum authoritate percurrere sumus polliciti; *Non Diana vel Apolline*, sed ipso Christo auspice ac favente.

§9

Cum itaque iam Griffinus puer morum probitate cultus, ac petulanter enutritus, adolescentiae annos attingeret materna in domo, interque cognatos: [21] saepe illi solebat mater referre, qualis, quantus[22] eius pater extiterat, quam ampla ditio, quamque celebre regnum ei iure haereditario debebatur, atque etiam quam crudelis iam tyrannus possideret. Quibus ille vocibus anxius, multoties animo subtristi multa secum versabat, tandem vero in curiam Murchathi regis profectus, querelas apud eum et reliquos Hyberniae reges effudit gravissimas, monstrando gentem extraneam eius paternam haereditatem occupare, humiliterque petendo, ut ei auxiliares copias subministrarent, quibus eam vel armis recuperaret. Consensum est in eius subsidium polliceturque quisque opportuno tempore ei suppetias ferre. Quo responso laetus summas gratias Deo illisque egit.

---

[18] *Lost in burnt corner of page but restored from the catchword at the bottom of the preceding page.*
[19] *Lost in burnt corner of page.*
[20] non sine *added above in later hand.*
[21] per a[...] *added in left margin.*
[22] que *added in later hand.*

§10

Et quum expectatum tempus advenerat, naves extructas conscendit, vela dat ventis, mareque Cambriam versus sulcat, appulitque in portum dictum Abermeney; atque in ea Cambriae parte, que Venedotiae[23] vocabatur, tunc principatum iniuste ac tyrannice gerebant Trahearnus filius Caradoci, et Kynwricus filius Rhiwallon regulus [fol. 135r] Powisiae, quam inter se sunt partiti. Ex hoc loco Griffinus nuntios misit ad[24] incolas Insulae Monae, et Arvoniae, et tres filios Merwydi in Llyno, viz. [25] Asserum, Meirianum, et Gwrganum, aliosque viros superiores, ut qua poterant celeritate ei occurrerent. Isti postposita omni cunctatione veniunt, salutant, adventus causas querunt. Quibus cum expossuisset, vehementius ab illis contendebat, ut eum adiuvarent in hereditate paterna vendicanda (siquidem ad illum iure spectabat in illos dominari) atque ut arma secum caperent, adversus eos qui in eius possessiones iniuste dominarentur, ex aliis locis quasi adventitios.

Ab hac congressione sic finita, concilioque hoc secreto absoluto, Griffinus rursum per mare iter arripit versus castrum de Rudlan, ad Robertum Baronem nobilem, et potentem, nepotem Hugonis Comitis Cestriae, ut auxilia vel precibus impetraret adversus hostes grassantes in avitas ditiones. Postquam vero cognovit Robertus quis esset, quam ob causam adventasset, et quid ab eo contenderet, amice pollicitus est se ei adiutorem futurum.

§11

Dum de hiis inter se colloquerentur, accessit ad Griffinum mulier prudens Tanguistela appellata, eius cognata, et uxor Lywarchi Olbiwch,[26] ut eum suum cognatum existentem salutaret, et bono quodam omine illi regnum praesagiret. Itaque dono illi obtulit camisiam praepulchram quam habuit optimam et tunicam ex yskin i. pelle Griffini filii Leolini Regis, filii Caecilii quondam Regis Cambriae confectam. Siquidem Lywarchus eius maritus, castri praefectus et quaestor fuit magnae existimationis et fidei apud Regem illum Griffinum filium Leolini.

§12

Hinc tandem conscensa navi Gruffinus in portum de Abermeney remigum viribus fretus revertitur. Ex quo loco milites armatos filiorum Merwydi, qui in asylum de Celynnawk propter metum et minas Powisianorum, aliorumque suorum cognatorum confugerant, necnon sexaginta alios selectissimos quos ante nominatus Robertus Rudlaniae praefectus sibi in auxilium ex Tegenia miserat cum quadraginta insulanis de Mona in cantredum de Llyn, ut Kynwricum oppressorem depugnarent. Isti animosi profecti, et in eum improviso securum, et nihil tale expectantem impetum facientes, eum et suorum maximam partem

---

[23] *Sic; the scribe misread Thelwall's note in Peniarth 434, p. 11.15.*
[24] misit ad *lost in burnt corner of page.*
[25] no viz. *lost in burnt corner of page.*
[26] r *added above with insertion mark after* w.

occiderunt. In statione apud Abermeney consederat Griffinus hoc tempore, rei eventum expectando, et illis felicia comprecando, cum ecce praecurrens iuvenis quidam Arvonensis, Anianus nomine, ut primus nuntium laetum portaret, viz. occubuisse Tyrannum, et inimicum suum, premiumque quasi omen reciperet, scilicet mulierem quandam [fol. 135v] speciosam,[27] Deladam vocatam, quae concubina prius fuerat Blethyni Regis Cambriae, quemadmodum olim iuvenis quidam Amalechita usque ad Philistim ex bello quod gestum fuerat in montibus Gelboae, ad David cucurrit, portans armillam, et sceptrum Saulis Regis cui David armillam dedit in premium tam laeti nuntii.

Jam reversi milites in expeditionem superiorem missi victoria ovantes, persuadent Griffino, ut ex hoc faelici omine progrederetur ad recuperandam Monam, Arvoniam, Leynam, et alios suos cantredos Anglie conterminos utque[28] populi sui submissionem, et indigenarum homagium acceptaret, totamque Venedotiam (illi hereditario iure debitam) circuiret, quam misericors iam illi Deus in suas manus obtulerat.

Hiis gestis exercitum copiosum in cantredum de Meirioneth ducit ubi Trahaernus tyrannorum alter morabatur; pugnaque commissa est in loco vallis Kyning, qui Cambrice dictus est Gwaeterw, vel ager sanguinis, in hunc usque diem. Ac Deus illi victoriam concessit eo tempore de inimicis suis, decideruntque plus quam mille ex parte Trahaerni, qui et ipse cum paucis vix elapsus aufugit conservatus ex bello, quem Gruffinus cum exercitu per deserta, et montes usque ad fines patriae suae persecutus est. Post hanc pugnam Griffini nomen percrebuit: rex Vendedotiae publice salutabatur, qui quasi gigas ad currendam viam exultans summa laetitia circumfusus est, quod Venedotiam ab iniquis et alienigenis dominis oppressam tam feliciter liberam fecisset: quomodo Judas ille Machabaeus olim terram Israel a dominatione regum infidelium, et gentibus conterminis liberasset, in eos irruendo saepissime. Itaque rebus ad hunc modum compositis, caepit regnum iure disponere, populum pacificare, universaque in virga ferrea gloriose in domino gubernare.

§13

Tempore iam modico interiecto, proborum hominum consilio, exercitum coegit numerosum, perrexitque versus Castrum de Rudlan, ut cum Roberto castri praefecto, et equitibus aliis Francis, et Normannis pugnaret, qui modo illuc ex Anglia deducti, inde in confinia Venedotiae ad habitandum commigrare ceperunt. Cum vero signo dato exercitum contra castrum eduxerat, usque ad muros cuncta vastat, ac incendit, spoliaque opima domum referens. Equites illi loricati galeatique e Francis complures lapsi ex equis in illa pugna ceciderunt, multi etiam peditum, ac vix pauci in turrim sese magna cum difficultate receperunt

---

[27] *Lost in burnt corner of page but restored from the catchword at the bottom of the preceding page.*
[28] utaque *written first and then deleted;* utque *written above in same hand.*

incolumes. Postquam reges, barones, cognatique Griffini in Hybernia res ab eo tam prosperrime gestas accepissent, ut [fol. 136r] qui apud eos natus, et enutritus fuerat, eius fortunae congratulabantur.

§14

At tres illi filii Merwydi, virique Lleyn universi, adversus Gruffinum[29] dominum suum legitimum latenter insurrexerunt, et nocte quadam intempesta, ex equitibus Hybernis, et satellitibus Gruffini, qui in illa regione diversabantur quinquaginta duos occiderunt. Cum huius discordiae inter Griffinum, ac suos subditos fama ad Trahaernum pervenisset, magnopere laetabatur, et tametsi iam victus esset, et fuga salutem quaeritans, statim Powisiae incolas adiit, rogatque ut secum adversus Venedotiam in ultionem mortis Kynwrici consanguinei sui cum expeditis militibus proficiscerentur. Hinc Gwrgeneus filius Caecilii[30] et regulus Powisiae, eiusque cohors una cum Trahaerno eiusque cohorte ad subiugandum Griffini regnum veniunt. Quod ubi tres filli Merwydi, virique Lleyn, et Evionith audivissent, ut periuri, foedifragi, et hostium adiutores perdere Griffinum dominum suum meditantur; hostiumque ductores fiunt. Simili se flagitio inquinaverunt duo fratres de Mona, Theodorus viz., et Gollwynus, accepto tamen prius a Griffino suo stipendio apud Kelliniawc vawr. Proditione hac cognita, hostiumque adventu, Griffinus de Mona, Arvonia, una cum Danis et Hybernis quos potuit, deducit secum in hostes; fit bellum crudele et atrox, utrimque decertatum est acerrime. At de exercitu Griffini interfecti complures iacebant, captique in praelio nonnulli. Sed Keritus, nutricius suus, et Varudrius Princeps Hybernorum, et dominus Cruc Brenan (qui locus est excelsus, divi Brendani heremitae admirabilis, novem cantredos circumiacentes habens) et de Optimatibus Monae septuaginta occubuerunt. Attamen Griffinus equo insidens inter confertissimos hostes gladio suo rapido quasi metere proditores ac inimicos videbatur, non aliter atque Agamemnnon Rex Graecorum olim preliabatur in bello Troiano. At cum Theodorus Monensis proditorum caput stricto gladio adcurrens Griffinum ex posteriori ephippii parte perfossurus erat; Gwynus vero Baro Monensis id conspicatus, adcurrens eum e proelio aufert et ad naves deduxit, quae in portu Abermeney in statione erant: et inde in insulam Adron (quae et phocarum insula dicitur) abierunt: indeque in Llwchgarmaw in Hybernia pertransierunt. Illa vero pugna loci nomine (in quo depugnatum est) celebratur,[31] usque ad hunc diem, Bron yr Erw, vel Erw yr allt, appellatur.

[136v] Nemo miretur has humanarum rerum vicissitudines, ut interdum vincere,[32] interdum fugere sit necesse; proditio siquidem regnat ab initio. Sic enim in manus Demetrii Regis infidelis populus Israeliticus Judam Maccabaeum

---

[29] ruf *lost in burnt corner of page.*
[30] filii Ithael, filii Gwerystan *in right margin in later hand.*
[31] *MS has* celebrantur *with* n *deleted.*
[32] vinc *lost in burnt corner of page.*

Regem, ac Principem suum tradiderunt: verum Bellator hic Dei, ut Gigas vel leo seipsum ultus est in utrosque.

Julius Caesar qui continuis bellis orbem terrarum sibi subiugarat a senatoribus Romanis in ipso Capitolio Romano proditione ac pugionibus confoditur. **Arthurus** etiam regum totius Britanniae[33] rex praenobilis, et fama nunquam intermoritura dignus duodecim bella contra Saxones ac Pictos gessit. In quorum primo fusus fugatusque erat ex proditione in civitate Llwyd Coet, quae et Llwyn Llwyt dicitur, hodie Lincolnia. At in reliquis de Saxonibus Pictisque subditorum suorum oppressoribus poenas dignas sumpsit, cui ne seni quidem resistere potuerunt.

§15

At Gruffinus[34] in Hyberniam appulsus de proditoribus, oppressoribusque acerbissime conquestus est coram regibus principibusque ibidem, qui tanta indignitate commoti persuadere conantur, ut statim in patriam navibus iam reparatis, rebusque necessariis reverteretur: quorum vocibus acquiescens cum triginta navibus Hybernorum Danorumque militibus plenis mare profundum sulcantibus in patrium solum vehitur, portumque Abermeney occupat, ubi Trahaernum dominantem reperit. Qui audito classis regiae adventu, caepit tristitia affici, suspiria alta ducere: timore et tremore contabescere, ac suos omnes, qui illi in Lleyno et Ardudio favebant pecunias suas ac facultates secum deducentes subito transmigrare fecit ad se in cantredum de Meirionyth. Cum ex adverso Griffinus eiusque exercitus partem reliquam Lleyni et Arvoniae in Monam transportat, ut ibi incolumes in eius tutela acquiescerent. At indignati auxiliarii Dani, suique satellites pretorii, quod promissa stipendia illis non sint persoluta, maximam Monae partem depopulati sunt, ac in patriam reverti navibus spoliis onustis festinant; ipsumque invito secum auferunt. Nec fuit haec domesticorum suorum ad Griffinum opprimendum proditio remissior, quam illa prius Cambrorum.

§16

Hinc mala innumera in Venedotia exorta sunt.

Ad has miserias accessit, quod paulo post Hugo Comes Cestriae, aliique belli duces, viz. Robertus de Rutlan, Gwarinus de Salopia, Gwalterus Herefordiae Comes, exercitum [fol. 137r] amplissimum equitum peditumque collegerunt, comitantibus etiam Gwrganeo[35] filio Caecilii, virisque Powisiae, et per montium iuga Lleynum usque[36] pervenerint. In quo cantredo ubi castra per hebdomadam posuissent, omnia longe lateque depopulantur, fundunt, fugant, et plena

---

[33] Arthurus *added in later hand in left margin.*
[34] Guffinus *MS.*
[35] wrganeo *lost in burnt corner of page.*
[36] que *lost in burnt corner of page.*

cadaveribus relinquunt, adeo ut octo annorum spatio desolata et inculta regio illa remansit; populusque a tanta clade relictus, miseria hac coactus in alienas terras perfugatus est, cuius maxima pars durissimam serviebant servitutem in exilio per multos annos, et vix quisquam in patriam unquam reversus est. Fuerat haec prima clades a Normannis illata, primusque eorum in Venedotiam ingressus, postquam in Angliam advenerint.

§17

Cum iam annis nonnullis in Hybernia Griffinus hospitio exceptus esset apud Diermit reges et alios viros nobiles, classem insignem in porta de Porthlarc rebus instruxit ad iter necessariis, quam dono regis acceptam Danis, Hybernis, ac Britannis onustam duxit prosperrimo per mare cursu, adspirantibus etiam secundis ventis in portum dictum Porth Cleis non longe a sede Archiepiscopali Menevensi. Ad cuius adventum Rhesus filius Theodori Rex australium Cambrorum, et Menevensis Episcopus, doctores, ac chorus universus Sti. Davidis, clericique omnes ecclesiae Menevensis in portum sunt profecti: Rhesusque primus Griffinum sic est allocutus: Salve Cambrorum regum Rex, ad te confugio, tibi genua flecto supplex, auxilium suppetiasque petens. Tum Griffinus: Quis tu? Et cuius huc advenisti causa? Rhesus (inquit): Sum filius Theodori huius nuper regionis dominus: nunc vero oppressus, profugus, ac pene obrutus, in sacro hoc delitesco loco. Quis (ait Griffinus) te in hoc fugere coegit? Domine (inquit ille) tres Cambriae reguli precipui, cum exercitibus suis in hunc principatum delati sunt, eius opes assidue exhaurientes. At quinam (ait Griffinus) tam potentes eges, qui hanc pervagantur dominationem tanta multitudine constipati. Caradocus (inquit ille) filius Griffini de Gwenta quae supra, et infra sylvam sita est, cum satellitibus suis, incolis de Morgannwc, cum plurimis aliis balistariis, et Normannis, Meiliricus filius Riwallani eum Powisianis, et Trahaernus Rex cum suis etiam Arustlianis.

Auditis vero nominibus eorum, qui Rhesi patriam tanta clade affecerunt, ira indignationeque exaestuans Griffinus, quaerit ab eo, quodnam illi laboris premium constitueret, si contra illos [fol. 137v] eius hostes[37] secum bellum gereret: Dimidium (inquit Rhesus) ditionis meae tibi[38] dabo, homagiumque tibi praestabo. Conditionem cepit Griffinus: aedemque D.[39] Davidi sacram ambo petunt, cum orandi tum foederis ineundi gratia.

---

[37] eius hostes *lost in burnt corner of page but restored from the catchword at the bottom of the preceding page.*
[38] *Lost in burnt corner of page.*
[39] *A new line is started here, leaving three-quarters of a line empty which is filled with line-filling marks.*

§18

Quo iureiurando confirmato, benedictioneque[40] interposita, statim Griffinus iter arripit sequentibus eum Danis, Hybernis, plurimisque Venedotis ad numerum centum et sexaginta, duce Cyndelo filio Comisi[41] Monensis. Rhesus cum perpaucis Australibus laetus simul proficiscitur; perbelle secum actum cogitans, quod tam opportunum auxilium nactus esset.

Longo iam itinere dimenso ad vesperam in montes perveniunt, ubi castra posuissent praedicti reges. Tum Rhesus Griffinum sic est allocutus: Domine, differamus prelium in crastinum,[42] quod iam advesperascit, et lux defectura est. Differ (inquit Griffinus) quousque tibi placuerit, ego vero cum ea quam paratam habeo cohorte in eos impetum faciam. Quod, ut dixerat, praestabat. Terrore ingenti conturbantur reges stupentque dum copias Griffini faeroces, constipata militum agmina, splendentia vexilla, Danos bipennibus armatos, Hybernos iacula ferreis cuspidibus cultellata ferentes, et hastatos scutatosque Venedotos contra se venire conspiciunt. Ipse vero Griffinus proelium primus irruit, non secus ac gigas vel leo indefessus cruento gladio inimicos prosternens, milites suos animose in hostes excitans, et ne terga adversariis darent alacriter exhortans. Fit bellum atrocissimum et cruentum, cuius famam post patrum mortem longe exaudient filii. Clamor proeliantium in celum usque ascendit: resonare visa est terra fremitu equorum ac peditum: pugnaces dimicantium voces longe lateque exaudiuntur, strepitus armorum ingens fuit. Tanta strages facta est, dum Griffini copiae hostes suos delerent, sibique cedere compellerent, ut sudoris et sanguinis flumina[43] decurrisse putarentur. Tandem Trahaernus effusis visceribus transfoditur, et terram pronus deiectus, quasi herbas viventes carpendo dentibus, et super arma palpare visus est. Cuius cadaver ut carmen suillam in lardum Gwcharkius Hybernus condidit; eodem in loco ceciderunt de stipatoribus eius equites 25, alii vero eorum primo agmine deleti sunt: multa suorum millia interficiuntur, reliquorum nonnulli terga verterunt, inque [fol. 138r] fugam se[44] precipitarunt. Griffinus vero victor more suo consueto eos[45] per silvas, valles, paludes, et montes tota illa nocte, lucente luna, et per totum diem posterum adeo acriter persecutus est, ut ex tanto numero vix unus aliquis in patriam sit reuersus.

Post hoc bellum terribile fortiter per Griffinum confectum, Rhesus ne[46] periculum proditionis a Griffino sibi intenderetur, subduxit sese sub crepusculum ab amicitia et consortio illius, nec in eius conspectum se postea dedit. Qua perfidia commotus Griffinus suos ditionem Rhesi depopulari iussit, quod et

---

[40] episcopi *added above in later hand.*
[41] Conusi *added in left margin as a correction.*
[42] castrinum *MS.*
[43] *MS has* flamina *corrected to* flumina; *cf. Peniarth 434, p. 26.10–11.*
[44] *Added above main text by main scribe with insertion mark after* fugam.
[45] sueto eos *lost in burnt corner of page.*
[46] *MS has* in *corrected to* ne.

factum est. Mons autem in quo hoc bellum gestum est, incolae montem Carn appellant, quod ibi garnedd, i. e. lapidum ingens cumulus congestus[47] sit, sub quo heroem aliquem multis antea seculis sepultum esse ferunt. Postquam vero hanc regionem maxima clade depopulationeque funditus devastasset, Griffinus in Arwystlensem pagum[48] copias duxit, in quo cede et flamma desaeviens, uxoribus virginibusque eorum in captivitatem ductis Trahaerni iniurias rursum in suorum capita persolvit. Postremo in Powisiam se contulit, ubi victoria potitus summa crudelitate in hostes usus est, adeo ut nec ecclesiis pepercerit. Ita tandem inimicis omnibus fusis, terraque eorum in solitudinem penitus redacta, in paternam hereditatem honorifice reversus est, ut eam quietam et pace faelicem redderet, ac gubernaret. Sic Venedotia magna tranquillitate ad aliquod tempus gavisa est.

§19

Dum ad hunc modum Griffinus regni sui deliciis frueretur, Meirianus Rufus, Baro suus, diabolico incitatus telo, eum coram Hugone comite Caestriae maliciose non solum accusavit, sed perdidit sic. Duos Comites Francos Hugonem scilicet prius nominatum, et Hugonem Salopiae filium Rogeri de Montegomerico iussit ut equites peditesque magno numero secum usque in locum Rvc dictum, in Edeyrnion ducerent. Tum proditor hiis adulatoriis verbis eum decepit: Salutant te (inquit) princeps magnifice comites duo illustres, qui tibi vicini ad confinia tui regni habitant. Hii summopere a te contendunt,[49] ut apud Ruc in Edeirnion ad colloquendum cum tuis auxiliariis et hospitibus venire digneris, interposita sponsione eundi redeundique sine periculo. Huius vocibus fidem adhibens Griffinus, in illum sui principatus locum profectus, ut in conspectum comitum venerat, compraehendi [fol. 138v][50] eum statim[51] mandarunt, et in publica foetentique custodia Cestriae ferreis catenis devinctum annis duodecim tenuerunt. Hospites vero eius tum etiam captos, amputatis singulorum pollicibus dextris, inhumanius afflictos liberos dimiserunt. Ceteri (audito tanto facinore) in varias regiones sunt dispersi, non aliter atque illud divinum oraculum habeat: 'Percutiam pastorem, et dispergentur oves gregis'.

§20

Amici ac domestici Griffini retulerunt eum fuisse staturae mediocris capillis flavis, cerebro calido, facie rotunda, et formosi coloris, oculis cum decore grandioribus, superciliis perpulchris, barba decora, collo subrotundo, carne candida, membris robustis, digitis longis, tibiis rectis, et speciosis pedibus;

---

[47]   congestum *MS.*
[48]   *Changed to* agrum *by later hand.*
[49]   *Preceded by* vp *deleted.*
[50]   Vita Griffini Regis Venedotiae *in top margin in a later hand.*
[51]   eum statim *lost in burnt corner of page but restored from the catchword at the bottom of the preceding page.*

peritum et externarum linguarum scientia excellentem; in milites clementem et munificum, in hostes magnanimum, et in proeliis fortissimum.

§21

Interim Hugo Comes Cestriae in ditionem eius copias ingentes adduxit, ac castella aliaque praesidia diversis in locis edificari curavit Francorum more, quo et terre illi facilius imperaret. Hoc tempore castellum in Mona constituit, aliud in Arvonia in antiqua urbe Constantini imperatoris filii Constantii Magni, aliud apud Bangor, aliudque in Meirionyth: in quibus ad eorum defensionem equites, pedites, sagittariosque collocavit. Qui tanta crudelitate tantisque malis patriae incolas affecerunt, quantam nulla unquam aetas viderat. At populorum clamor ad Deum ascendebat, ipseque illis opportuno tempore subsidium tulit.

§22

Siquidem post sedecim annorum spatium e carcere Griffinus liberatus est, idque sic evenit. Juvenis quidam Ederniensis Kynwricus Longus nomine una cum paucis sodalibus Cestriam veniens ad necessaria coemenda, conspicit forte in palatio civitatis suum regem vinculis astrictum, quem in dorso abreptum clam e civitate subduxit, iterque in patriam vespere cum sociis conficit, civibus iam caenantibus, atque domi apud se tacite diebus nonnullis aluit. Quibus elapsis valetudineque recuperata, latenter noctu Griffinum in Monam deduxit, ubi Sandevus filius Ayrei clanculum ei necessaria subministrauit: verum non multo post, conscensa navi, in Hyberniam transfretare tentavit: at ventus adversus eum in portum Hodni in australibus partibus Walliae coegit. Inde pedestri itinere pergens novem electissimis amicis tantummodo comitatus (quorum [fol. 139r][52] nonus ibi occubuit), tribus vicibus uno, eodemque die, praesidiariis[53] militibus illius regionis pugnavit, terque eos superavit, quum octo tantum[54] illi superessent[55] comites: unumque ipse ex adversariis generis nobilitate in illa regione praestantem interfecit, sicque ex illorum manibus evasit.

Iter hoc[56] in Ardudwy usque confecit, incertus quo pergeret, ne proderetur a Francis. Tandem filii Collwini Egimirus, Gellanus, Merwydus, ac Edenyvedus eum ad se compassione moti receperunt, rebusque necessariis in desertis latibulis sustentarunt. Post aliquot menses sexaginta viros ad illum coegerunt, ac per Venedotiam de loco in locum <palantes[57]> diversa loca peragrant, damna inferentes non modica dum Hugo Comes vixit: ut olim David filius Isai Bethleemita in terra *Judaea* tempore *Saulis* regis.

[52] Vita Griffini Regis Venedotiae *in top margin in a later hand.*
[53] iariis *lost in burnt corner of page.*
[54] tan *lost in burnt corner of page.*
[55] supessent *MS with two letters deleted between* e *and* s; *the abbreviation for* per *has been misunderstood.*
[56] *Glossed* inde *by later hand.*
[57] *Added in gap by later hand; possibly missed by the main scribe who misunderstood Thelwall's gloss in Peniarth 434, p. 32.6.*

Cum vero Franci, qui in praesidiis morabantur, eum tanta mala operantem senserant, ipsi milites in defensionem patriae relicti, eum per sylvas, perque agros, ut canes venatici defessum cervum indagare et persequi student. Itaque sublata omni spe evadendi, naviculam Cannonicorum de Aberdaron conscendit, in qua remigum importunis laboribus in Hyberniam tandem pervenit. Inde infra mensem reversus in eadem navicula, in flumine a quo solvebat stationem reperit, et inde mox in Hyberniam reversus est.

§23

A qua in Insulas Daniae maturiori capto consilio ad Gothreum regem familiarem suum adnavigavit, ut ab eo[58] naves aliaque ad res suas necessaria impetraret. Quodque tunc primum ad eum confugerat, confisus se subsidia accepturum. Cuius adventu contristatus rex, compati, atque condolere crebris eius miseriis coepit. Ad extremum Griffinus inde cum classe sexaginta navium sibi in subsidium concessa Monam appulit, ut cum Francis castella tutantibus ipse quique cum eo ex insulis devenerant, preliaretur. At incolae summo illi impedimento fuere. Bellum gestum est saevum et crudele ab aurora usque ad vesperam; multique utrinque ceciderunt, quique animo forti praestabant in primo impetu.[59] Tum Griffinus in confertissimos hostes prorupit,[60] seque in primum agmen dat, ut Francos loricatos et galeatos sua bipenni armatus prosterneret, ut David rex inter Philistheos. Nox proelium diremit, navesque auxiliariae[61] in Insulas sunt profectae. At ipse in quandam insulam (quae phocarum vel vitulorum marinorum Insula vocatur) [fol. 139v] cum vna solummodo[62] navi secessit, ex qua navem e Cestrensi portu vectam[63] occisis nautis depraedatus est: ac postero die Leynum versus vela dans, in portum Nevin salvus cum suis omnibus intravit. Quod ubi ad cantredorum incolas fama detulisset, convolarunt statim ex singulis regni partibus, scilicet homines de Leyno, Evyonith, Ardudwy, Arvonia, Rossia, et Dyffrynclwyt (.i. valle Cluydana) qui ad sui legitimi principis obsequia exequenda fidem suam tradunt. Collecto sic ingenti exercitu confirmatus Griffinus, adiuvante eum Deo opt. max., copias duxit adversus castellum quod superius diximus in Mona exaedificatum esse, quod ad aliquot dies oppugnauit. At Franci obsessi e muris, propugnaculis, et turribus in eos iacula torserunt, sagittas[64] emiserunt, saxa balistis deiecerunt, aliisque sese instrumentis bellicis defensitarunt: donec tandem quotidiana et assidua Cambrorum oppugnatione cedere sint coacti,

---

[58] *MS has* abeo *deleted and* ab eo *written above.*
[59] occubuere *added as gloss in later hand.*
[60] *Abbreviation for* pro *deleted and* pro *added above in later hand.*
[61] r *added above.*
[62] cum vna sol *lost in burnt corner of page but* cum vna *restored from the catchword at the bottom of the preceding page.*
[63] am *lost in burnt corner of page.*
[64] saggitas *written first and deleted, and* sagittas *written after it.*

ceciditque eorum dux, vel Senescallus, cuius erat hoc castellum, aliique sexaginta quatuor cum eo. Hoc castello flammis consumpto hostibusque expugnatis, tanto successu laetus Griffinus, adversus reliqua in eius regno castella pergit: quae pugnando cepit, diruit, ac incendit, populumque in ipsis universum gladio occidit. Ad hunc modum adversariis omnibus devictis Venedotiam a castellis liberam reddidit, et suum principatum denuo recepit, de suis hostibus condignas sumens poenas. Ac sic Venedotia per biennium pace ac tranquillitate usa est. Nec praetereundem videtur, quod cum Griffinus apud Aberllienawc in Mona pugnaret centum viginti militibus, iuvenibusque strenuis quatuor decim,[65] ac castellum incenderat, ac omnia penitus devastasset, multosque ex castellanis peremisset, ad aliud Monae latus proficiscitur, ubi naves eius tres in anchoris starent, subito alii castellani una cum inhabitantibus Monam, eum adoriuntur, toto illo die persequuntur, eiusque postremum agmen sepius ad prelia provocant: attamen, ut antea, Griffinus ad coeptum iter progreditur, spolia aufert, Francos ac Saxones vinctos secum, et captivos deducit, insidiatorum horum renovata pugna quam plurimos interfecit. In hoc proelio cadit Gellanus Cytharedus, i. archimusicus Penkerd, iuxta naves ex parte Griffini. Paternus fortasse qua scientiarum varietate ac quo eloquentiae splendore excelluit, Griffini egregia facinora ac res preclare gestas in Cambria, Hybernia, Insulis Daniae [140r] subiectis, aliisque diversis nationibus enarrare posset; ego ingenue fateor[66] deesse mihi facultatem, immo nec tanto oneri posse me esse parem,[67] si vel soluta oratione[68] Tullii eloquentia pollerem, vel adstricta numeris poesi Maronem vincerem.

§24

Dum variis fortunae fluctibus iactaretur Griffinus, modo prosperis, modo adversis, in uxorem accepit Angharatam filiam Oweni filii Edwini principis Tegeniae (nunc Englefelde), quam huius provinciae prudentiores referre soliti sunt, faeminam nobilem fuisse, ingenuae staturae, capillis candidis,[69] subgrandioribus ac splendentibus, accipitrino vel erecto corpore. Singulas etiam corporis partes habuisse ad proportionem compositas quam aptissime, tibias rectas, pedes concinnos, digitos longos, ungues tenerrimos; affabilem praeterea fuisse tradiderunt, ae sermone elegantem, cibi et potus largitione liberalem, perspicacem, cautam, in consiliis prudentem, in familiares clementem, et in egenos liberalem, et ad res praeclaras omnes instructissimam. Ex hac octo suscepit liberos, filios tres, scilicet Cadwallanum, Owenum, et Cadwalladerum, filias vero quinque, viz. Gwenllianam,

---

[65] comitatus *added above in later hand.*
[66] enue fateor *lost in burnt corner of page.*
[67] arem *lost in burnt corner of page.*
[68] aratione *MS.*
[69] oculis *added above in later hand with insertion mark before* subgrandioribus.

Marretam, Raynyldem, Susannam et Agnetam: fuere etiam illi ex concubinis liberi aliquot.

§25

At ubi Willelmus longa spatha rex Angliae bellicas expeditiones, fortitudinem et sevitiam Griffini in Francos accepisset, aegerrime tulit, ac totius regni vires in eum commovit, et in Venedotiam equitum, peditumque varias turmas duxit, quibus incolas omnes funditus destruere et pessundare proposuit, ut ne canem quidem ullum vivum relinqueret. Aggressus est sylvas, ac lucos omnes succidere et evertere, ut ne vel umbra quidem, qua se Gwyndyt, i. Venedoti tutarentur, deinceps superesset. Hic primum castra ad locum vocatum Castellum muratum posuit. Atque huius expeditionis Cambrorum nonnulli et auctores et ductores erant. Audito tanto belli apparatu Griffinus copias totius sui principatus collegit, ac adversus Regem Gulielmum eduxit, in angustiis viarum insidias collocans, in quas subito inciderat a montibus descendens exercitus Regis. Has Anglus reformidans per regionem mediterraneam Cestriam exercitum reduxit: in quo eius itinere nec incolae damnis quae minatus esset afficiebantur, nec perfidi ductores laborum fructus quos sperabant perceperunt, nisi forte unica sit quisque vacca dona[fol. 140v]tus.[70] At Anglus equitum maximam partem, armigeros, famulos, equosque[71] quam plurimos amisit. Ita Francorum iactantia concidit, ad nihilumque devenit: quum copiae Griffini modo anticipare, modo subsequi modo a dextris, modo a sinistris, illis esse solebant, ne eius subditis nocerent nimium. Quod si Griffinus suos, dum abditos lucos pertransirent, in eos immisisset, postremum illum diem Anglus ac Franci sensissent, verum cohibuit suorum faerociam Griffinus, ut olim *David* se gessit erga *Saulem*.

§26

Rebus ad hunc modum non succedentibus, Hugo Comes Cestriae (de quo supra) malorum omnium architectus (ut anteactis temporibus Antiochus) classem militibus onustam parat, ut quem ceperat intimum doloris sensum ex presidiariorum suorum trucidatione, dirutis funditus castellis et equitibus mala morte multatis, iam saltem in Cambros ulcisceretur. Ad hanc rem paratum habuit Hugonem alterum comitem viz. Salopiae una cum sua cohorte, ut simul proficiscentes multimodas iniurias a Griffino illatas, innumeraque accepta incommoda illi reponerent. Itaque tandem phalanges suas in terras Griffini classe ducunt, praeeuntibus cum suis asseclis ac copiis Oweno filio Edwini et Uchtredo fratre suo. Res[72] haec ubi patefacta fuerat, Venedoti ac Powisiani in unum convenerunt, ut illis totis viribus ne subiugarentur, resisterent. Cuius rei

[70] tus *lost in burnt corner of page but restored from the catchword at the bottom of the preceding page.*
[71] *Lost in burnt corner of page.*
[72] *Followed by* omnes *which was then deleted.*

causa Powisiae principes, viz. Caduganws, et Maredithus eius frater traduxerunt
res suas omnes in patriam Griffini: maturoque ibi capto consilio, sese ambo in
Monam cum Griffino receperunt: quo in loco, quasi in firmissima civitate
altissimo pelago undique cincta, conquieverunt, idque maxime quod naves longae
sexdecim de Hybernia in subsidium Griffini mittebantur, quibus adversus
Comitum classem maritimo bello decertarent. Comites huius rei certiores facti,
nuntios clam ad classis Hybernicae praefectos destinant, ut amplissimis muneribus
pollicitis rogarent, quatenus a Griffino in eius summis periculis, maximisque
angustiis deficerent, auxilioque omni destitutum relinquerent, quod effectum
praestiterunt. Siquidem Francorum dolis delusi, totam insulam (fracta fide
Griffini data), vacuam praesidiis in direptionem hostibus tradiderunt. Hac
Francorum fallacia, Griffinus in summam animi aegritudinem coniectus,
consilii [fol. 141r] dubius, quid adversus vim Francorum, vel classis suae[73]
auxiliariae defectionem, opus esset facto. Itaque re pr[...][74]cum suis deliberata,
arrepta quadam navicula, una cum Cadwgano filio Blethyni, suo genero in
Hyberniam transfretavit, populum, suaque bona Dei voluntati ac protectioni
commendans, qui subvenire cunctis cum angustiis maximo premuntur,
clementiae, et bonitatis suae non oblitus consueverit. At plebs multis modis
miserabilis, eius absentiam sentiens, fuga sibi salutem quaesivit, ac in specubus
subterraneis, alnetis,[75] sylvis, lucis, filicetis, montium iugis, locisque praecipitibus,
palustribus, et incultis, locisque aliis inaccessis absconderet, qui se latitabat, ac
sese occultabat, Judaicorum scilicet Francorum, aliorumque barbarorum metu,
qui in eorum perniciem advenerant. Quoniam (ut divinum dicit eloquium)
cecidit populus sine duce. Non fuit difficile iam Comitibus eorumque exercitui
per totam insulam longe lateque eodem illo die pervagari, populum concidere,
aliquorum bona diripere, aliorum membra detruncare, donec nox eos a
persequendo retardaret.

§27

Verum ecce postero die inexpectato singulari Dei providentia, regalis quaedam
classis appropinquans sese in conspectum obtulit, qua animadversa contristati
sunt Franci, ac foedifragi illi Dani qui a[76] Griffino defecerant. At Franci vero
ad consuetas sibi fallendi artes se contulerunt. Atque ex Cambris confederatis
emiserunt quosdam ad insulanos, qui eos ad concordiam hortarentur,
persuaderentque statim securitatem ac pacem accipere quibus possent optime
rationibus. Nam timebant Franci, ne ex utraque parte simul urgerentur, viz. ne
eodem tempore et cum Cambris profugis ex una, et cum hac regia classe ex
altera parte simul dimicandum foret, quod, ut sperabant, effectum est. Hac ratione

---

[73] is suae *lost in burnt corner of page.*
[74] prius *deleted and followed by* pr[...]; *end of word lost in burnt corner of page.*
[75] aluetis *MS.*
[76] *Added above by later hand.*

fallaces Franci miserrimos Cambros huius insulae carceribus circumsessos in fraudem pellexerunt, tantam tamque immanem cladem perpessos, quantam ne posteri quidem post multas maiorum aetates oblivioni tradere poterint.

§28

Veruntamen classem, quam superius inopinate conspectam diximus, ad Regem Llychlynij vel Noruegiae[77] spectantem, divini numinis misericordia singularis in Monam dirigere est dignata, ut plebem suam miseriis involutam tandem liberaret. Siquidem [fol. 141v] ad dominum[78] suum ex infinitis suis calamitatibus, et malis clamavit, et exaudivit[79] eam Deus.

Cum vero regi, qui huic classi prefuit, per interpretes monstraretur, que haec esset insula, quis eius princeps, quantae ibi caedes fierent, quam dira persequutio, quique essent tam cruentae stragis authores, condolere coepit ac fremere: itaque naves tres ad littus tendere praecepit. Quod cum Franci perceperunt, quamvis timidiores mulierculis, loricati, et pro more suo in equis sedentes ad pugnandum cum rege cum suis classicis pugnatoribus procedunt. Rex vero eiusque nautae fortiter ex adverso cum eis dimicarunt. Cadunt Franci ex equis, ut ficus de arboribus ficiferis, alii mortui, alii vulnerati crebris ictibus Norvegensium vel Lychlynensium. At rex ipse magnanimus e puppi sagittam torquens Hugonis Comitis Salopiae oculum perfodit, qui in terram exanimis ex equo suo armato cadit ac super arma aliquandiu luctatur moribundus. Franci vero ex hoc eventu in fugam versi Lychlynensium ictibus terga ostendunt. Rex autem classem inde statim subduxit, quia cum ingenti militum manu iter hoc suscepisset, ad perscrutandas insulas Britanniae[80] ac Hyberniae, quae extra orbis terminos habentur, ut Ferillus[81] dixit: Britannos a toto orbe penitus esse divisos.

§29

At Hugo Comes Cestriae aliique Franci ob discessum Magni regis Noruegensium laetitia perfusi captivos Venedotos, et suas praedas in tutiora loca Cantredi de Rhossia deduxerunt, Griffini adventum de hora in horam metuentes; quo in loco cuiusque[82] animalia capta, reliquasque praedas omnes numerabant, ac in duas partes sunt partiti, quorum dimidiam partem secum Cestriam transportavit Comes.

Tum aderant etiam Dani illi periuri proditores qui Griffinum prodiderant, quam Hugo illis prolixe promiserat virorum, mulierum, servorum, virginum captarum portionem in suae perfidiae premium accepturi, persolvebat ille quidem

---

[77] Rex Lychlynij vel Noruegiae *added in right margin by later hand.*
[78] ad dominum *lost in burnt corner of page but restored from the catchword at the bottom of the preceding page.*
[79] et ex *lost in burnt corner of page.*
[80] Brittanniae *MS with second* t *deleted.*
[81] Virgilius *in left margin in later hand.*
[82] *Written twice and first instance deleted.*

illis ut fidelis infidelibus, ut illud Divinum confirmaret. Nam postquam ex singulis
partibus collegisset, cunctas amiculas edentulas, incurvas, claudas, monoculas,
inutiles et impotentes, obtulit has Danis in mercedem proditionis. Quam
mancipiorum squalentem catervam ubi vidissent, sublatis anchoris, in [fol.
142r] altum solverunt Hyberniam versus. At qui tunc temporis[83] ibi imperabat
poenas de illis sumpsit gravissimas, mulctando[84] alios morte, alios membrorum
abscissione, aliosque in exilium perpetuum ex toto suo regno exterminans.

§30

Atque ecce, eodem tempore Griffinus antiqua sua consuetudine de Hybernia
reversus, universam patriam in solitudinem redactam, subditosque suos in alia
loca traductos invenit. Itaque legatos ad Hugonem Comitem Cestriae mittit,
quorum opera effectum est, ut in pacis conditiones inter eos sit conclusum.
Inde in illo Cantredo de Rossia concessae sunt illi villae tres.

§31

Ab hoc tempore per annos complures Griffinus vitam tenuem duxit, curisque
variis distentam, spe tamen meliori, ac divina providentia se consolando. Transacto
tandem annorum aliquot spacio, in curiam Henrici Regis Angliae qui fratri
successit se contulit: a quo Ervinii Bangorensis episcopi interventu, salutem,
amorem, et sermonis gratiam est consequutus. Cui etiam Rex summa cum pace
ac gratia concessit cantredos de Lleyn, Eivionyth, Ardudwy, et Arllechwedd,
una cum incolis eorum, ac praedis universis. Ut vero in patriam est reversus
Griffinus a curia Regis, suos subditos in illarum terrarum possessionem
adducit, Deo gratias agens, qui deponit divites superbos de firmis suis sedibus,
et humiles in eorum locos exaltat: qui egenum facit potentem, et qui hominem
humiliat, eundem ad honores evehit. Deinceps omnia Griffino prospere
paulatim succedunt, quia in Domino spem fixam habuerat. Confugiunt ad eum
quotidie reliqui de Rossia cum rebus suis, non expectata vel petita Comitis
Cestriae licentia, sicque populorum multitudine augere coepit.

Anno sequenti in Monam ipse cum suis profectus ibi imperabat: indeque in
alios commotas se contulit: hoc modo in Venedotia suis viribus[85] imperium, ac
pristinum statum recuperavit, ut *Maccabaeus* filius *Mattathiae* olim in *Israel*.
Subditis etiam singulos gravissimo servitutis iugo, qui propter superiores
bellorum necessitates in exilium adacti fuerant, liberavit totamque Venedotiam
opibus ac gaudio replevit, ut Israelitae e captivitate Babylonica reversi.

---

[83] mporis *lost in burnt corner of page.*
[84] tando *lost in burnt corner of page.*
[85] vi *deleted and* iu *added above in later hand.*

§32

At Comes moleste tulit, quod se invito ditionem suam sic occupaverat Griffinus, [fol. 142v] immo rex[86] Angliae eius hoc facinus admiratur. Itaque aerarium suum recondit,[87] sumptusque ingentes in equites ac pedites fecit. Regem etiam Scotiae,[88] Scotos[89] ac Australes Cambros secum adduxit. Cum hiis copiis in Griffini principatum ingressus est, positis castris apud Murcastell. Ipse vero Griffinus bellorum stratagemata ac pericula sepius expertus, ex adverso castra metatur in nivosi montis Eryri bracchiis. Quibus ex locis legati utrinque sepius sunt missi, atque tandem post inducias, in pacis formam est consensum. Sicque Henricus in Angliam revertitur, ac Griffinus in propriam ditionem redit.

At rursum Henricus Rex transacto temporis perbrevi spacio, exercitum magnum ductans venit, castraque in eodem loco (quo prius), in ipsis montibus posuit, hoc consilio, ut iam tandem Griffini principatum funditus everteret: subditosque eius omnes in ore (ut dicam) gladii perderet, mactaret, et ad extremam internecionem redigeret. Hoc audito Griffinus suos in aciem collegit, et ut in more illi erat, in eius occursum dirigebat, transmissis tamen prius domesticis suis, ac colonis una cum uxoribus ac liberis in solitudines montium Eryri, ubi extra omnem periculi metum forent. Quibus rebus evenit, ut Rex metuens, ne in manus Griffini incideret, cum in valles a montium cacuminibus discenderet,[90] in Angliam pace facta se recepit.

O Deus bone, quoties Griffinum subvertere conati sunt comites Cestriae, ac non poterant. Quoties aggressi sunt fallacis Trahaerni viri, at non poterant insidioso suo proposito omnino perficere.

§33

Post tantos hosce exantlatos labores, Griffinus per annos complures divitiis regnabat, regumque vicinorum familiaritate cum summa concordia est usus, viz. Henrici Regis Angliae, Marchathi Regis Hyberniae, Regisque qui insulis Daniae praeerat: fuitque celebre eius nomen, non solum in regnis adiacentibus, verum etiam in remotissimis terris.

Jam per Venedotiam coeperunt bonarum omnium rerum incremeneta fieri; iam coepit populus ecclesias fundare, glandes seminare, arbores plantare, pomaria et hortos colere, ac fossis et sepibus munire, murataque aedificia extruere, frumenta ac terrae fructus Romanorum more in alimenti usum convertere. Basilicas vero erexit Griffinus iuxta palatia sua, quae [fol. 143r] maximis sumptibus construxerat, ac honorifica conviviorum liberalitate[91] assidue celebrabat. Quid referam amplius.

---

[86] immo rex *lost in burnt corner of page but restored from the catchword at the bottom of the preceding page.*

[87] condit *lost in burnt corner of page.*

[88] Sc *lost in burnt corner of page.*

[89] scotos *deleted and* Scotos *added above in later hand.*

[90] *Sic MS.*

[91] *Lost in burnt corner of page.*

Venedotia tunc dealbatis[92] ecclesiis splendescebat non aliter quam firmamentum stellis: populum suum virga ferrea gubernabat, concordiam ac pacem cum regnis sibi finitimis conservans, filios adhuc iuvenes extremis regni Cantredis praeposuit, ut populum regere discerent, ac quasi moenia immobilia essent adversus extraneas nationes, illosque barbaros, qui nova contra se molirentur. Reguli vero minores ad eius curiam, ac patrocinium sepius confugiebant, auxilii ac consilii sui impetrandi causa, quoties eos alienorum iniuriae urgerent.

§34

Ad extremum iam longa senectute confectus, et oculorum lumine amisso, operibus se misericordiae, ac pietatis totum dedit, animo secum revolvens, quod ex rebus militiae gestis memoriam iam reliquisset perpetuam. Propositum etiam habuit in secretiorem ac solitarium quemdam locum secedere, ut divinarum rerum contemplationi intentius vacaret, ac vitae sanctius ducendae incumberet, dominationibus terrenis penitus contemptis et abiectis. Atque ubi iam vitae terminum appropinquare intellexit, liberos convocari precepit, ut quae a morte sua fieri et observari vellet illis exponeret, quemadmodum aliquando *Ezechias* Rex olim fecerat. Itaque substantiam suam omnem distribuit: cuius iustitia in aeternum permanebit. Ecclaesiae Christi apud Dublinum viginti solidos donavit, quo in loco et natus et nutritus fuerat. Singulisque cathedralibus ecclesiis Hyberniae: necnon Ecclesiae Menevensi, abbatiis Cestriae, et Salopiae tantundem: Ecclesiae Bangorensi plus legavit. Ac Ecclesiae Caercybi decem solidos: ac tantundem ecclesiis Penmonae, Gelynnawc, Enlli, Meivot, Sti. Germani, ac Dinerthi, multisque aliis principalibus ecclesiis. Bona illa quae episcopo, archidiacono, presbyteris, clericis, doctoribus, Christianisque egenis dedit, ego Sti. Spiritus protectioni commendabo, qui omnia scrutatur et cognoscit.

§35

Ad eum iam in extremis agentem, vitaeque finem expectantem, accesserunt ex omni eius principatu viri celebres et prudentissimi, viz. David episcopus Bangor, Symeon archidiaconus, vir aetate ac prudentia maturus, prior Monasterii Cestriae, compluresque alii presbyteri ac scholastici, ut oleo consecrato eius corpus inungerent, iuxta praeceptum Jacobi [fol. 143v] Apostoli.[93]

Erant[94] una eius filii, quibus ille benedicendo predixit, quales viri postea[95] eventuri essent, ad similitudinem Jacobi Patriarchae, qui filiis in[96] Aegypto benedixisset: atque in mandatis dedit, ut fortiter se gererent, inimicisque magno animo resisterent, ut ille postremis suis temporibus egerat.

---

[92] albatis *lost in burnt corner of page.*
[93] *Lost in burnt corner of page but restored from the catchword at the bottom of the preceding page.*
[94] *Lost in burnt corner of page.*
[95] *Lost in burnt corner of page.*
[96] *Lost in burnt corner of page.*

Aderat etiam eodem tempore Regina Ancharat eius uxor cui dimidiam omnium bonorum suorum partem, duo mesuagia, vel patrimonia, cum porthmiis de Abermeney legavit.

Necnon filie eius presentes erant, ac nepotum nonnulli, atque horum singulis partem rerum suarum tribuit, qua commodius post eius mortem ducere vitam possent.

Cambri, Hyberni, ac Dani, Griffini obitum magno maerore ac luctu persequuti sunt, non secus atque Judeei Josue filium Nun olim lugebant.

Cum duos et octoginta annos[97] Griffinus complevisset, ex hac vita discessit. Sepultusque est in ecclesia Bangorensi, splendida erecta tumba ad sinistram altaris magni partem: praecemurque nos Deum ut eius anima cum aliorum bonorum ac praeclarorum Regum animabus in Domino conquiescat. Amen.

---

[97] annorum *82 in left margin in later hand.*

Bibliography

Primary sources

Alfred the Great: Asser's Life of King Alfred and Other Contemporary Sources, trans. S. Keynes and M. Lapidge (London, 1983).

Am ddiwedd Arthur, ed. from BL Cotton Vitellius C.ix by D. S. Evans, 'Dau gopi o destun', *Trivium,* 3 (1968), 30–47 (at pp. 39–43).

Annales Cambriae: A Version, ed. E. Phillimore, 'The *Annales Cambriae* and the Old-Welsh genealogies from Harleian MS. 3859', *Y Cymmrodor,* 9 (1888), 141–83 (repr. in Morris, *Arthurian Sources,* V, 13–55); A, B, and C Versions, ed. J. Williams ab Ithel, *Annales Cambriae* (London, 1860); A, B, and C Versions (682–954): ed. D. N. Dumville, *Annales Cambriae, A.D. 682–954: Texts A-C in Parallel* (Cambridge, 2002).

Annales Cestrienses: Chronicles of the Abbey of St. Werberg at Chester, ed. R. C. Christie (Lancashire and Cheshire Records Society, 14; 1886).

Armes Prydein: The Prophecy of Britain from the Book of Taliesin, ed. I. Williams, trans. R. Bromwich (Medieval and Modern Welsh Series, 6; Dublin, 1972).

Asser's Life of King Alfred, ed. W. H. Stevenson (Oxford, 1901).

The Autobiography of Edward, Lord Herbert of Cherbury, ed. S. L. Lee (London, 1886).

Biblia Sacra Vulgata: Biblia Sacra iuxta Versionem Vulgatam, ed. R. Weber et al. (Stuttgart, 1969).

Brenhinedd y Saeson or the Kings of the Saxons, ed. and trans. T. Jones (Cardiff, 1971), references are to the page and line numbers of this edition.

Brut y Tywysogyon, Peniarth MS. 20, ed. T. Jones (Cardiff, 1941), references are to the page, column and line numbers of this edition; trans. by T. Jones in *Brut y Tywysogyon or the Chronicle of the Princes, Peniarth MS. 20 Version* (Cardiff, 1952), references are to the page and line numbers of this edition.

Brut y Tywysogyon or the Chronicle of the Princes, Red Book of Hergest Version, ed. T. Jones (Cardiff, 1955), references are to the page and line numbers of this edition.

A Catalogue of the Manuscripts in the Cottonian Library deposited in the British Museum (London, 1802).

The Chartulary or Register of the Abbey of St. Werburgh, Chester, ed. J. Tait, 2 vols. (Chetham Society, NS, 79 (1920), 82 (1923)).

Cronica regum Mannie et Insularum, ed. G. Broderick, 2nd edn (Douglas, 1995).

Collectio Salernitana, ed. S. de Renzi, 5 vols (Naples, 1852–9).

Commentarioli Britannicae descriptionis fragmentum auctore Humfredo Lhuyd (Cologne, 1572).

Cronica Regum Mannie et Insularum. Chronicles of the Kings of Man and the Isles, ed. G. Broderick (Douglas, 1979; 2nd edn 1995).

Cyfreithiau Hywel Dda yn ôl Coleg yr Iesu LVII, ed. M. Richards, 2nd edn (Cardiff, 1990).

The Diaries of John Dee, ed. E. Fenton (Charlbury, 1998).

The Dictionary of Medieval Latin from British Sources, ed. R. E. Latham and D. R. Howlett (Oxford, 1975).

The Dictionary of Welsh Biography down to 1940 under the Auspices of the Honourable Society of the Cymmrodorion, ed. J. E. Lloyd et al. (London, 1959).

William Dugdale, *Monasticon Anglicanum* (London, 1665–73); repr. ed. J. Cayley, H. Ellis and B. Bandinel, 8 vols (London, 1817–30).

Early Welsh Genealogical Tracts, ed. P. C. Bartrum (Cardiff, 1966).

Einhard, *Vita Karoli Magni: The Life of Charlemagne*, ed. E. S. Firchow and E. H. Zeydel (Dudweiler, 1985).

Episcopal Acts and Cognate Documents relating to Welsh Dioceses, 1066–1272, ed. J. C. Davies, 2 vols. (Cardiff, 1948–53).

Die Gesetze der Angelsachsen, ed. F. Liebermann, 3 vols. (Halle, 1903–16).

Geiriadur Prifysgol Cymru, ed. R. J. Thomas et al. (Cardiff, 1952–2002).

Gildas, *De Excidio Britanniae*, ed. M. Winterbottom (Chichester, 1978).

Giraldus Cambrensis, *Descriptio Kambriae*, in *Giraldi Cambrensis Opera*, ed. J. S. Brewer, J. F. Dimock and G. F. Warner (London, 1861–91), VI, 155–227.

Giraldus Cambrensis, *De Invectionibus*, in *Giraldi Cambrensis Opera*, ed. J. S. Brewer, J. F. Dimock and G. F. Warner (London, 1861–91), III, 1–96 (books 1–4), I, 123–96 (books 5–6).

——, *Itinerarium Kambriae*, in *Giraldi Cambrensis Opera*, ed. J. S. Brewer, J. F. Dimock and G. F. Warner, (London, 1861–91), VI, 3–152.

Handlist of Manuscripts in the National Library of Wales (Aberystwyth, 1940–).

Historiae Brytannicae Defensio, Ioanne Priseo … authore (London, 1573).

Historia Gruffud vab Kenan, ed. D. Simon Evans (Cardiff, 1977).

The History of Gruffydd ap Cynan: The Welsh Text with Translation, Introduction and Notes, ed. A. Jones (Manchester, 1910).

The History of the Gwydir Family written by Sir John Wynn of Gwydir, ed. J. Ballinger (Cardiff, 1927); *The History of the Gwydir Family and the*

Memoirs of Sir John Wynn, ed. J. G. Jones (Llandysul, 1990). References are to Jones's edition.

John Dee's Library Catalogue, ed. Julian Roberts and Andrew G. Watson (London, 1990).

The Latin Texts of the Welsh Laws, ed. H. D. Emanuel (Cardiff, 1967).

Lhuyd, Edward, *Parochialia: Being a Summary of Answers to 'Parochial Queries in order to a Geographical Dictionary, etc. of* Wales', ed. R. H. Morris, 3 vols (London, 1909–11).

The Life of Edward, First Lord of Cherbury, Written by Himself, ed. J. M. Shuttleworth (Oxford, 1976).

'Life of Griffith ap Cynan', ed. R. Williams, *Archaeologia Cambrensis*, 3rd series, 12 (1866), 30–45, 112–31.

Llyfr Blegywryd, ed. S. J. Williams and J. E. Powell (Cardiff, 1942).

'Llywelyn's Charter to Cymer Abbey in 1209', ed. K. Williams-Jones, *Journal of the Merioneth History and Record Society*, 3 (1957–60), 45–78.

A Mediaeval Prince of Wales: The Life of Gruffudd ap Cynan, ed. D. Simon Evans (Felinfach, 1990).

The Merioneth Lay Subsidy Roll, ed. K. Williams-Jones (Cardiff, 1976).

Orderic Vitalis: *The Ecclesiastical History of Orderic Vitalis*, ed. M. Chibnall, 6 vols. (Oxford, 1969–80). Not all books are subdivided into section; reference is to book number and page and line reference to Chibnall's edition.

Oxford Dictionary of National Biography, ed. H. C. G. Matthew and B. Harrison (Oxford, 2004), *www.oxforddnb.com.*

Oxford Latin Dictionary, ed. P. G. W. Glare (Oxford, 1982).

Pedeir Keinc y Mabinogi, ed. I. Williams (Cardiff, 1930).

Peniarth Estate Papers, vol. III (Aberystwyth, 1997).

Record of Caernarvon: Registrum vulgariter nuncupatum 'the Record of Caernarvon' e codice msto Harleiano 696 descriptum, ed. H. Ellis (London, 1838).

Rhagymadroddion, 1547–1659, ed. G. H. Hughes (Cardiff, 1951).

Rhigyfarch's Life of St. David, ed. J. W. James (Cardiff, 1967).

Schedule of Peniarth Manuscripts and Documents (Aberystwyth, 1959).

The Song of Dermot and the Earl, ed. G. H. Orpen (Oxford, 1892; repr. Felinfach, 1994).

Suger, *Vie de Louis VI le Gros*, ed. H. Wacquet (Paris, 1964).

Trioedd Ynys Prydein: The Welsh Triads, ed. R. Bromwich, 2nd edition (Cardiff, 1978).

Vitae Sanctorum Britanniae et Genealogiae, ed. A. W. Wade-Evans (Cardiff, 1944).

The Welsh Life of St David, ed. D. S. Evans (Cardiff, 1988).

Welsh Medieval Law, being a Text of the Laws of Hywel the Good, namely the British Museum Harleian MS. 4353 of the 13th Century, ed. A. W. Wade-Evans (Oxford, 1909).

Ymborth yr Enaid, ed. R. I. Daniel (Cardiff, 1995).

Secondary literature

Ballinger, J., *Katheryn of Berain, as a Study in a North Wales Family History* (London, 1929).

Bartrum, P., 'Was there a British "Book of Conquests"?', *BBCS*, 23, (1968–72), 1–6.

Bensley, E., 'Catalogue of Peniarth Manuscripts which are wholly or partly in Latin' (typescript in the National Library of Wales, Aberystwyth, n.d.).

Berschin, W., *Biographie und Epochenstil im lateinischen Mittelalter*, 3 vols (Stuttgart, 1986–91).

Blom, A., 'The Chronicles of the Kings of Mann and the Isles' (unpublished M.Phil. dissertation, University of Cambridge, 2003).

Bradley, K. R., *Suetonius' Life of Nero: A Historical Commentary* (Brussels, 1978).

Briquet, C. M., *Les Filigranes: Dictionnaire Historique des Marques du Papier dès leur Apparition vers 1282 jusqu'en 1600. A facsimile of the 1907 edition with supplementary material contributed by a number of scholars*, ed. A. Stevenson. 4 vols (Amsterdam, 1968).

Broderick, G., 'Irish and Welsh strands in the geneaology of Godred Crovan', *Journal of the Manx Museum*, 8 (1980), 32–8.

Charles-Edwards, T. M., *Early Irish and Welsh Kinship* (Oxford, 1993).

——, 'Some Celtic kinship terms', *BBCS*, 24 (1971–2), 105–21.

——, M. E. Owen, and P. Russell (eds.), *The Welsh King and his Court* (Cardiff, 2000)

——, and P. Russell, 'The Hendregadredd Manuscript and the Orthography and phonology of Welsh in the early 14th century', *NLWJ*, 28 (1993–4), 419–62.

Davies, C., *Latin Writers of the Renaissance* (Cardiff, 1981).

——, 'The sixteenth-century Latin translation of *Historia Gruffud vab Kenan*', in Maund, *Gruffudd ap Cynan*, 157–64.

Davies, L. M., 'The Tregaer manuscript: an elegy for Charles I', *NLWJ*, 31 (1999–2000), 243–70.

Davies, R. R., *Conquest, Co-existence, and Change: Wales 1063–1415* (Oxford and Cardiff, 1987).

——, 'Henry I and Wales', in H. Mayr-Harting and R. I. Moore (eds), *Studies in Medieval History Presented to R. H. C. Davis* (London and Ronceverte, 1985), 132–47.

Davies, S., and P. W. Thomas (eds), *Canhwyll Marchogyon: Cyd-destunoli Peredur* (Cardiff, 2000).

Duffy, S., 'The 1169 invasion as a turning-point in Irish–Welsh relations', in B. Smith (ed.), *Britain and Ireland 900–1300: Insular Responses to Medieval European Change* (Cambridge, 1999), 98–113.

——, 'Irishmen and Islesmen in the kingdoms of Dublin and Man, 1052–1171', *Ériu*, 43 (1992), 93–133.

——, 'Ostmen, Irish and Welsh in the eleventh century', *Peritia*, 9 (1995), 378–96.

——, review of Maund, *Gruffudd ap Cynan*, *CMCS*, 38 (Winter 1999), 102–3.

Dumville, D. N., 'Celtic–Latin texts in northern England, *c*.1150–*c*.1250', *Celtica*, 12 (1977), 19–49; reprinted in D. N. Dumville, *Histories and Pseudo-Histories of the Insular Middle Ages* (Aldershot, 1990), XI.

——, 'Ireland and Britain in *Táin Bó Fraích*', *Études celtiques*, 32 (1996), 175–87.

Dunbabin, J., 'The Maccabees as exemplars in the tenth and eleventh centuries', in K. Walsh and D. Wood (eds), *The Bible in the Medieval World: Essays in Memory of Beryl Smalley* (Oxford, 1985), 31–41.

Etchingham, C., 'North Wales, Ireland and the Isles: the Insular Viking Zone', *Peritia*, 15 (2001), 145–87.

Evans, J. G., *Report on Manuscripts in the Welsh Language*, 2 vols (London, 1898–1910).

Evans, M. D., 'Vaughan, Robert Powell (1591/2–1667)', *ODNB www.oxforddnb.com/view/article/28141*

Flanagan, M. T., '*Historia Gruffudd vab Kenan* and the Origins of Balrothery', *CMCS*, 28 (Winter 1994), 71–94.

——, *Irish Society, Anglo-Norman Settlers, Angevin Kingship: Interactions in Ireland in the Late 12th Century* (Oxford, 1989).

French, P., *John Dee: The World of an Elizabethan Magus* (London, 1972).

Gransden, A., *Historical Writing in England, I, c.550–c.1507* (London, 1996).

Hanning, R. W., *The Vision of History in Early Britain: From Gildas to Geoffrey of Monmouth* (New York, 1966).

Harris, B. E., *A History of the County of Cheshire*, II (Oxford, 1979).

Honigmann, E. A. J., *Shakespeare: The 'Lost Years'* (Manchester, 1985).

Hudson, B. T., 'The changing economy of the Irish Sea province: AD 900–1300', in B. Smith (ed.), *Britain, in Britain and Ireland 900–1300: Insular Responses to Medieval European Change* (Cambridge, 1999), 39–66.

Huws, D., *Medieval Welsh Manuscripts* (Cardiff and Aberystwyth, 2000).

——, 'Robert Vaughan', in Huws, *Medieval Welsh Manuscripts*, 287–302.

——, 'Texts: ii. the manuscripts', in T. M. Charles-Edwards, M. E. Owen, and D. B. Walters (eds), *Lawyers and Laymen* (Cardiff, 1986), 119–36.

Jesch, J., 'Norse historical traditions and *Historia Gruffudd vab Kenan*: Magnús berfœttr and Haraldr hárfagri', in Maund, *Gruffudd ap Cynan*, 117–48.

Jones, J. G., *The Wynn Family of Gwydir. Origins: Growth and Development, c.1490–1674* (Aberystwyth, 1995).

Jones, N. A., '*Historia Gruffudd vab Kenan*: the first audience', in Maund, *Gruffudd ap Cynan*, 149–56.

——, 'The Mynydd Carn "Prophecy": a reassessment', *CMCS*, 38 (Winter 1999), 73–92.

Jones, T., '"Cronica de Wallia" and other documents from Exeter Cathedral library, MS. 3514', *BBCS*, 12 (1946–8), 27–44.

Keen, M., *Chivalry* (New Haven, 1984).

Kettle, A. J., 'The Abbey of Chester', in *A History of the County of Cheshire*, III, ed. B. E. Harris (Oxford, 1980), 132–46.

Knowles, D., C. N. L. Brooke and V. C. M. London, *The Heads of Religious Houses, England and Wales, I, 940–1216* (Cambridge, 2001).

Lambert, P.-Y., 'Two Middle Welsh epithets for horses: *trybelid* and *ffraeth* (Breton *fraez*)', *CMCS*, 44 (Winter 2002), 103–6.

Leo, F., *Die griechische-römische Biographie* (Leipzig, 1901).

Lewis, C. P., 'Gruffudd ap Cynan and the Normans', in Maund, *Gruffudd ap Cynan*, 61–77.

——, 'Gruffudd ap Cynan and the reality and representation of exile', in L. Napran and E. van Houts (eds), *Exile in the Middle Ages: Selected Proceedings from the International Medieval Congress, University of Leeds, 8–11 July 2002*, (Turnhout, 2004), 39–51.

Lewis, T., 'Bibliography of the laws of Hywel Dda', *Aberystwyth Studies*, 10 (1928), 151–82.

Lloyd, J. E., *A History of Wales from the Earliest Times to the Edwardian Conquest*, 3rd edn, 2 vols (London, 1939).

Lloyd, N., 'Meredith Lloyd', *Journal of Welsh Bibliographical Society*, 11 (1975–6), 133–92.

Lloyd-Jones, J., *Geirfa Barddoniaeth Gynner Gymraeg*, 2 vols (Cardiff, 1931–63). A–H only.

——, '*Rôn*', *BBCS*, 15 (1952–4), 200–2.

Llwyd, A., *A History of the Island of Mona* (Rhuthin, 1833).

Mac Cana, P., 'The conjunctive pronouns in Welsh', in M. J. Ball, J. Fife, E. Poppe and J. Rowland (eds), *Celtic Linguistics. Ieithyddiaeth Geltaidd. Readings in the Brythonic Languages. Festschrift for T. Arwyn Watkins*, (Amsterdam and Philadelphia, 1990), 411–33.

McLeod, W., '*Rí Insi Gall, Rí Fionnghall, Ceannas nan Gàidheal*: sovreignty and rhetoric in the late medieval Hebrides', *CMCS*, 43 (Summer 2002), 25–48.

Maginn, C., 'Herbert, Sir William (*c.*1553–1593)', *ODNB www.oxforddnb.com/view/article/13056*

Maund, K. L. (ed.), *Gruffudd ap Cynan: A Collaborative Biography* (Woodbridge, 1996).

——, '"Gruffudd, grandson of Iago": *Historia Gruffud vab Kenan* and the construction of legitimacy', in Maund, *Gruffudd ap Cynan*, 109–16.

——, *Ireland, Wales and England in the Eleventh Century* (Woodbridge, 1991).

——, 'Trahaearn ap Caradog: legitimate usurper?', *WHR*, 13 (1986–7), 468–76.

——, *The Welsh Kings: The Medieval Rulers of Wales* (Stroud, 2000).

Meyer, K., 'Zur keltische Wortkunde', *Sitzungsberichte der königliche preussische Akademie der Wissenschaften*, 6 (1914), 939–58.

Moore, D., 'Gruffudd ap Cynan and the mediaeval Welsh polity', in Maund, *Gruffudd ap Cynan*, 1–59.

Morgan, T. J. and P. Morgan, *Welsh Surnames* (Cardiff, 1985).

Morris, J., *Arthurian Sources*, 6 vols (Chichester, 1995).

Ní Mhaonaigh, M., 'Tales of three Gormlaiths in medieval Irish literature', *Ériu*, 51 (2002), 1–24.

Orlandi, G., '*Clausulae* in Gildas' *De Excidio Britanniae*', in M. Lapidge and D. Dumville (eds), *Gildas: New Approaches* (Woodbridge, 1984), 129–49.

Ovenden, R., 'Jaspar Gryffyth and his books', *British Library Journal*, 20 (1994), 107–39.

Owen, E., *A Catalogue of the Manuscripts Relating to Wales in the British Museum*, Part I (London, 1900).

Owen, M. E., 'The laws of court from Cyfnerth', in Charles-Edwards, et al. (eds), *The Welsh King and his Court*, 425–77.

Parry, G., *A Guide to the Records of Great Sessions in Wales* (Aberystwyth, 1995).

Phillips, J. R. S., *The Justices of the Peace in Wales and Monmouthshire, 1541–1689* (Cardiff, 1957).

Pryce, H., 'British or Welsh? National identity in twelfth-century Wales', *EHR*, 116 (2001), 775–801.

——, 'The church of Trefeglwys and the end of the "Celtic" charter tradition in twelfth-century Wales', *CMCS*, 25 (Summer 1993), 15–54.

——, 'Gruffudd ap Cynan (1054/5–1137)', *ODNB www.oxforddnb.com/view/article/11693*

Richards, M., *Atlas Môn* (Llangefni, 1972).

——, *Enwau Tir a Gwlad* (Caernarfon, 1998).

Richter, M., *Giraldus Cambrensis: The Growth of the Welsh Nation*, revised edn (Aberystwyth, 1976). Originally in *NLWJ*, 16 (1969–70), 193–252, 293–318; 17 (1971–2), 1–50.

Roberts, B. F., 'Personal names in the *Historia Regum Britanniae*', *BBCS*, 25 (1972–4), 274–90, 282.

——, '*Ystoria*', *BBCS*, 26 (1974–5), 13–20.

Roberts, R. J., 'John Dee and the matter of Britain', *Transactions of the Honourable Society of Cymmrodorion* (1991), 129–43.

——, 'Dee, John (1527–1609)', *ODNB www.oxforddnb.com/view/article/7418*

Roderick, A. J., 'A dispute between Llywelyn ap Gruffydd and Gruffydd ap Gwenwynwyn', *BBCS*, 8 (1935–7), 248–54.

Russell, P., *Celtic Word-Formation* (Dublin, 1990).

——, '"Divers evidences antient of some Welsh princes": the Welsh manuscripts and books of Dr John Dee', *Journal of Celtic Studies*, 5 (2005), forthcoming.

——, *The Prologues to the Medieval Welsh Lawbooks* (Cambridge, 2004).

——, 'Scribal (in)competence in thirteenth-century north Wales: the orthography of the Black Book of Chirk (Peniarth MS 29)', *NLWJ*, 29 (1995–6), 129–76.

——, 'What did medieval Welsh scribes do? The scribe of the Dingestow Court manuscript', *CMCS*, 37 (Summer 1999), 79–96.

Sherman, W. H., *John Dee: The Politics of Reading and Writing in the English Renaissance* (Amherst, 1995).

Sims-Williams, P., *The Celtic Inscriptions of Britain: Phonology and Chronology, c.400–1200* (Oxford, 2003).

——, 'Clas Beuno and the Four Branches of the Mabinogi', in B. Maier and S. Zimmer (eds) *150 Jahre 'Mabinogion': Deutsch-Walisische Kulturbeziehungen* (Tübingen, 2001), 111–27.

——, 'Edward IV's confirmation charter for Clynnog Fawr', in C. Richmond and I. Harvey (eds), *Recognitions: Essays Presented to Edmund Fryde* (Aberystwyth, 1996), 229–41.

——, 'Historical need and literary narrative: a *caveat* from ninth-century Wales', *WHR*, 17 (1994), 1–40.

——, 'Old Irish *feda* (gen. *fedot*): a "puzzling" form in the *Cambrai Homily* and its implications for the apocope of /i/', in P. Anreiter and E. Jerem (eds), *Studia Celtica et Indogermanica: Festschrift für Wolfgang Meid* (Budapest, 1999), 471–4.

——, 'Some functions of origin stories in early medieval Wales', in T. Nyberg, I. Piø, M. Sørensen and A. Trommer (eds), *History and Heroic Tale, A Symposium. Proceedings of the Eighth International Symposium organized by the Centre for the Study of Vernacular Literature in the Middle Ages. Held at Odense University on 21–22 November, 1983*, (Odense, 1985), 97–131.

Smith, J. B., 'The Age of Princes', in J. B. Smith and Ll. B. Smith (eds), *The History of Merioneth, II, The Middle Ages* (Cardiff, 2001), 1–59.

——, *The Sense of History in Medieval Wales. Yr Ymwybod â Hanes yng Nghymru yn yr Oesoedd Canol* (Aberystwyth, 1991).

——, 'Treftadaeth Deheubarth', in N. A. Jones and H. Pryce (eds), *Yr Arglwydd Rhys* (Cardiff, 1996), 18–52.

Thomas, P. W., 'Cydberthynas y pedair fersiwn ganoloesol', in Davies and Thomas, *Canhwyll Marchogyon*, 10–43.

Thornton, D. E., 'The genealogy of Gruffudd ap Cynan', in Maund, *Gruffudd ap Cynan*, 79–108.

G. Townend, B., 'Suetonius and his influence', in *Latin Biography*, ed. T. A. Dorey (London, 1967), 79–111.

Van Hamel, A. G., 'Norse history in Hanes Gruffydd ap Cynan', *RC*, 42 (1925), 336–44.

Williams, G., 'Kyffin, Maurice (*c.*1555–1598)', *ODNB www.oxforddnb.com/view/article/15817*

Williams, I., 'Llywelyn Foelrhon', *BBCS*, 10 (1939–41), 242.

Williams, J. E. C., 'Meilyr Brydydd and Gruffudd ap Cynan', in Maund, *Gruffudd ap Cynan*, 165–86.

Wormald, P., *The Making of English Law: King Alfred to the Twelfth Century, I, Legislation and its Limits* (Oxford, 1999).

Woudhuysen, H. R., *Sir Philip Sydney and the Circulation of Manuscripts, 1558–1640* (Oxford, 1996).

Wyatt, D., 'Gruffudd ap Cynan and the Hiberno-Norse World', *WHR*, 19 (1998–9), 595–617.

Zimmer, S., 'A medieval linguist: Gerald de Barri', *EC*, 35 (2003), 313–50.

Concordance

The text of *VGC* has been divided into sections corresponding to those in *HGK*. The following table provides an easy mode of cross-reference between *VGC*, *HGK* and *MPW*.

VGC (§ number)	Peniarth MS 434 (page, line number)	*HGK* Welsh text (page, line number)	*MPW* English trans. (page, line number)	Chapter heading in *MPW*
1	1. 1	1. 2	53. 1	His birth
2	1. 3	1. 7	53. 8	His parents
3	1. 10	1. 12	53. 15	His pedigree on his father's side
4	3. 11	2. 16	54. 30	His pedigree on his mother's side
5	4. 4	3. 1	55. 10	Harald Haarfagar and his brothers
6	7. 12	4. 22	56. 34	His pedigree on his grandmother's side
7	9. 2	5. 14	57. 26	His pedigree in relation to God
8	9. 12	5. 20	58. 1	Myrddin's prophecy
9	10. 10	6. 7	58. 21	His youth
10	11. 11	6. 21	59. 7	He sails for Gwynedd
11	13. 6	7. 20	60. 1	The prophecy of Tangwystl
12	13. 15	8. 1	60. 11	Gwynedd subdued
13	16. 15	9. 21	62. 1	An attack on Rhuddlan castle
14	17. 11	10. 5	62. 17	The battle of Bron yr Erw

15	21.1	12.4	64.20	Another expedition
16	22.4	12.25	65.14	The Normans ravage Gwynedd
17	23.3	17.13	66.1	An alliance with Rhys ap Tewdwr
18	24.17	14.20	67.9	The battle of Mynydd Carn
19	28.9	16.27	68.17	The imprisonment of Gruffudd
20	29.14	17.18	70.6	His person
21	30.5	18.1	70.16	Earl Hugh in Gwynedd
22	30.15	18.10	70.29	He escapes from prison: reaches Ireland
23	33.1	19.20	72.8	He regains Gwynedd
24	37.1	21.21	74.6	His wife and children
25	37.18	22.9	74.23	The expedition of William Rufus
26	39.12	23.10	75.26	The expedition of the earls
27	42.8	25.5	77.11	The appearance of King Magnus
28	43.5	25.18	77.28	The death of Hugh, earl of Shrewsbury
29	44.12	26.23	78.25	The Normans and the traitors
30	45.17	27.17	79.12	He makes peace with Hugh, earl of Chester
31	46.9	28.1	79.21	He consolidates his position in Gwynedd
32	47.17	29.1	80.18	The expeditions of King Henry
33	49.14	30.3	81.20	Peace and prosperity
34	51.7	31.5	82.15	He retires and distributes his wealth
35	52.15	32.8	83.7	Gruffudd's death

Index of names

The items are listed in English alphabetical order. Names beginning in *I-* and *J-* have been merged, as have been those beginning with *C-* and *K-*. The references are to the paragraph and sentence numbers of the main text edited in this volume. The forms of the names recorded are those in the Latin text; they may not take the same form in the English translation. An italicized reference means that that occurrence of the name comes from the sections of text taken from Cotton Vitellius C.ix. Where the name itself is italicized, the name only occurs in text from Cotton Vitellius C.ix.

Index of biblical references

The following index contains all the biblical passages referred to in the Introduction and notes. Reference to a biblical passage does not imply direct quotation in the text. The references are to the paragraph and sentence numbers of the main text edited in this volume. The books are listed in biblical order. The Bible used for all quotations is the *Biblia Sacra Vulgata*.

Old Testament

Genesis 49	35/2
Exodus 17.13	32/7
Numbers 21.24	32/7
Deuteronomy 13.15	32/7
Deuteronomy 20.13	32/7
Deuteronomy 20.17	32/7
Judges 1.8	32/7
Judges 1.25	32/7
Judges 4.15	32/7
Judges 6.2	26/10
Judges 18.27	32/7
Judges 20.37	32/7
Joshua 6.21	32/7
Joshua 10.30	32/7
Joshua 10.32	32/7
Joshua 10.35	32/7
Joshua 10.37	32/7
Joshua 10.40	32/7
Joshua 23–24	35/5
Joshua 24.9	35/5
1 Samuel 13.6	26/10
1 Samuel 15.8	32/7
1 Samuel 22.19	32/7
1 Samuel 24.1–8	25/9
1 Samuel 25.22	25/1
1 Samuel 25.34	25/1
1 Samuel 31	12/4
2 Samuel 1	12/4
2 Samuel 15.14	32/7

1 Kings 14.10	25/1
1 Kings 16.11	25/1
1 Kings 21.21	25/1
2 Kings 9.8	25/1
2 Chronicles 29–32	34/2, 35/2
2 Chronicles 32.27–9	34/2, 35/2
Judith 7.17, 15.6	32/7
Psalms 81.6	7/1
Isaiah 39.2	34/2, 35/2
Jeremiah 21.7	32/7
Jeremiah 29.17	28/6
Nahum 3.12	28/6
Zachariah 13.7	26/10
1 Maccabaeus 1.11	26/1
1 Maccabaeus 3.3–4,	14/14, 18/8
1 Maccabaeus 3.28	32/2
1 Maccabaeus 5.51	32/7
1 Maccabaeus 7.28–29	19/3–4
1 Maccabaeus 9.20	35/5

New Testament

Matthew 26.31	19/7, 26/10
Luke 1.52–3	29/3
Luke 21.24	32/7
John 19.38	26/10
John 20.19	26/10
John 7.13	26/10
1 Corinthians 14.22	29/3
2 Corinthians 6.15	29/3
James 5.14	35/1

Index of manuscripts